CREATIVE HARMONY
and MUSICIANSHIP

An Introduction to the Structure of Music

PRENTICE-HALL MUSIC SERIES
Douglas Moore, Editor

CREATIVE HARMONY
and MUSICIANSHIP

An Introduction to the
Structure of Music

by HOWARD ANSLEY MURPHY

Professor of Music and Music Education
Teachers College • Columbia University
New York City

and

EDWIN JOHN STRINGHAM

Former Faculty Member of Columbia University
(Teachers College); Juilliard School of Music;
Union Theological Seminary; Queens College
of the City of New York • Head of Music
Department of U. S. Army University (Biarritz,
France) • Guest Professor with University of
California at Los Angeles and University of Tex-
as • Author of "Listening to Music Creatively"

PRENTICE-HALL • INC.
New York   1951

Printed in the United States of America

FOREWORD TO TEACHERS

THE TRUE PURPOSE of "theoretic" study, as conceived by the authors, is to foster the growth of musicianship through the acquisition of insights and skills needed to meet individual needs. For its realization, the philosophy of this text is based upon three fundamental tenets:

First: That so-called "theory" should be an explanation of the *structure of music* for appreciative, executive, and creative purposes. Music literature of the classic and romantic periods is the field of investigation, and hence the learning sequence should conform to the harmonic usage or chord frequency as found in music literature of these periods.

Second: That general principles of structure should emerge from this study of literature and be applied directly through specific techniques that are learned only when needed for growing insight and understanding.

Third: That all phases of study (written and keyboard facility, and aural and visual perception) be coordinated into *a single unified conception of musical structures* to meet the practical needs of the performer, creator, or listener.

Such a different approach raises many new problems; it is the purpose of this Foreword to discuss and, if possible, to solve them.[1]

The Scope and Organization of the Text

The first general problem deals with the quantity and order of the material. Broadly speaking, the book contains the material presented in first year college harmony, keyboard, ear-training and music-reading classes. If the book is used in high school, at least two years would ordinarily be required to complete this material.

---

[1]Further see Howard A. Murphy, *Teaching Musicianship.* New York: Coleman-Ross Company, Inc., 1950

The book consists of four parts and is divided into thirty chapters (one for each academic week) and four summaries. Each chapter contains expository material, questions for review and for further study, and assignments for writing, playing, listening, and analysis. The melodies in the *Assignment for Writing* may be used also for music reading.

Preliminary Requirements and Rudiments

Only a knowledge of notation and of keyboard design is necessary as a basis for Chapter I. They are summarized in the Appendix, page 595. Other rudiments (scales, key signatures, and intervals) are explained in the text as need for understanding them arises from the music being examined. (See Analytic Table of Contents, pages xvi-xix.) The Key of C major is used for Chapters I — VIII, in order to provide the student with an adequate harmonic vocabulary quickly, free of technical details that can be more easily and appropriately learned later in their musical context. Needless to say, if the student is already familiar with other keys he should use them from the outset.

Beginning in Chapter IX all major and minor keys and signatures are presented through modulatory examples from literature. Intervals are introduced in Chapter VII, *as parts of chords,* when it is necessary to understand and recognize the qualitative difference between major and minor triads. Thus both key signatures and intervals are learned, not as isolated facts before contact with music, but as technical aspects of real music requiring explanation for further insights and skills. In other words, these phases of rudiments are treated functionally rather than theoretically.

Expository Material

Each chapter is based on an example from music literature, which is analyzed for the desired technical information. As far as possible the student is encouraged to make his own deductions from the excerpt quoted. This process requires careful guidance by the instructor and continuous class participation involving the following class procedures:

1. *Performance.* It is suggested that, whenever possible, the complete composition cited in the text be performed in class either by being played, sung, or heard through recordings.

2. *Participation.* It is important that the class sing all new chords, using numbers and letters, and all harmonic passages in four parts.

3. *Experimentation.* When alternative choices are suggested, as in the case of multiple basses for a melody, the class itself should decide on the preferable solution based on the hearing of the various possibilities.

Two technical points in the text are left to the discretion of the instructor: the explanation of both the occasional use of chromaticism in the examples and the distinction between the real meter versus the time signature. In the latter case the true meter is indicated in parenthesis thus: $\frac{3}{4}$ $\left(\frac{6}{4}\right)$

Review and Suggestions for Further Study

The expository material in each chapter closes with a series of questions related to the material presented. The answers to those titled *Review* are to be found in the text itself, but the *Further Study Questions* involve reasoning either from facts presented or from outside reading, the purpose being to focus more sharply the material presented and to stimulate class discussion. The *Review* might conceivably be used as a weekly quiz.

Assignments

The four assignments following the *Review* and *Further Study Questions* represent, with music reading, the basic areas for application of the expository material. There is no particular significance in the order of these assignments. Quite logically, the order might be listening, analysis, playing, and writing.

A word needs to be said regarding the quantity of material in these assignments. Since an awareness of the structure of music through the study of music literature is a basic philosophy of this text, an unusual wealth of reference material has been included. However, this quantity of material is cited in order to give the text *flexibility* and the instructor and student *freedom of choice*. It is not intended that all, or even a large portion, of this material be used in any one class. Rather it is felt that all concerned will profit by selecting only the material that is of interest to them or that is available at the time. Care has been taken to include *all types of music literature* in order to make the book adaptable to the special interests of various groups — pianists, singers, instrumentalists, and listeners. When work is assigned, it is assumed that the student will solve only *one problem* in each division. It would even be possible, in cases of special interest, to omit entirely one or more of the four areas presented. Thus, for a class piano group, attention could be focused on the expository and keyboard sections, or a class in General Music or Appreciation might use only the descriptive and the analytic portions. In general, however, a single problem from each of the four sections should suffice for a week's work. Another reason for the variety of material is that it is advisable for the instructor to permit the student himself to select any problem in a given area, rather than to assign the same problem to all.

1. *Writing.* This section consists of three types of problems: writing simple melodies for poems, original instrumental compositions, and the harmonization of melodies for piano and later for two, three, or four voices. Beginning in Chapter XXI a few figured and unfigured basses with given soprano are included, largely to illustrate the concept of figured bass without stressing its use. The setting of words to music is an essential part of the student's technical and musical growth and as such merits special consideration and emphasis. Probably both the setting of words and harmonization could be included in a weekly assignment. Especially at the beginning, when the principles of phrase and period forms have been assimilated and a feeling for them developed, the creative writing could be either instrumental or vocal at the option of the student.

2. *Playing.* Keyboard application of technical knowledge is second only to aural experience in developing musicianship. Some keyboard experience is urged for all students, the extent of which is dependent upon individual proficiency. *A steady tempo is essential in keyboard work.* For nonpianists some keyboard experience, such as finding scales and types of chords, harmonizing of simple folk songs by ear, and playing the melody alone in the right hand and the chords in block form with the left hand, is desirable. In many cases application of material learned also can be applied directly to the student's own instrument. It will be noted that the student is directed to repeat certain chord patterns in piano style. This procedure is a valuable link in learning to improvise. The chord pattern is to be broken up in any type of practical pianistic figuration.

3. *Listening.* The development of aural sensitivity is of prime importance in the growth of musicianship. Work in this area is divided into two parts, oral and written. The oral dictation may be given on a number of levels. For example, as the passage is played, the student recognizes (1) consonance and dissonance, (2) major, minor, or dissonant quality, (3) letter and quality names of chords, (4) fundamental or inverted chords, and finally (5) such specific details as inversions, and nonharmonic tones. Thus the student may operate on any one of at least five levels depending upon his aptitude and training. On all these five levels, however, it is essential that the student develop an awareness of *general* musical balance and style as related to specific structural elements.

The skills in the second type of dictation (written) may be broken down into the same patterns. When the final stage is reached the student should *memorize* first the melody, then the bass, and next indicate chord quality and name, the latter being done as the passage is played. It is important for the student to form a general concept of the music by frequent repetitions before notating specific details. The purpose of dictation is to increase aural sensitivity rather than notational skill. Hence the element of phrase-wise attention and musical memory are of primary importance.

4. *Analysis.* Analysis of music should be both aural and visual. The material in this section, *after being heard,* can be used for class discussion. The term "analysis" includes all aspects of structure — form, chords, and nonharmonic tones. The simpler excerpts can be used for transposition in keyboard work.

5. *Music Reading.* Although not selected primarily for music reading, or so titled, the melodies in the Assignments for Writing and for Playing can also be used for music reading, especially since they are directly related to the harmonic content of the chapter. The reading of music through singing can be greatly facilitated by relating the melody to its harmonic background. For this reason it is desirable for the instructor to outline this background as the melody is sung by the class.

6. *Creative Work.* As musical taste is developed and as basic skills are mastered all possible encouragement should be given to individual creative experimentation. The student should be led, through the study of music literature, *to think after the composer* and to recreate this thought for himself. But recreation is not enough. The student should be encouraged and guided in *self expression* — in learning to create for himself. Such self expression can function from the beginning — limited only by the student's capabilities and interest, not by his technical equipment. However, since all students are not equally capable or interested in creative expression, partially solved problems for completion are included in addition to purely creative problems. It is important that creative work be evaluated by the class through performance. Ensemble combinations formed in the class can be utilized. Regular programs of student compositions are also a stimulus to creative writing. In keyboard work, especially when beginning improvisation, one student can play a predetermined chord pattern while others improvise melodies for it. The experienced instructor undoubtedly has used or can invent many similar devices for arousing and stimulating innate originality.

In conclusion, the text itself is experimental in concept and method. In its original form it has been widely used in high schools and colleges and has been modified considerably as a result of varied experiences and criticisms. If there is one significant conclusion that has emerged from these years of testing it is to teach the *art of music,* not theory, for the enrichment of life, through the stimulation of creativity and the clarification of insights for the performer and listener.

H. A. M.
E. J. S.

ACKNOWLEDGMENTS

THE AUTHORS gratefully acknowledge criticism and help in the preparation of the manuscript from Professor John Castellini, Walter E. Nalbin, Mrs. Nathan Dane II, and Dr. Marjorie Walthall.

In addition, the authors are indebted for permission from the publishers to quote melodies from the following material: Hall & McCreary Company, Chicago, *The H & M Auditorium Series Nos. 5, 11, 12, 17, 20* and *The H & M Choral Collection No. 12;* Oxford University Press, New York, *The Folk Song Sight Singing Series;* American Book Company, New York, *Hollis Dann's Junior Songs* and *The Foresman Series* (Child's Book, Manual for First Grade, and the Second through the Sixth Book of Songs); A. G. Comings & Son, Oberlin, Ohio (Victor Lytle) *96 German Chorales.*

All portions of the *Leiderschatz* and *Meisterchorales* are reprinted with the authorization of the copyright owner, C. P. Peters Corporation, Carnegie Hall, New York City. The authors also gratefully acknowledge permission to quote from the several works of *The Concord Series,* published by the E. C. Schirmer Music Co. of Boston. Acknowledgment of permission to use other copyrighted music and poems will be found in the text where the material appears.

TOPICAL TABLE OF CONTENTS

Part I
Basic Chords in One Tonality. Single Melodic Line

CHAPTER		PAGE
I	THE I AND V CHORDS	3
II	THE V₇ CHORD	19
III	THE IV CHORD	30
IV	THE II₆ CHORD	46
V	THE CADENTIAL I$^6_4$ CHORD	62
VI	THE I₆ CHORD	76
VII	THE VI CHORD	90
VIII	THE II AND III CHORDS	107
	SUMMARY I	125

Part II
Basic Inverted Discords. The Major Mode (Modulation).
Two-and Three-voice Writing

IX	MODULATION TO THE DOMINANT KEY	131
X	THE V$^6_5$ CHORD	148
XI	THE V$^6_5$ CHORD (Continued)	168
XII	THE V$^4_3$ CHORD	188
XIII	THE VII₆ CHORD	207
XIV	THE V$^4_2$ CHORD	226
XV	THE V$^4_2$ CHORD (Continued)	243
XVI	IMPLIED MODULATION TO THE DOMINANT KEY	260
	SUMMARY II	280

Part III
Basic Inversions. The Minor Mode.
Four-Voice Writing

XVII	THE MINOR MODE: PARALLEL AND RELATIVE SCALES	287

CHAPTER   PAGE

XVIII   THE HARMONIC MINOR SCALE: DOMINANT
          MODULATIONS 302

 XIX   THE MELODIC MINOR SCALE: RELATIVE
          MODULATIONS 319

  XX   THE NATURAL MINOR SCALE: MEDIANT
          MODULATIONS 338

 XXI   FOUR-PART VOCAL WRITING 361

 XXII   THE V₆ CHORD 383

XXIII   THE IV₆ AND OTHER CHORDS OF THE SIXTH . . 402

XXIV   THE II₅⁶ CHORD 423

 XXV   EMBELLISHING ₄⁶ CHORDS (THE IV₄⁶) 447

XXVI   PASSING ₄⁶ CHORDS (THE V₄⁶) 470

        SUMMARY III 491

Part IV
Secondary Discords. Enharmonic Scales

XXVII   THE II₇ AND OTHER SECONDARY SEVENTH
          CHORDS 499

XXVIII THE II₃⁴ AND II₂⁴ CHORDS 525

XXIX   THE V₉ CHORD 546

 XXX   THE VII₇ CHORD 571

        SUMMARY IV 592

        APPENDIX — SUMMARY OF NOTATION . . . 595

ANALYTIC TABLE OF CONTENTS

ANALYTIC TABLE OF CONTENTS

Chapter	Chords	Intervals	Keys*	Inharmonic Tones	Form	Vocal Writing
Part I						
I	I, V		C major		Phrase; period; perfect, semi-cadences	Solo voice; setting of words
II	V_7	Definition				Optional accompaniment
III	IV			Neighboring and passing tones	A-B-A plagal cadence	
IV	II_6			Suspension (retardation)		
V	Cadential I_4^6				Inversion	
VI	I_6					
VII	VI	Perfect fifth; major and minor thirds		Anticipation	Extension by evaded or imperfect cadence	
VIII	II, III				The sequence	

Part II	Major scale pattern	Major and minor seconds	C-G; modulation to dominant			Two-voice; soprano, alto; the round
IX						
X	V_5^6		G-D, key signature		A-B	
XI	V_5^6 (*con't*)	Major and minor sevenths	D-A	Appoggiatura; acciaccatura		Three-voice: soprano I, soprano II, alto
XII	V_3^4		A-E			
XIII	VII$_6$	Augmented fourths; diminished fifths	F-C			
XIV	V_2^4		B-flat, F			Soprano, alto baritone
XV	V_2^4 (*con't*)		E-flat, B-flat			
XVI			A-flat, E-flat; implied modulation to dominant	Echappée		Soprano, alto, bass

Summary of Part II

XVII

---
*In this table capital letters refer to major keys and small letters to minor keys.

ANALYTIC TABLE OF CONTENTS (CONTINUED)

Chapter	Chords	Intervals	Keys*	Inharmonic Tones	Form	Vocal Writing
Part III XVII	The minor mode		F-f, key signatures; parallel and relative scales			
XVIII	Harmonic minor	Augmented seconds	f-c; dominant modulation			
XIX	Melodic minor		c-E-flat; relative modulation			
XX	Natural (pure) minor		g, B-flat; mediant modulation; summary of modulation			
XXI			d			Four-voice (mixed voices)
XXII	V₆		a		Summary of A-B-A forms	
XXIII	IV₆; other chords of the sixth		e			
XXIV	II$_{6}^{5}$		b	Pedal point		

	embellishing $^6_4$ chords				
XXVI	V^6_4 passing $^6_4$ chords		c sharp		
Summary of Part III					
Part IV XXVII	II_7; other secondary seventh chords		B (C-flat); enharmonic notation		Summary of A-B
XXVIII	II^4_3-II^4_2		G-flat (F sharp)		Antecedent and consequent groups
XXIX	V_9		D-flat (C sharp); circle of major keys	Double neighboring tones	
XXX	VII_7	Diminished sevenths	e-flat (d sharp); enharmonic minor keys; circle of minor keys		
Summary of Part IV					

*In this table capital letters refer to major keys and small letters to minor keys.

Part I

BASIC CHORDS IN ONE TONALITY
SINGLE MELODIC LINE

Preliminary Requirements

A knowledge of the rudiments of music (with the exception of key signatures and intervals) is necessary as a basis for Chapter I. However, if the student lacks this foundation, a summary of notation may be found in the Appendix, page 595.

This preliminary information should be deduced from an examination of literature used by the student rather than learned as an isolated body of facts unrelated to real music. The time required for assimilation of this basic material will vary with the age level, maturity, and experience of the student.

Chapter I

THE I AND V CHORDS

Harmony deals with the structure and relationship of tonal combinations known as *chords*. Principles of harmony are based primarily upon musical practice as found in the works of great composers. In this study we shall discover some of these principles and develop skills in their application in order to understand and express more intelligently the meaning that great music has for everyone.

Our conception of harmony, however, will include more than techniques of writing. It will also include hearing, singing, and playing what is written and the understanding of structural growth through analysis and creative writing.

Since, then, this study of musical structures will be based upon musical practice, let us begin by singing the following melody:

Ex. 1

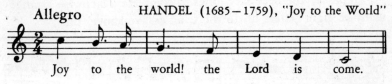

Repeat this melody in fragments of one, two, and three measures, starting each time from the beginning. None of these fragments sounds complete. Obviously it is necessary to continue to the final C for a completely satisfactory ending. All these tones seem drawn to this C as to a magnet. For this reason all these tones are said to be related to C and, consequently, to each other. Any group of tones thus drawn to a central tone is called a *key,* and the point of complete repose at the end is called the *key tone.* This relationship of the tones of a key to their key tone establishes the accepted

3

principle of *tonality* in music. The negation of this principle in some contemporary music is known as *atonality*.

Sing the following melody[1] and find its point of repose, or key tone.

Ex. 2   DANIEL DECATUR EMMETT, *Dixie*

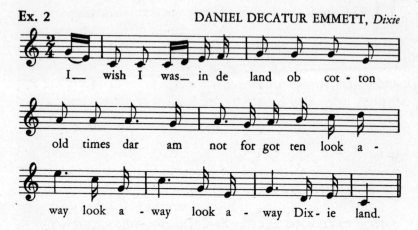

I— wish I was— in de land ob cot - ton old times dar am not for got ten look a - way look a - way look a - way Dix- ie land.

Using this key tone as a starting point, select from the melody (Example 2) the necessary tones to complete a stepwise arrangement of eight letters up to the C an octave above, thus:

Ex. 3

C	D	E	F	G	A	B	C
1	2	3	4	5	6	7	8
do	re	mi	fa	sol	la		ti	do

When the tones of the key are arranged stepwise, beginning with the key tone, they form a *scale*, so called from the Latin word *scala*, a ladder. This scale is called *major* because of its individual tone

---

[1] See also the initial phrase of *The First Nöel*.

pattern. (See Chapter IX.) Now compare the pitches of the two melodies in Examples 1 and 2. Evidently they are made up of the same tones, the white keys of the piano. These white keys, then, represent both the key of C major and the scale of C major, having C as their common center or point of repose.

Consider again the first three notes of *Dixie* in Example 2:

Ex. 4

Played or sung together, they form a *chord,* a combination of three or more tones that can be arranged on adjacent lines or spaces. Arrange measures 5 and 6 in the same way, thus:

Ex. 5

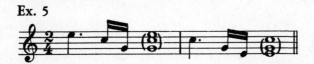

Note that the chords in Examples 4 and 5 are made up of the same letters, C–E–G, arranged differently. Such three-tone chords are called *triads,* and it should be noted that the letters of chords (for example, C–E–G) are always named in ascending order so that the first note mentioned will be the lowest on the staff. When the three tones of a triad are as close together as possible, that is, on consecutive lines or spaces (Example 4), the lowest tone is called the *root,* and the chord is named from this *root tone.* The different positions of the chord, as in Example 5, continue to be named from this same root even when the tones are differently spaced. Hence, these are all C chords in different positions. These chords can obviously be arranged in still other ways, using wider spacing between the tones, as, for example, C–G–E, G–E–C. Comparable chords can be built on other notes of the scale, as, D–A–F, B–D–G.

In addition to the letter name, a chord also has a number name that corresponds to the scale number of its root. Since a triad may be built on each tone of the scale, in the key of C major the C triad is I because C is the key tone of that scale, the D triad is II because D is its second note, and so on. Since there are seven tones in the scale, there will therefore be seven possible triads in any given scale.

The I chord is the basis for our feeling of key or tonality in music. Compositions usually begin and end on this chord. Test this by deciding whether the first and the last tones of the following melodies are parts of the I chord (*i.e.* 1, 3, or 5 of the scale — do, mi, or sol): *America, The Star Spangled Banner, Annie Laurie,* and other familiar tunes. Note also that these and all other melodies are made up of only three kinds of progressions — steps (scale), skips (chord), or repeated tones used either alone or in combination. These progressions are illustrated in the following melodies:

Ex. 6

(a) Scale

(b) Chords

(c) Repeated tones

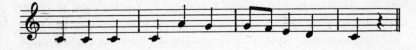

However, most melodies are constructed of scale progressions with an occasional skip.

Sing this melody from Schubert's Song Cycle, *The Maid of the Mill:*

Ex. 7

This fragment is made up chiefly of skips that suggest a definite harmonic background. Outline the passage thus:

Ex. 8

The root of the first chord is C and that of the second chord G. Since C and G are 1 and 5 in the scale (that is, the first and fifth tones of the scale of C), the chords built on these tones also are designated I and V. These chords form the harmonic background of the melody. Remember the I and the V, for they are the most frequently used chords in music. The themes of many works in musical literature consist of skips between tones of these chords.

But there are other interesting points about this melody, aside from its harmonic background, dealing with the *form,* or arrangement, of the musical material. Note that the melody begins and ends on tones of the I chord. It is four measures in length and expresses a complete musical thought. These four measures comprise a *phrase* in music; in this case the phrase is repeated for the sake of emphasis and clarity.

The end of a musical phrase is called a *cadence,* from the Latin word *cadere* (to fall), referring to the inflection of the voice at the end of a sentence. Cadences usually occur on an accented beat of the measure, as does this one. Experiment by ending this melody on 3 or 5 of the scale and compare each with Schubert's ending. Explain the relative value of each ending.

There are various types of cadences in music. This cadence is called a *perfect authentic cadence* — perfect because the melody comes to complete repose on the key tone C, and *authentic* because the chords V–I definitely establish the tonality or key. Compositions usually end thus, although other melodic and harmonic endings are possible.

In writing songs, the composer must first determine where the accented syllables occur in the words of the poem. Recite some poetry rhythmically, exaggerating or emphasizing the stressed syllables. This emphasis on accents is called scanning, or *scansion,* which can be indicated in music by note values. Both are illustrated in the following example:

Ex. 9   *(a)*   ᴜ — ᴜ — ᴜ — ᴜ —
Good people all, of every sort,
ᴜ — ᴜ — ᴜ — (ᴜ —)
Give ear unto my song;
ᴜ — ᴜ — ᴜ — ᴜ —
And if you find it wondrous short —
ᴜ — ᴜ — ᴜ — (ᴜ —)
It can not hold you long.

— *Oliver Goldsmith*

(b)

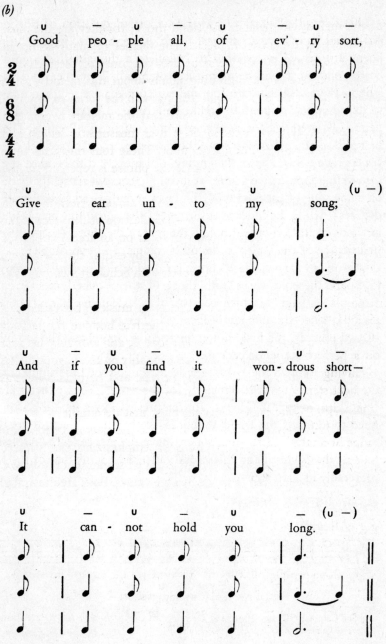

These considerations lead to the important question of poetic *meter* and its relation to musical *form*.[2] Note that two lines of the poem are generally required to complete a thought that would correspond to a phrase in music, commonly four measures in length. Note also that two four-measure phrases are required here to express the complete thought. This form in music is called a *period*. It is equivalent to a compound sentence in English. The first phrase of a period is termed the *antecedent,* and the second, the *consequent phrase*. Since the ending, or cadence, at the end of the second line should give a sense of incompleteness, it is usually made on some tone of the V chord (the fifth, seventh, and second scale degrees), while the cadence at the end of the fourth line may be on any tone of the I chord, although the root of the chord (that is, the first degree of the scale) is the most common. The incomplete cadence, on any tone of the V chord, is called a *half-* or *semi-cadence*. Compare these cadences with those of the Schubert melody in Example 7, page 7, which consists of a repeated phrase (not a period), since the melody is identical. The period, then, consists of two phrases, the first ending on a semi-cadence, and the second on a perfect authentic cadence.

Having scanned the poem and decided upon the time signature, the next step is to write a melody for the words, using either scale line, skips, or repeated tones. For the present, skips should be confined to tones of the I and V chords. Determine a practical vocal range by analysis of familiar songs. Make the first cadence on some tone of the V chord and the second cadence on some tone of the I, preferably its root, thus:

Ex. 10

Allegretto

Good peo-ple all of ev'- ry sort, Give ear un-to my song;

---

[2] See Calvin S. Brown, *Music and Literature: a Comparison of the Arts*. Athens, Ga.: The University of Georgia Press, 1948.

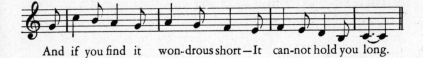

And if you find it won-drous short—It can-not hold you long.

It would also have been possible to make the second phrase a repetition of the first phrase with a new ending, thus:

Ex. 11

And if you find it won-drous short—It can-not hold you long.

Note that these two phrases form a *period.* When the two phrases of a period begin alike, the period is said to be *parallel* as in Example 11; when they begin differently, the period is said to be *contrasting* as in Example 10.

To summarize: the melody may be made either from consecutive scale tones, chord tones, or repeated tones or a combination of these progressions. Scanning the words will indicate the poetic meter, which may be expressed by several different time signatures. The cadences, of course, will occur at the end of the second and the fourth lines in simple four-line stanzas. These cadences are the punctuation marks of music and occur naturally at the end of the thought expressed by the words. For present purposes an incomplete cadence may be defined as a pause on some tone of the V (G) chord, and a complete cadence as a pause on some tone of the I (C) chord, preferably its root (the key tone of the scale). However, it should be noted that the third or the fifth of the scale is used sometimes as either an incomplete or complete cadence.

Probably the simplest melody is one made up entirely of chord skips, but some scale progressions and repeated tones are usually necessary for variety and balance. Experiment with various kinds of melodic progressions until this balance is achieved. The ear is the final arbiter.

Review:

1. What a key and scale are.
2. How the tones of the key and scale are related.
3. What the central tone or point of repose in a key is called.
4. What chords and triads are.
5. What the basic tone of a chord is called.
6. How a chord or triad is named.
7. Two ways of naming a chord.
8. What chord is the basis for our feeling of key or tonality.
9. What are the most frequently used triads in music.
10. What form in music is.
11. Why a cadence is so named.
12. The difference between a semi- and a perfect cadence.
13. How to scan a poem for musical setting.
14. What a phrase and a period are.
15. What makes a period parallel or contrasting.
16. Three types of melodic progressions.

For Further Study, Determine:

1. The difference between a key and a scale.
2. On what scale tones familiar melodies begin and end.
3. The distinction between chord and triad.
4. The difference between key tone and root.
5. How to find the root of a chord.
6. Why compositions usually begin and end on the I chord.
7. Which tone of the I chord makes the most complete ending for a melody.
8. Why music has form.
9. How to choose the best time signature for a melody.
10. The difference between a period and a repeated phrase.
11. The range and cadences of familiar tunes.
12. Cadences that differ from those described above.

I — Assignment for Writing

1. Scan the following stanzas and write melodies for one or more of them in either $\frac{2}{4}, \frac{4}{4}, \frac{6}{8}$ in the key of C major or other familiar keys. Use the scale, repeated tones, or skips in the I and V chords.

(*a*)   In Islington there was a Man,
        Of whom the world might say,
     That still a godly race he ran
        Whene'er he went to pray.
   Elegy on the Death of a Mad Dog — Oliver Goldsmith

(*b*)   John Gilpin was a citizen
        Of credit and renown,
     A train-band Captain eke was he
        Of famous London town.
          John Gilpin — William Cowper

(*c*)   No stir in the air, no stir in the sea,
     The ship was still as she could be;
     Her sails from heaven received no motion;
     Her keel was steady in the ocean.
          Inchcape Rock — Robert Southey

(*d*)   O suns and skies and clouds of June,
        And flowers of June together,
     Ye cannot rival for one hour
        October's bright blue weather.
     October's Bright Blue Weather — H. H.

(*e*)   I come from haunts of coot and hern,
        I make a sudden sally,
     And sparkle out among the fern,
        To bicker down a valley.
          The Brook — Alfred, Lord Tennyson

(*f*)   The splendor falls on castle walls
        And snowy summits old in story:
     The long light shakes across the lakes,
        And the wild cataract leaps in glory.
          Blow, Bugle, Blow — Alfred, Lord Tennyson

(*g*)   Little one, come to my knee!
        Hark, how the rain is pouring
     Over the roof, in the pitch-black night,
        And the wind in the woods a-roaring!
          A Night With A Wolf — Bayard Taylor

2. Make a list of ten songs indicating, by number or syllable, the first and last tone of each.

3. Write some original instrumental melodies in repeated phrase or period form, using only quarter and eighth notes, except in the last measure. (Optional.)

II — Assignment for Playing

1. Play familiar melodies by ear in the key of C major. (Other keys optional.)

2. Improvise simple melodies in period or repeated-phrase form in the key of C major. (Other keys optional.)

3. Play the I–V–I chords in the key of C major, or other familiar keys, with the root in the left hand and the three upper voices in the right hand. Play in three positions with the root, third, and fifth in the soprano.

4. Harmonize one of the following tunes, using only the I and the V chords, one or two chords to each measure, thus:

Fine (feé-nay), from the Italian, meaning *end* or *close.*
**D.C., *Da capo* (dah-kah'-po), from the Italian, meaning *from the beginning.*

Andante — German Folk Song

(c)

Reprinted by permission from 140 Folk-Songs, Concord Series No. 3. Published and copyrighted by the E. C. Schirmer Music Company.

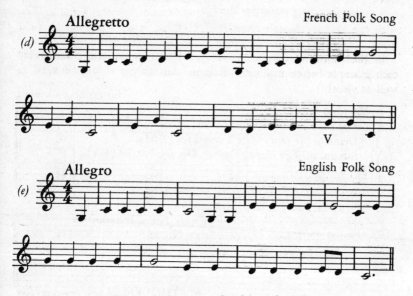

Allegretto — French Folk Song

(d)

Allegro — English Folk Song

(e)

III — Assignment for Listening

1. *Oral dictation.*

Note to the instructor. The following melodies are cited primarily for recognition of cadences and form. One or more of the simpler melodies might also be written by the class from memory in order to emphasize points of melodic and formal construction. Numbers in parentheses refer in all cases to measures, numbering the first complete measure as one.

140 Folk-Songs. Concord Series No. 3. Nos. 2, 7, 27, 29.

Folk Song Sight Singing Series: Book I, Nos. 16, 23, 25, 33, 45, 50, 71.

Mendelssohn, *The Stormy Spring*, Op. 71, No. 2 (1-4).
Beethoven, *Third Symphony*, Op. 55, Allegro con brio (1-6).

2. *Written dictation (melody, bass, and name of chord).*

Note to the instructor. In dictating it is essential to play the music in phrase lengths and have the class memorize the complete musical thought before writing the bass and soprano. The name of the chord may be written as the chord is being played. Observe an even tempo in playing.

Wagner, *Parsifal*, Faith Motive.
Beethoven, *Fidelio Overture* (1-4).
Schubert, *The Sailor* (4-12).
See also *Assignment for Analysis.*

IV — Assignment for Analysis

In the following passages identify cadences, form, and chords. Play each example before making a decision. All analysis should be aural as well as visual.

1. *For form only:*
   The Blue Bells of Scotland (1-8).
   Drink to Me Only With Thine Eyes (1-8).
   Schumann, *The Happy Farmer*, Op. 68, No. 10 (1-4).

2. *For chords and form:*
   Beethoven, *Fidelio Overture*, principal theme.
   Wagner, *Parsifal*, Faith Motive.
   Mendelssohn, *Song Without Words*, No. 3, Introduction.
   Zelter, *Folk Song (Liederschatz)*, No. 88.
   Brahms, *Sapphic Ode* (1-4).

BEETHOVEN, *Fidelio Overture* [E]*

Allegro

(a)

* The letter in brackets indicates the original key.

WAGNER, *Parsifal,* Faith Motive [A♭]

Lento

(b)

MENDELSSOHN, *Song Without Words,* No. 3 [A]

Molto allegro e vivace

(c)

Allegro

MOZART, *Rondo*

(d)

ZELTER, Folk Song

Chapter II

THE V₇ CHORD

Ex. 12
Moderato

German Folk Song

SING, or play, this folk song and identify the accompanying chords. Spell each chord upward from its root and place the appropriate Roman numeral under its bass tone. In measure 3, an F is added to the G chord, thus:

Ex. 13

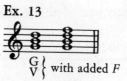

$\begin{smallmatrix}G\\V\end{smallmatrix}$ with added *F*

Compare these two chords by singing them in parts, noting their relative tension. Clearly the added F gives to the chord a sense of greater activity·or expectancy that demands satisfaction. Such a group of active tones is *dissonant* and may be satisfied, or *resolved,* by moving to a group of inactive, or *consonant,* tones. Dissonant combinations form *discords* and consonant combinations form *concords* in music. In this case the dissonant G–B–D–F chord is resolved by progressing to the nearest tones of the consonant C–E–G chord. Note especially the tendency of the chord seventh (F) to move down to the third (E) of the I chord.

This new combination of tones (G–B–D–F) is one of the most frequently used chords in music, especially as a substitute for its triad (G–B–D). It will be recalled that three-tone chords (made of alternate staff letters) are called *triads*. The staff distance between each tone is an *interval*, which is named by counting upward from its lowest tone as 1. Thus the staff distances or intervals in the G triad would be a third (G–B) and a fifth (G–D). The added F would be a seventh above the root G, thus:

Ex. 14

The chord G–B–D–F is called a *seventh-chord*, as the seventh (G–F) is the largest interval that it contains. It would be symbolized G_7, or V_7, in the key of C major.

Experiment by adding a seventh to each triad in the C major scale. Note that they are all dissonant chords demanding resolution. Other seventh chords will be discussed and used later, but, for the present, only the extension of the V triad, namely the V_7 chord, will be used.

Sing these two melodies and determine the chord background of each measure. Locate the cadences and name the form of each melody.

Ex. 15

MOZART, *Piano Sonata*, K547

Allegro

(a)

Lively   American Folk Song, *Ain't Gonna Rain* (1870)*

(b)

*There are many Negro and mountain versions of this Iowa and Nebraska dance song, which originally came west from Kentucky and other southern states. See Carl Sandburg, *American Songbag*. New York: Harcourt, Brace and Company, 1927.

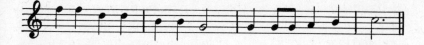

Returning to Example 12, page 19, note that the tones of the chord in the bass are arranged in a pattern or design called an *accompaniment figure*. This figure supplies the harmonic and rhythmic background, which enhances the effect of the melody. Recall other accompaniment figures frequently used for the march, waltz, tango, and other dances. Find examples of these rhythms and note how important the accompaniment is in carrying out the mood of the melody.

All chord progressions can be arranged as accompaniment figures. One of the simplest figures is made by using the tones of the chord consecutively instead of simultaneously, as in Example 12, page 19. Accompaniment figures are often given to the left hand while the right hand plays the melody. At present, it is advisable to keep the original accompaniment pattern without change for the entire melody.

Continuing the melody of Example 12, the implied chords should first be sketched, then arranged as an accompaniment figure, thus:

Ex. 16

Note that the D of the G₇ chord is omitted in the bass of measure 1 since the accompaniment is only a three-note figure. Here the missing tone D occurs in the melody. However, the chord's fifth is often omitted in a seventh chord as it adds less to the tonal color than the chord's third or seventh does. Note also that the preliminary beat, before measure 1, is not harmonized. Further, observe that the grouping of the accompaniment figure precludes the use of more than two chords to a measure.

It is also desirable, in writing an accompaniment, to connect the chords smoothly by moving to the nearest possible position of the chord desired. To facilitate this smoothness, the third of any chord may be omitted in the accompaniment when it is present in the melody, thus:

Ex. 17

Sing the following melody, noting its harmonic background. The fifth (C–G) is used as an accompaniment to suggest the sound of the Scottish bagpipes, thus:

Ex. 18   Scotch Folk Song

The Camp-bells are com-ing O - ho, O-ho! The

IV   (See Chapter III)

The melody tones, marked * in Examples 17 and 18, do not belong to the chord of the measure. Note that they are between two chord tones and adjacent to them on the staff. These unaccented tones, which are foreign because they do not belong to the chord, will be discussed more fully in Chapter III. For the present, in harmonizing melodies, choose chords for the accented beats only.

Review:

    1. How the V₇ chord is constructed.

    2. What is meant by consonance and dissonance.

    3. What is meant by resolution and how the chord seventh usually resolves.

    4. Why G–B–D–F is called the G₇ chord.

    5. What tone of the V₇ chord may be omitted.

    6. What is meant by an accompaniment figure.

    7. The function of an accompaniment figure.

    8. How the tones of an accompaniment figure are determined.

    9. When the chord third or fifth may be omitted.

    10. What is meant by a "foreign tone."

    11. What tones, foreign to a chord, may be used against it in a melody.

For Further Study, Determine:

    1. Some distinctions between triads and seventh-chords.

    2. Different kinds of accompaniment figures.

    3. One of the functions of foreign tones.

    4. The relation of melodic skips to the harmonic background.

    5. Why the fifth, C–G, suggests the bagpipes.

    6. How to name the chord G–B–D–F–A.

I — Assignment for Writing

    1. Scan the following stanzas and write melodies for one or more of them in ²⁄₄, ⁴⁄₄, or ⁶⁄₈ in the key of C major. (Other keys optional.) Skips in the melody will consist of the scale, repeated tones, or the I, V, or V₇ chords.

        (*a*)   Ye mariners of Spain,
               Bend strongly on your oars,
               And bring my love again, —
               For he lies among the Moors!
       Song of the Galley — Spanish Ballads, 16th Century
                   (Translated by John Gibson Lockhart)

        (*b*)   If thou art sleeping, maiden,
               Awake and open thy door.
            'Tis the break of day, and we must away
               O'er meadow, and mount, and moor.
              Song — Gil Vicente, 16th Century
            (Translated by Henry Wadsworth Longfellow)

(*c*) Gladly to Allah's dwelling
       Yonder would I take flight;
       There will the darkness vanish,
       There will my eyes have sight.

       Allah — Siegfried Mahlmann
       (*Translated by H. W. Longfellow*)

(*d*) Is this the way I was going?
       Whither, O brooklet, say!
       Thou hast, with thy soft murmur,
       Murmured my senses away.[1]

       Whither? — Wilhelm Muller
       (*Translated by H. W. Longfellow*)

(*e*) Out of my own great woe
       I make my little songs,
       Which rustle their feathers in throngs
       And beat on her heart even so.

       Proem — Heinrich Heine
       (*Translated by Elizabeth Barrett Browning*)

2. Write some original instrumental melodies (for piano, violin, or other instruments played by members of the class).

3. Harmonize at least one of the following melodies, using the style of accompaniment in Example 12, page 19.

<hr>

[1] This is part of Schubert's song, *Whither?*, the beginning of which was quoted in Example 7.

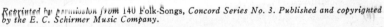

II — Assignment for Playing

1. Play the melody of *Three Blind Mice* by ear in the key of C major. Harmonize it with the I and V₇ chords, using the accompaniment of Example 12.

2. Improvise simple melodies in period or repeated-phrase form in the key of C major (other keys optional). See Example 15.

3. Play the I–V₇–I chords in all the melodic positions as given below. Note the omitted fifth in the V₇ chord.

(possibly)

4. Harmonize one or more of the melodies in the *Assignment for Writing* (3) above, or select from the following melodies, using the style of accompaniment in Example 12.

> *140 Folk-Songs.* Concord Series No. 3. Nos. 9, 19, 24 (1-8), 27, 75, 80.
>
> *Folk Song Sight Singing Series:* Book IV, Nos. 80-86.

III — Assignment for Listening

1. *Oral dictation:* harmonic recognition only. Identify chords by letter and Roman numeral.

> Kuhlau, *Sonatina,* Op. 55, No. 1, Vivace (1-8).
> Schubert, *The Linden Tree* (9-16),
> > *Wandering* (1-7),
> > *German Dance,* Op. 33, No. 7 (1-8).
> Chopin, *Preludes,* Nos. 7 and 15;
> > *Waltzes,* Op. 34, No. 1, D flat (1-8),
> > Op. 69, No. 1 (65-72),
> > Op. 70, No. 1 (1-16),
> > Op. 70, No. 3 (49-56);
> > *Mazurka,* Op. 50, No. 2, D flat (1-8).
> Haydn, *Surprise Symphony,* Menuetto (1-8).
> Mozart, *Piano Sonata, F Major,* K322, Finale (15-22).
> Beethoven, *Symphony III,* Op. 55, Trio (1-31);
> > *Symphony IV,* Op. 60, Menuetto (1-4);
> > *Symphony V,* Op. 67, Finale (26-34).

2. *Written dictation* (*bass, melody, and name of chord*). Transpose all examples to C major.

> *Golden Book: Alouette,* p. 128;
> > *Farewell to Summer,* p. 91.
> *Sing!: Michael Finnigan,* p. 79.
> Beethoven, *Symphony V,* Op. 67, Finale (1-4).
> Mozart, *Marriage of Figaro,* No. 25, $\frac{3}{4}$ section (1-4).

IV — Assignment for Analysis

Kuhlau, *Sonatina,* Op. 55, No. 1, Allegro and Vivace.
Wagner, *Flying Dutchman Overture,* Senta Motive.
Schubert, *Unfinished Symphony,* First Movement, subordinate theme.
Brahms, *Sapphic Ode* (1-4).
Beethoven, *Symphony V,* Op. 67, Finale (1-4).

In the following passages identify cadences, form, and chords:[2]

BEETHOVEN, *Fifth Symphony,* Op. 67, Finale

Allegro

SCHUBERT, *Unfinished Symphony* [G]

Allegro moderato

WAGNER, *Flying Dutchman,* Motive of Redemption [F]

Andante

---

[2] These passages contain some foreign (nonharmonic) tones to be discussed in subsequent chapters beginning with Chapter III.

Allegretto   MOZART, *Jupiter Symphony*, K551, Trio

(Chap. X)

Vivace   KUHLAU, *Sonatina* Op. 55, No. 1, Finale

Chapter III

THE IV CHORD

Ex. 19

HANDEL (1685–1759) [D]

THESE ARE the concluding chords of the "Hallelujah Chorus" from Handel's oratorio, *Messiah*. Sing them in parts, noting the strong cadential effect. Determine the roots of these chords, find the scale number of each root, and give the letter and number names of both chords. This use of the IV–I is known as the *perfect plagal*[1] *cadence.* Here it serves as a substitute for the usual perfect authentic cadence. It is added to the ending of hymns for the word "amen," and is, therefore, also known as the *amen cadence.* Compare it with the perfect authentic cadence by singing both in parts, thus:

Ex. 20

---

[1] From the Greek *plagios,* meaning sidewise and, hence, indirect.

The difference in effect is due to the first chord in each cadence. Obviously the dissonant V_7 chord creates more tension than the consonant IV chord.

The IV chord is perhaps more often used during a phrase than in a cadence, as shown in this Haydn minuet from his fourth *London Symphony*.[2]

Ex. 21

Allegro   HAYDN, *Fourth London Symphony*, Minuet [Bb]

Sing the phrase in two parts — the melody an octave lower, and the bass as written. Name the chords by letter and number, noting especially the chord in measure 2.

This new IV (F) chord, with the I and V, are the most frequently used chords in music, possibly because they are the determinate chords of tonality (referred to in Chapter I), and, as such, are known as tonal chords. Their relationship may be likened to the sides of a triangle, of which the I chord is the base and the IV and V chords are the two sides, thus:

Ex. 22

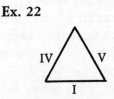

---

[2] So called because it was the fourth in a set of twelve symphonies written for the London Philharmonic Orchestra in 1792 and 1794. They are also known by the name of the orchestra's manager, Salomon.

It will be found later that all other chords are classified as belonging to the I, IV, or V types, according to their use.

All combinations of the I–IV–V chords are possible. However, when the IV and the V chords are used together, the IV chord usually precedes the V. Observe that in the IV–V progression (Example 21, measures 2, 3) the melody moves in contrary motion to the bass. This is also true of the V–IV progression.

The following lively Polish dance contains some interesting new points.

Ex. 23

Vivo e risoluto   CHOPIN, *Mazurka*, Op. 17, No. 1 [B♭]

Sing the melody (an octave lower) with the chord roots as before. Note that the tones marked thus * do not belong to the chord of the measure. Such foreign, or *nonharmonic,* tones are frequently used for embellishment and are named according to their usage. In measure 1, the foreign tones return to the same chord tone; they are then called *neighboring tones.* In measure 3, they pass on to the next chord tone, and are then known as *passing tones.* Since both neighboring and passing tones are adjacent to chord tones, they can be distinguished only by their resolution. They may be either single tones, as the A in measure 1, or thirds and sixths, as the other non-harmonic tones in this passage.

Observe that in measure 1, the lower neighbors (D–F) use accidentals. Note that in playing the passage without the accidentals an equally satisfactory effect may be achieved. Both forms are therefore possible, but, since Bach's time (1685-1750), composers have generally used accidentals for lower neighbors, making them a half step below chord tones.[3]

Music using accidentals foreign to the scale is called *chromatic* (from *chromo,* meaning color), because these alterations add new tonal tints. Music made up entirely of scale tones without additional accidentals is called *diatonic* (from *dia,* meaning through or related to the tonic, which is another term for the key tone of the scale to be discussed in Chapter IX).

Identify the use of passing and neighboring tones in the following folk song:

Ex. 24

In Example 24, compare measures 1 and 2 with measures 3 and 4, and also 5 and 6 with 7 and 8, noting the effect of the different embellishments. Experiment in using accidentals for the lower neighbors (A–C) in measure 2. Are they an improvement? Evidently their use is entirely optional. Observe also the scales in

---

[3] The only exception being in cases where the lower half-step neighbor is also a scale step, as, for example, C–B–C and F–E–F.

measures 3 and 7 formed by using passing tones in the I and the V chords, two of the passing tones being consecutive. Are these non-harmonic tones accented (on the beat), or unaccented (between the beats)? Clearly their rhythmic location is also optional.

Consider the following melody in relation to the use of the IV chord and nonharmonic tones:

Ex. 25
Moderato   German Folk Song

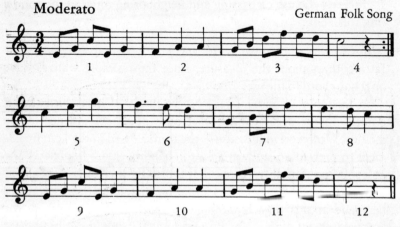

Hear the melody and determine the chords outlined by its skips. In the first and last phrases, the harmonic background is clearly I–IV–V₇–I, using one chord for each measure. The skip, D–G, (measures 6 and 7), suggests this solution for the second phrase: I–V₇–V₇–I. Test this by singing the chord roots as the melody is played or sung. In contrast to this harmonic background, the non-harmonic tone E (measures 3, 6, and 11) stands out clearly. What other nonharmonic tone occurs in measure 8? Note that the skips in this melody outline the chords of its harmonic background. This is a basic principle of harmonization whose application will aid greatly in the solution of future problems.

Continue by writing an accompaniment for the melody, using the following waltz pattern.

Ex. 26

Melody

Chords

Accompaniment

C I   IV

In the waltz accompaniment, the *first* bass note is regarded as lasting throughout the measure, since most simple waltzes have only one chord to the measure.

In Example 26, measure 1, observe that the chord-third (E) is omitted in the accompaniment because of its prominence in the melody. However, in measure 2, the third is used in the accompaniment to prevent an awkward shift in hand position. In general, the best solution is usually the one that avoids these changes of register. There are so many possibilities that no unqualified statement can be made at this time regarding the spacing of the tones in the accompaniment figure. In most instances it will be a matter of taste rather than of rule.

Study this completed accompaniment (Example 27) carefully and decide why the tones of the accompaniment figure are arranged thus:

Ex. 27

Moderato

I   IV   V₇   I   *Fine*
C   F   G₇   C

It is important to note the directions *fine* and *D.C. al fine* at the end of the phrases, which mean, in this case, that phrase 1 is played again after phrase 2. Play the dance both with and without this final repetition of phrase 1. The repetition of the phrase at the end gives a greater degree of satisfaction, and creates one of the basic patterns of musical form to be found in the simplest folk song and the most elaborate symphony. It is called the *A–B–A* form because of the arrangement of the phrases — statement, contrast, and re-statement. Including all repetitions, the form of this folk song (Example 27) would be symbolized *A* (*A*)–*B–A*. This design is also known as a *ternary* form or a *three-part* song form.

To summarize the material of this chapter: the IV is used to harmonize the fourth, sixth, or eighth scale step. It may be used in any combination with the I and V or V_7 chords. The melody and roots of chords built on adjacent staff degrees should move in contrary motion. This, at present, applies to the IV–V and V–IV progressions.

Melodies are often embellished by nonharmonic tones called *passing* or *neighboring tones*, so named from their different step-wise resolutions. Chord skips may be filled in with passing tones, and repeated tones embellished by upper and lower neighboring tones. The rhythmic location of these foreign tones and the use of accidentals for lower neighbors are both optional.

Diatonic music consists predominantly of scale tones, whereas chromatic music uses many accidentals foreign to the scale.

The *A–B–A* form (statement, contrast, and restatement) is the most frequently used form in music, probably because of its satisfactory balance.

Review:

1. What the plagal cadence is and how it is used.
2. What scale steps the IV chord harmonizes.
3. The relative importance of the IV chord in the key.
4. The function of nonharmonic foreign tones.
5. The distinction between passing and neighboring tones.
6. What is meant by diatonic and chromatic music.
7. When to make embellishments chromatic.
8. How to write a waltz accompaniment.
9. The principle of the *A–B–A* form.
10. Another name for the plagal cadence.
11. The rhythmic location of nonharmonic tones.

For Further Study, Determine:

1. Whether the plagal cadence must be preceded by the authentic cadence.
2. Which cadence is most used as an ending.
3. Two other names for the *A–B–A* form.
4. Why the *A–B–A* is the most satisfying form.
5. Which are more dissonant, accented or unaccented nonharmonic tones, and why.
6. Why the melody tones of chords built on adjacent staff degrees usually move in contrary motion to their roots.
7. What pattern results from inserting passing notes between the tones of the I chord.
8. Between what tones of a chord consecutive diatonic passing tones are possible.

I — Assignment for Writing

1. Scan the following stanzas and write melodies for one or more of them in $\frac{2}{4}$, $\frac{4}{4}$, $\frac{6}{8}$, or $\frac{6}{4}$ in the key of C major (other keys optional). Aside from scale passages and repeated tones, the melodies may skip in the I, V, V_7, or IV chords. (Piano accompaniment optional.)

> (a) Who has seen the wind?
> Neither you nor I:
> But when the trees bow down their heads,
> The wind is passing by.
> *Who Has Seen the Wind? — Christina Rosetti*

(*b*)   The morns are meeker than they were,
        The nuts are getting brown;
        The berry's cheek is plumper,
        The rose is out of town.

                        Autumn — Emily Dickinson[4]

(*c*)   I am fevered with the sunset,
        I am fretful with the bay,
        For the wander-thirst is on me
        And my soul is in Cathay.

                        The Sea Gypsy — Richard Hovey[5]

(*d*)   The day is done, and the darkness
        Falls from from the wings of Night,
        As a feather is wafted downward
        From an eagle in his flight.

                        The Day Is Done — H. W. Longfellow

(*e*)   Oh, I'm in love with the janitor's boy,
        And the janitor's boy loves me;
        He's going to hunt for a desert isle
        In our geography.

                        The Janitor's Boy — Nathalia Crane[6]

2. Experiment with writing instrumental melodies in phrase and period form. Use neighboring and passing tones. Accompaniment optional.

3. Harmonize at least one of the following melodies, using the accompaniment figure of Example 27, page 35:

Moderato   SCHUBERT, *Valses Nobles*, Op. 77, No. 6 [C]

*Suspension, a delayed chord tone (see Chapter IV).

---

[4] From *Poems and Poems*, published by Little, Brown & Company, Boston.
[5] Reprinted by permission of Dodd, Mead & Company, Inc.
[6] From *The Janitor's Boy and Other Poems* by Nathalia Crane, published by Albert and Charles Boni, 1924.

Moderato   Folk Song

Andante   MOZART, *Berceuse* [F]

(See Ex. 12)

Moderato   German Folk Song

SCHUBERT, *Valse Nobles*, No. 12
Vivo
(i)

WEBER, *Invitation to the Dance*
Allegro vivace
(j)

See also:
> *140 Folk-Songs.* Concord Series No. 3. Nos. 22, 70, 77, 105, 108,
> 123.
> *Foresman III,* p. 94, 95, 103.
> *Folk Song Sight Singing Series:* Books I-III.
> Melodies in *Assignment for Playing* below.

II — Assignment for Playing

1. Improvise phrases in ¾. Experiment with passing and neighboring tones, first in quarters and then in eighth notes. Use this chord background:

2. Play all the possible connections of the I, IV, and V_7 chords. The right hand should move stepwise, if possible; otherwise not more than a third, thus:

Note that (*a*) and (*b*) are alike except that (*b*) eliminates the middle tonic chord. Play these progressions in two other positions, and embellish stepwise melodic progressions with the neighboring tone corresponding to the direction of the melody.

3. Improvise melodies in period form as directed in Chapter I.

4. Play by ear the melody of *Santa Lucia*. Repeat with waltz accompaniment.

5. Harmonize one or more of the melodies in the *Assignment for Writing* (3) or select from the following melodies, using the style of accompaniment in Example 27, page 35.

> *140 Folk-Songs.* Concord Series No. 3. Nos. 78, 97, 117, 123, 140.
> *Folk Song Sight Singing Series:* Book I, Nos. 82, 83, 86, 95, 102, 105, 110.
> *Folk Song Sight Singing Series:* Book II, Nos. 3, 7, 11, 12, 37, 39, 48, 57, 64, 67, 78.

Using style of accompaniment in Example 12, page 19:

> *140 Folk-Songs.* Concord Series No. 3. Nos. 33, 80, 113, 122, 137.
> *Foresman III,* Nos. 50, 52, 63, 66, 85.

III — Assignment for Listening

1. *Oral dictation:* recognition only. Identify chords by letter, and Roman numeral.

> Weber, *Invitation to the Dance,* principal theme. (1-24)
> Bach, *Two-Part Invention No. 8* (1-2).
>> *Well-Tempered Clavier,* Vol. I, Fugue 3, subject.
> Mozart, *Jupiter Symphony,* Trio (1-8).
>> *Twelve Variations on a Minuet by Fischer.*
> Beethoven, *Minuet in G* (1-4).
> Kuhlau, *Sonatina,* Op. 20, No. 1, Rondo.
> *Golden Book: Dixie* (1-8), p. 10;
>> *There's Music in the Air,* p. 34;
>> *Flow Gently, Sweet Afton* (1-8), p. 35;
>> *Old Black Joe,* p. 25;
>> *The Bird's Return,* p. 91.
> Diller, *First Studies in Harmonic Analysis,* Nos. 9, 32, 33.
> See also the Strauss waltzes, *Blue Danube,* etc.

2. *Written dictation (bass, melody, and name of chords).*

> *Green Book Twice 55: Steal Away* (1-4), No. 49.
> *Golden Book: We Three Kings of Orient Are* (1-8), p. 74.
> *Foresman V, Speed Away,* p. 186.

Wagner, *Rheingold,* Walhalla Motive;
  Siegfried's Funeral March (C Major section).
Beethoven, *Egmont Overture,* Op. 84, second theme (1-4).
Folksongs of Many Peoples I: The Christ is Coming, p. 127;
    Glory to the Lord, p. 89.

IV — Assignment for Analysis

Analyze form, chords, and nonharmonic tones. Have each example played before deciding these points. After hearing the music, check the details by looking at the score.

Martini, *Gavotte* (1-8) (Note canon).
Chopin, *Mazurkas,* Op. 7, No. 1, p. 162, part 1,
    Op. 7, No. 3, p. 166, D flat section (1-4),
    Op. 30, No. 3, p. 188 (1-4);
  Polonaise, Op. 26, No. 2, D flat section (1-8).
Schubert, *Impromptu,* Op. 90, No. 4 (47-50),
    Op. 94, No. 3, D flat section (1-8);
  Valse Nobles, Op. 77, Nos. 1, 2.
Beethoven, *Bagatelle,* Op. 33, No. 2, Trio (1-7), p. 8;
  Egmont Overture, Op. 84, subordinate theme (1-4).
Schubert, *G Major Piano Sonata,* Op. 78, First Movement (1-4);
  Impromptu, Op. 142, No. 1 (45-50);
  The Wanderer, poco più mosso (1-4);
  Moment Musical, Op. 94, No. 6.
Haydn, *Symphony in C,* No. 7 (Peter's edition), Finale (1-4);
  Symphony in D, No. 10 (Peter's edition), Trio, part III.
Rossini, *Barber of Seville,* Largo al factorum (37-21 from end).
Schumann, *Vienna Carnival Scenes,* Op. 26, Scherzino (1-4).
Dvořák, *Humoresque,* Op. 101, No. 7 (1-8).
Wolf, *Weyla's Song* (1-4).

The following passages, for analysis, have been selected from the preceding list:

PADRE MARTINI, *Gavotte* [F]

(a) Grazioso

CHOPIN, *Waltz*, Op. 34, No. 1 [Ab]

Vivace

(b)

SCHUBERT, *Impromptu*, Op. 90, No. 4 [Ab]

Allegretto

(c)

BEETHOVEN, *Sonata*, Op. 2, No. 3, First Movement

Allegro con brio

(d)

SCHUBERT, *Impromptu,* Op. 142, No. 1 [F]

Allegro moderato

(e)

*Chromatic embellishment

SCHUMANN, *Vienna Carnival-Scene,* Op. 26, Scherzino [B♭]

Allegro grazioso

(f)

Poco lento e grazioso   DVOŘÁK, *Humoresque* [G♭]

(g)

Chapter IV

THE II₆ CHORD

Ex. 28

Moderato · German Folk Song

(a)

HAYDN (1732—1809), *Surprise Symphony*, (1791)

Andante

(b)

THESE PHRASES contain several new points of melodic and harmonic interest. Both are similar in motive development and harmonic background, but they differ in type of melodic progression and accompaniment figure. Explain both the similarities and differences.

Analyze the harmonic background of the folk song (Example 28 [*a*]) by spelling the chord of each measure upward from its lowest note. The chord of measure 1 is an incomplete C–E–G (I) chord, the missing E occurring in the melody. The chord in measure 2, however, is obviously not an F–A–C (IV) chord. To determine

46

the root in this case, it is necessary to arrange the letters of the chord in thirds, D–F–A (named the root, third, and fifth of the chord respectively). Hence, it is a D chord, although F appears as the lowest tone. When the lowest tone of a chord is any other than its root, the chord is said to be *inverted*. (See Chapter I, Example 5.) Since the third is the first chord tone above the root, this D chord is said to be in the *first inversion*. A triad in the first inversion is also called a *chord of the sixth,* because the distance from the bass tone up to the root (F to D) is an interval of a sixth, or six letters, irrespective of the actual distance, thus:

Ex. 29

Consequently, it is symbolized D_6 or II_6 in the key of C major. Since the remaining chords are in the fundamental position — that is, have the chord root in the bass — the chords of the entire phrase would be named thus: C–D₆–G₇–C, or I–II₆–V₇–I. Name the chords in the Haydn excerpt in the same manner.

In measure 2 of the folk song, page 46, substitute the F chord for the D_6. Compare the F and the D_6 chords, singing their tones consecutively, then simultaneously, thus:

Ex. 30

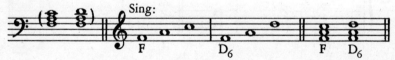

Observe that each of these chords, though similar, has a distinctive color or quality that will be discussed in Chapter VIII, page 107. On the basis of their similarity in construction and usage, they are classified in the same chord group. Thus the II_6 (F–A–D) may often be substituted for the IV (F–A–C). This is frequently done before the perfect authentic cadence, as in the following example.

Ex. 31

IV V₇ I   II₆ V₇ I   IV V V₇ I   II₆ V V₇ I

Sing the following vocal arrangement several times until the difference in quality between the IV and the II₆ chords is clear. Note especially the difference at (*b*), where the same melody tones are used for both chords:

Ex. 32

Soprano
Alto

Tenor
Bass

What chord follows the II₆ in Example 32 above? Try resolving the II₆ immediately to the IV and to the I chords. Which of these progressions (II₆–V, II₆–IV, II₆–I) sounds the most satisfactory? The II₆–IV gives the effect of a passing note in the melody, and the II₆–I is less satisfactory than the II₆–V. For the present then, we will follow the II₆ only by the V or V₇, as in Examples 28, 31, and

32. Note that the chords in Examples 31 and 32 are identical. Example 31 is in *close harmony* because the three upper tones of the chord are grouped within an octave. Otherwise, the grouping is called *open harmony,* as in Example 32. Open harmony, used in four-part vocal writing, will be discussed and will be used by the student beginning with Chapter XXI.

But the use of the II₆ is not the only new point in Example 28, page 46. Compare the tones in the melody with the harmonic background. Find those in the treble staff that do not belong to the chords outlined in the bass staff.[1] In measure 2, the first tone, E, is a foreign, or nonharmonic, tone. Show how its status changed in respect to the harmony after it was repeated from measure 1. Such a delayed tone, which does not change when the chord changes, is called a *suspension.* Locate suspensions in the following melodies:

Ex. 33

Moderato [A]   SCHUBERT, *Who is Sylvia?*

Largo [G]   HANDEL, *Xerxes*

Moderato   *Annie Laurie*

---

[1] The last tone (E) in measure 2 (Example 28, page 46) is a "free" nonharmonic tone and need not be discussed at present.

In *Annie Laurie,* note that the suspension (*b*) in measure 2 is made by holding over a passing tone instead of a chord tone. Recall other melodies containing suspensions.

Composers use suspensions, like passing and neighboring tones, as melodic embellishments. Suspensions heighten the effect of the proper chord by delaying its full realization temporarily. Here is how Haydn uses them in a variation of the melody from the *Surprise Symphony* (Example 28, page 46):

Ex. 34

melody shifted to bass

(If possible, study Haydn's use of embellishments in this entire movement. Note also the beautiful chromatic harmonization at the end.)

Try omitting suspensions in Examples 33 and 34, by playing the expected chord tone instead of the foreign tone. This simple alteration completely changes the character of the melody.

In all these examples, the suspensions resolve down stepwise. Ascending suspensions, called *retardations,* are comparatively rare. (See Beethoven, *Violin Sonata,* Op. 12, No. 1, Variation 4; Beethoven, *Piano Sonata,* Op. 26, Variations 3 and 4.)

Now consider how a composer chooses chords and uses the various types of nonharmonic tones in a melody. In case there is a choice of chord, the composer is guided largely by his ear. Through it he senses the need of harmonic variety. He may also prefer the color or quality of certain chords, as in the closing measures of the

Andante of Haydn's *Surprise Symphony*. The tones of the melody may strongly suggest the harmonic background. Thus, if the melody tones are C–E–G, he would naturally hear the C chord as the harmonic background unless he desired some special effect. All these factors influence his choice of chords in general. The same principles apply to a decision between the IV and the II₆.

There is, however, another vital factor considered by the composer in choosing chords, namely the *tempo* of the melody. This relation between tempo and chord might be termed *harmonic rhythm*.[2] Thus the composer is concerned not only with the quality of chords, but also with their rate of change within a given tempo. This principle has been observed in the previous use of accompaniment figures. In Chapter II the tempo, meter, and general character of the melodies suggested an accompaniment figure that permitted the use of two chords in each measure. Had the tempo been very slow, as many as six chords in the measure of $\frac{6}{8}$ would have been possible. In Chapter III waltz melodies that utilized one chord in each measure were considered. Conversely, a slower tempo would undoubtedly have required three or more chords in each measure. This is the problem of harmonization: to determine the number as well as the quality of chords to be used. It can be solved only by considering the tempo and mood of the melody in question. The general principle involved can be stated thus: use more chords in a slow tempo than in a fast one.[3]

As regards the use of nonharmonic tones, their location and type are defined by the chords chosen. In other words, they are always dependent on, and secondary to, the harmonic background and fit, like pieces of mosaic, into the general chord scheme after it has been selected.

Sing the melody in Example 35 and apply these principles to its harmonization.

---

[2] Cf. Walter Piston, *Harmony* (New York: W. W. Norton and Co., 1941), Chapter V.

[3] This new principle of harmonic rhythm has not as yet been universally accepted or applied.

Ex. 35

Begin by analyzing the form of the melody. Although the imperfect cadence in measure 4 is concealed by continuous eighth notes, the entire passage is undoubtedly a contrasting period ending with a perfect authentic cadence in measures 7 and 8. Considering the fairly rapid tempo, use only one chord for each measure. The skip, G–E, in the first measure suggests the C (I) chord which could be continued through measure 5. However, variety demands an earlier change of chord. The repeated tones in measures 2 and 3 can be heard as suspensions. Hence the problem is to find a chord for the second tones, D and B, of these measures. The G chord could be used for both, but it would be more interesting to use the D_6 for measure 2 and save the G for measure 3. Return to the C chord for measures 4 and 5. In measure 6, the skip, F–D, suggests the D_6, and this would be especially effective followed by the G_7 as a part of the perfect authentic cadence in measure 7.

To summarize, the following chords have been chosen:

Ex. 36

Sing the bass and melody together in the most convenient register. Experiment with other solutions. When the harmonic background has been definitely chosen, turn it into an accompaniment, using the figure in Example 28 (*a*), page 46, thus:

Ex. 37

Note how the spacing in the left hand is adjusted to the melody; note, too, that in all broken-chord accompaniment figures the lowest tone is regarded as the bass for the entire figure. (Measure 5 would probably sound better if the first tone in the left hand were E, making the chord C₆. See Chapter VI, page 76).

This type of broken chord accompaniment may also be modified for different meters, thus:

Ex. 38

These accompaniment figures are widely used for different tempi and types of melodies. Experiment in original work with these rhythmic variations and also with the use of suspensions by inserting repeated tones when the melody descends stepwise.

Review:

1. How a chord is inverted.
2. What the chord is called when the third is in the bass.
3. Another name for the first inversion of triads.
4. Where the II₆ is often substituted for the IV chord.
5. What chords usually precede and follow the D₆ (II₆).
6. What a suspension is.
7. How to make suspensions in a melody.
8. The effect of suspensions and why they are used.
9. Factors that influence composers in choosing chords.
10. Explain the meaning of "harmonic rhythm."

For Further Study, Determine:

1. Why chords are inverted.
2. How many inversions are possible for a triad; for a seventh chord.
3. Whether the bass and the root are always synonymous terms.
4. Points of similarity and difference between the suspension and other nonharmonic tones studied.
5. How familiar melodies containing suspensions would sound without them.
6. Other ways of breaking up chords into accompaniment figures.
7. How to choose a suitable accompaniment figure for a melody.

8. Why it is usually better for the accompaniment figure to remain unchanged in a short composition or in a complete section of a longer one.

9. Whether it is necessary to know the chord background of a melody in order to identify its nonharmonic tones.

10. An example of a retardation other than those cited in the text.

I — Assignment for Writing

1. Scan the following stanzas and write melodies for one or more of them in $\frac{2}{4}$, $\frac{3}{4}$, $\frac{4}{4}$, $\frac{6}{8}$, or $\frac{6}{4}$. In order to use $\frac{3}{4}$, scan first in $\frac{2}{4}$ or $\frac{4}{4}$, use the same position of bar lines, and adjust note values in each measure to fit $\frac{3}{4}$ meter. If an accompaniment is added, sketch the chord background first, using the new II as a substitute for the IV in addition to the I, V, or V₇. Otherwise, the melody may be entirely free. Experiment with suspensions. Two-stanza poems are best set as A–B forms (see page 151).

(a)   The nightingale has a lyre of gold,
         The lark's is a clarion call,
      And the blackbird plays but a boxwood flute,
         But I love him best of all.

      For his song is all of the joy of life,
         And we in the mad, spring weather,
      We two have listened till he sang
         Our hearts and lips together.
                    The Blackbird — W. E. Henley[*]

(b)   The night has a thousand eyes,
         And the day but one;
      Yet the light of the bright world dies
         With the dying sun.

      The mind has a thousand eyes,
         And the heart but one;
      Yet the light of a whole life dies
         When love is done.
                    Light — F. W. Bourdillon

(c)   Break, break, break,
         On thy cold gray stones, O Sea!
      And I would that my tongue could utter
         The thoughts that arise in me.
                Break, Break, Break — Alfred, Lord Tennyson

---

[*] From *Poems by William Ernest Henley*, used by permission of Charles Scribner's Sons.

(*d*)   O sailor, come ashore,
        What have you brought for me?
        Red coral, white coral,
        Coral from the sea.

Coral — Christina Rossetti

(*e*)   Locust, locust, playing a flute,
        Locust, locust, playing a flute!
        Away up on the pine-tree bough,
          Closely clinging,
          Playing a flute,
          Playing a flute!

The Coyote and the Locust — Zuni Tribe, American Indian[5]

2. Experiment writing melodies for various instruments in phrase and period form, including the material of this and preceding chapters (accompaniment optional).

3. Harmonize at least one of the following melodies for piano, using the accompaniment figures of Examples 12, page 19; 27, page 35; 28 (*a*), page 46; and, possibly, 38, page 54:

(c) Lively — English Singing Game

II₆   V₇

(d) Moderato — German Folk Song

II₆

(e) Allegro — KÜCKEN

(f) Andante — English Folk Song

1. only

2.

⌣. Fine   D.C. al Fine

(g) Moderato — German Folk Song (1825)

(Use figure of Ex. 38 a)

Fine

D.C. al Fine

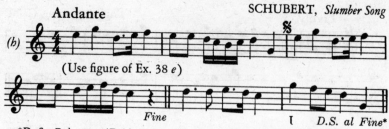

Andante   SCHUBERT, *Slumber Song*

(*b*)

(Use figure of Ex. 38 *e*)

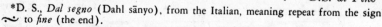

Fine   *D.S. al Fine**

*D. S., *Dal segno* (Dahl sānyo), from the Italian, meaning repeat from the sign ⁓ to *fine* (the end).

II — *Assignment for Playing*

1. Learn the following chord progressions and embellish descending stepwise melodic progressions with suspensions:

I   IV   V₇   I   I   II₆   V₇   I

2. Play by ear the melody of *My Bonnie Lies Over the Ocean*, in the key of C major. Harmonize it with the waltz accompaniment using the I, IV, II₆, and V₇ chords.

3. Improvise melodies in period form as directed in Chapter I.

4. Improvise phrases over this accompaniment figure:

(or IV)

5. Play the II₆ chord thus:

6. Harmonize one or more of the melodies in the *Assignment for Writing* (3), or select from the following melodies, using the style of accompaniment in Example 27, page 35, or Example 37, page 53:

Diller, *First Studies in Harmonic Analysis,* Nos. 43, 44, 49.
140 Folk-Songs. Concord Series No. 3. Nos. 4, 32, 52.
Foresman Manual (Child's Book), pp. 42, 52, 54, 56, 62, 73, 112, 124, 131, 132 (dance), 134, 138, 143, 145.
Folk Song Sight Singing Series: Book III, No. 86.

III — Assignment for Listening

1. *Oral dictation:* harmonic recognition only. Identify chords by letter and Roman numeral.

Foresman III, Minuet, p. 98.
Gounod, *Sing, Smile, Slumber.*
Beethoven, *Six Easy Variations in G,* theme (12-16).
Mozart, *Don Giovanni,* No. 7 (1-8).
See also *Assignment for Analysis* below.

2. *Written dictation (bass, melody, and name of chords).*
Sing!: Listen to the Mocking Bird (4-8).
Diller, *First Studies in Harmonic Analysis,* Nos. 47, 56, 65.
Beethoven, *Sonata,* Op. 28, Scherzo (5-8).

IV — Assignment for Analysis

Chopin, *Waltz,* Op. 70, No. 1, G flat section (1-8) ;
Mazurka, Op. 33, No. 2 (1-8).
Mozart, *Les Petits Riens,* K 299, Gavotte (1-4) ;
Haffner Symphony, K 385, Minuetto (1-8);
D Major Symphony, K 250, Trio I, Part III only.
Diabelli, *Sonatine,* Op. 151, No. 4 (1-4).
Beethoven, *Symphony IV,* Finale (1-4) ;
Sonata, Op. 28, Scherzo (1-8).
Rossini, *Barber of Seville,* Largo al factotum (last 20 measures).

The following passages, for analysis, have been selected from the above list. Identify cadences, form, chords, and nonharmonic tones.

CHOPIN, *Waltz,* Op. 70, No. 1 (1835) [G♭]

MOZART, *Haffner Symphony,** K385 [D]

Menuetto

(b)

*Why was this called the *"Haffner"* Symphony?

DIABELLI, *Sonatine,* Op. 151, No. 4
See Chapter XVI, Ex. 126

Allegro moderato

(c)

BEETHOVEN, *Fourth Symphony,* Finale [B♭]

Allegro ma non troppo

(d)

l.h.

BEETHOVEN, *Sonata*, Op. 28,* Scherzo [D]

Allegro vivace

*This sonata is sometimes called the *Pastoral Sonata*.

Chapter V

THE CADENTIAL I_4^6 CHORD

Ex. 39

HAYDN (1732–1809), *Military Symphony* (1794), Trio [G]

T HIS GAY dance melody is typical of one aspect of Haydn's style — inexhaustible humor. But his style embraced much more: sanity, clarity, exalted feeling, and superb craftsmanship. The latter characteristic especially is shown by the organization of this Trio.[1]

---

[1] Trio is here the middle portion of a minuet, scherzo, or march. The name apparently refers to the old custom of the trio being played for contrast by three instruments, rather than by the full orchestra or band.

After a contrasting section, beginning with the same figure, thus:

Ex. 40

the first four measures return with this new phrase added:

Ex. 41

The return to the beginning makes the entire Trio an *A–B–A* (or three-part) song form, which is one of the basic designs of all the arts — statement, departure, and return.

Ex. 42

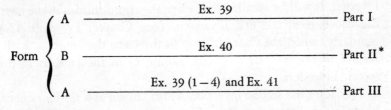

*Part II usually begins and ends on the V or V₇ chord.

Listen again for the cadences and form of parts I and III. Identify the cadences in measures 4 and 7 and 8 of each. The cadence in measure 4 is a half- or semi-cadence (V), and that in measures 7 and 8 is a complete, or perfect authentic, cadence (V₇–I). Note that the two phrases of each part begin similarly. These two phrases establish the period form.

Part I is undoubtedly a parallel period (See Chapter I, page 11). Part III is also a period, but is it parallel or contrasting in construction? Its second phrase (Example 41) consists of the same little figures as that of the first phrase (Example 39), except that the direction is revesed. When the consequent phrase is thus made of the same material used in the opposite direction (inverted), the resulting period is called *parallel by inversion*.

In Example 39 note that the cadence chord (V) occurs on the second beat of measures 4 and 7. Obviously, Haydn wished to delay the entrance of the cadence chord by substituting a closely related chord on the first beat. Spell the chords upward from the bass tone, G in measure 4, G–C–E followed by G–B–D, and, in measure 7, G–C–E followed by G–F–B–D. Arranged in thirds, they read C–E–G, moving to G–B–D–(F) in both measures, thus:

Ex. 43

Since the root of the C chord is not in the bass, this chord is inverted. It will be recalled that when the chord-third is in the bass, the chord is in the first inversion. (See Chapter IV, page 47.) Similarly, when the chord-fifth is in the bass, the chord is in the *second inversion*. The C chord, having G in the bass, is in the second inversion.

A triad in the second inversion is also known as a *six-four chord*, because the distance on the staff from the bass to the other chord tones is six and four staff degrees respectively, as in the following example.

Ex. 44

Hence, it is written C⁶₄, or I⁶₄, in the key of C major. The cadence chords for measures 4 and 7 and 8 would be named thus: I⁶₄–V, and I⁶₄–V₇–I.

Play measure 4, Example 39, omitting the C⁶₄ chord and going directly to the G chord. Obviously, the general effect is much the same, whether or not the C⁶₄ is used.

Therefore, it can be concluded that a triad in the second inversion lacks strong harmonic individuality. In the case of the cadential I⁶₄, there is a tendency to accept the bass tone as a root (rather than a fifth), because the ear anticipates the V₇ chord which the I⁶₄ displaces rhythmically. For this reason, the tones of the I⁶₄ gravitate to other tones, forming the triad, or seventh-chord, built on the bass tone. In Example 39, measure 4, therefore, the tones C–E, in the I⁶₄, merely give the effect of accented passing tones connecting the D₆ and G chords, thus:

Ex. 45

The I⁶₄, when used before the V₇ in a cadence, is called a *cadential ⁶₄ chord*. It usually occurs on a strong beat of the measure, and, as you will observe, is preceded by some chord other than the V₇.

Name all the chords and nonharmonic tones in Examples 39 and 41. What chord is suggested in the first measure of each — the C or G? Test by substituting first the C chord, and then the G chord in the left hand.

How could the I⁶₄ best be used in the following melody?

Ex. 46

Alla marcia   French Folk Song (Condensed)

Sing this stirring march tune. Locate its cadences and identify the type of period. The general harmonic background is strongly suggested by the melodic skips. In measure 3, the chords are C and D$_6$, moving over the bar to the C$_4^6$ and G$_7$ in measure 4. The second phrase begins with the I chord followed by the D$_6$ in measure 6. This chord leads naturally to the I$_4^6$–V$_7$ in measure 7. The E at the end of measure 7 is a *free* tone over the G$_7$, anticipating the C chord in measure 8. (See Chapter XVI, Example 126.

Sing the bass and melody together, imagining the sound of the chords suggested by the bass.

Ex. 47

Consider other possibilities for the bass, testing their effectiveness.

Select a type of accompaniment suitable for this martial melody. Perhaps one of the best and simplest is to use repeated chords suggesting the regular rhythm of marching feet.

Ex. 48

Alla marcia

Note how the spacing in the left hand is adapted to the melody by using a consistent register. As is usual in instrumental music, the preliminary beat of the phrase is left unharmonized. This example shows the utility of the cadential I⁶. Observe, also, how the style of accompaniment intensifies the mood of the melody. Compare Examples 39, page 62, and 48, above, in this respect. Although the opening rhythmic figures are similar, the different accompaniments create an entirely different mood. Thus, both the rhythmic and harmonic factors of a melody are important in bringing out its musical and aesthetic possibilities.

Review:

1. When a period is parallel by inversion.
2. What is meant by the three-part form.
3. What the triad is called when its fifth is in the bass.
4. Why the second inversion of a triad is called a $\frac{6}{4}$ chord.
5. One use of the I_4^6.
6. What chord follows the cadential I_4^6.
7. Why $\frac{6}{4}$ chords lack harmonic independence.
8. On what part of the measure the cadential I_4^6 usually occurs.
9. How to space the accompaniment figure to fit the melody.
10. The importance of the accompaniment figure (rhythmic background) in harmonizing a melody.
11. Why the upper tones of the cadential I_4^6 sound like foreign tones.

For Further Study, Determine:

1. What chords may precede the I_4^6.
2. Why the cadential I_4^6 resolves so naturally to the V.
3. What the words *"trio"* and *"dolce"* mean when applied to music.
4. What a *minuet* is and how it came to be included in the symphony.
5. Why Italian terms are so generally used in giving directions about music.
6. Whether all composers use Italian words for directions.
7 How many movements a symphony usually has.
8. Whether part II of a three-part form must be based on a different figure from part I (see Example 40, page 63).
9. Whether part III is ever based on a new figure.
10. Two meanings of the term "inversion" in music.

I — Assignment for Writing

1. Scan the following stanzas and write melodies for one or more of them in $\frac{2}{2}$, $\frac{2}{4}$, $\frac{3}{8}$, $\frac{3}{4}$, $\frac{4}{4}$, $\frac{6}{8}$, or $\frac{6}{4}$. In choosing a metric signature, it is best to choose one that will make each phrase four measures in length. (Accompaniment optional.)

> (*a*)   Hark! I hear the tramp of thousands,
>   And of arméd men the hum;
>   Lo! a nation's hosts have gathered
>   Round the quick alarming drum.
>
>   *The Reveille — Bret Harte*

(*b*)   The sun descending in the west,
        The evening star does shine;
        The birds are silent in their nest.
        And I must seek for mine.

                        Night — William Blake

(*c*)   The moon on the one hand, the dawn on the other;
        The moon is my sister, the dawn is my brother.
        The moon on my left hand, the dawn on my right:
        My brother, good morning: my sister, good night.

                The Early Morning — Hilaire Belloc[2]

(*d*)   Gayly bedight,
        A gallant knight,
        In sunshine and in shadow,
        Had journeyed long,
        Singing a song
        In search of Eldorado.

                    Eldorado — Edgar Allan Poe

(*e*)   We are the music-makers,
            And we are the dreamers of dreams,
        Wandering by lone sea-breakers,
            And sitting by desolate streams;

                Ode — Arthur O'Shaughnessy

(*f*)   Under the wide and starry sky
        Dig the grave and let me lie:
        Glad did I live and gladly die,
            And I laid me down with a will.

        This be the verse you grave for me:
        Here he lies where he long'd to be;
        Home is the sailor, home from sea,
            And the hunter home from the hill.

                Requiem — Robert Louis Stevenson

2. Experiment writing original instrumental melodies (accompaniment optional). For example, write a march in *A–B–A* form, each part a phrase in length, using Example 48 as a model for rhythm only.

---

[2] From *Sonnets and Verses*, published by Medell McBride & Company.

3. Harmonize at least one of the following melodies for piano, using the accompaniment figure of Example 48, page 67, and those of previous lessons:

CARON (1806)

(a) Alla marcia

KUHLAU, *Sonatina*, Op. 55, No. 5

(b) Tempo di marcia

MOZART, *Marriage of Figaro*

(c) Allegro

Moderato   Spanish Folk Song

(d)

(Use accompaniment figure of Ex. 38 b)

Allegro

(e)

Andante   Folk Song (1849)

(f)   V$_7$ (V$_9$)

II$_6$

Moderato   Folk Song

(g)

II$_6$ I$_4^6$

Andante   MEHUL (1807)

(h)

II — *Assignment for Playing*

1. Harmonize one or more of the melodies in the *Assignment for Writing* (3) or select from the following melodies, using any of the preceding styles of accompaniment:

   140 Folk-Songs. Concord Series No. 3. Nos. 1, 10, 22, 56, 57, 68, 72, 85, 90, 93, 94, 102, 110, 124, 126.

2. Improvise melodies in period form as directed in Chapter I.

3. Improvise melodies in period form over this accompaniment figure:

Alla marcia

4. Play by ear the melody of *Old Folks at Home* in the key of C major. Add an accompaniment using the I, IV, II$_6$, V$_7$, and cadential I$_4^6$ chords.

5. Play the I$_4^6$ chord thus:

6. Learn the following cadence formulae, and embellish descending stepwise melodic progressions with suspensions:

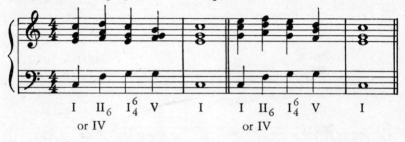

III — Assignment for Listening

1. *Oral dictation:* harmonic recognition only. Identify chords by letter, and Roman numeral.

Yankee Doodle
Foresman Manual (Child's Book), *I Saw a Ship A-sailing*, p. 88.
Mozart, *Piano Sonata*, K457, Adagio (1-4).
Beethoven, *Symphony I*, Op. 21, Finale, Coda.
Chopin, *Mazurka*, Op. 7, No. 5 (5-12).
Mendelssohn, *Songs Without Words*, No. 9 (1-3), No. 28 (1-4),
   No. 41 (1-4).

2. *Written dictation (bass, melody, and name of chords):*
Golden Book: *Battle Hymn of the Republic*, p. 12 (1-8);
          Jesus, Lover of My Soul, p. 61;
          Silent Night, p. 67;
          The Cuckoo, p. 85.
Green Book, *Twice 55:* No. 77, *Joy to the World* (1-4).
Sing!: Old Aunt Jemima (1-6), p. 84

IV — Assignment for Analysis

Mozart, *Violin Sonata*, K303, Minuet.
Chopin, *Mazurka*, Op. 24, No. 3 (1-12).
Meyerbeer, *Coronation March*, second theme (last 8 measures).
Schubert, *Violin Sonatina*, Op. 137, No. 1, Andante (1-8).
Beethoven, *Sonata*, Op. 49, No. 2, Minuet, C Major section.
The following passages for analysis have been selected from the above list. Identify cadences, form, chords, and nonharmonic tones.

MOZART, *Violin Sonata*, K303

Tempo di menuetto

CHOPIN, *Mazurka*, Op. 24, No. 3 [A♭]

Moderato con anima

MEYERBEER, *The Prophet*, "Coronation March" [F]

Molto maestoso

Chapter VI

THE I₆ CHORD

Ex. 49　　　　　　HANDEL (1685 – 1759), *Messiah* (1741) [D]

HEAR, by singing or playing, the opening phrase of the "Hallelujah Chorus" from Handel's oratorio, *Messiah,* quoted above. Recite the words alone to the rhythm of the music. This gives the effect of *choral speech,* and shows Handel's skill in suggesting a series of exultant shouts through the rhythm. Sing it again, noting how the pitches heighten the rhythmic effect of the words.

This phrase is characteristic of Handel's simple, forceful style of vocal writing. Note the feeling of dignity and power combined with exultation. One of the principal factors is the integrated effect of simple chords repeated in a vital, rhythmic pattern. Observe how relatively unimportant the melody is; in fact, the tenor part is much more expressive melodically than is the soprano. In addition to the rhythmic and harmonic simplicity, another important factor is the structural unity secured through the repetition of the initial figure. Are the three repetitions exact or modified? Identify the only nonharmonic tone in the entire phrase.

Repeat the first measure slowly, listening to the chord changes.

Ex. 50   Soprano   Alto

Tenor   Bass

Compare the first two chords. The root of the second chord is C. Since the chord-third (E) is in the bass, the chord is in the *first inversion*. It is symbolized I₆ or C₆. Name the other chords in the passage. The first chord in measure 4 (B₆) will be discussed in Chapter XIII, page 207.

The substitution of the I₆ for the fundamental I chord in this passage gives melodic interest to the bass line. This is one of the chief functions of the I₆. Observe its use in the following excerpt from the Finale of Haydn's *Drumroll Symphony:*

Ex. 51   HAYDN

Allegro con spirito

This is an unusual example since the first chord of the composition is a I₆. The first four measures are a kind of motto which Haydn uses for the entire movement. Note the jolly *obbligato* melody added in measures 5 to 8. This added melody is an example of *counterpoint*,[1] which means the art of combining melodies. Examine the entire "Hallelujah Chorus" for examples of counterpoint.

A composer's choice of the I or I₆ chords depends on the effect which he desires (see Example 51, page 77). The fundamental I has a feeling of finality or completeness because there is nothing inherent in the chord that suggests further movement. In other words, its effect is static. On the other hand, the first inversion (I₆) seems unstable and wants to move to a new chord. Thus, it may be said to be more dynamic than the fundamental position of the I. Composers utilize these static and dynamic qualities in composition. If a definite cadential close is desired, the composer would not use the inverted I for the final chord. Conversely, he would use inverted chords during the phrase to give the sense of harmonic motion or progression.

Reference to the passages for analysis at the end of this chapter will show that, in general, the I₆ is used as a substitute for the fundamental I except in a perfect cadence. Consequently, the I₆ is preceded and followed by the same chords as the fundamental I.

Since the I₆ is substituted, then, for the fundamental I to give harmonic variety to the phrase and melodic interest to the bass, determine how it could be used in the folk song that follows.

Ex. 52

German Folk Song

---

[1] From the Latin *punctus contra punctum* (point against point), that is, note against note. *Point* was the medieval term for *note*.

Sing one bass note for each measure beginning while the melody
is being played or sung, thus:

Ex. 53
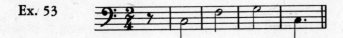

This bass line could be improved by using both the I and I₆ in
measure 1, thus:

Ex. 54

Compare this accompaniment figure with that of Example 37,
page 53. Note that Example 54, above, has certain advantages:
the two bass notes in each measure give greater flexibility by
allowing a change of chord within the measure, and the double
notes make the chords more complete than in Example 37. Note,
also, how the accompaniment figure is altered at the cadences. In
which cadence does the accompaniment figure sound more complete, and why?

This accompaniment figure can be modified for use in various
meters, thus:

Ex. 55

In the same manner, study carefully the following possibilities for the use of first inversions in this folk melody, testing each one by ear. Do not use more than two chords in each measure.

Ex. 56

German Folk Song

Identify by Roman numerals and letters the chords indicated by each of these basses and the resultant nonharmonic melodic tones. Bass 3 uses more than two chords in each measure through an application of contrapuntal principles; but, because of this, it must be harmonized by chords in the treble, not by an accompaniment figure in the bass, thus:

Ex. 57

Use the I₆, II₆, and I⁶₄ in your own work to give a distinct melodic character to the bass. Try various possibilities until you find one that is satisfying both harmonically and melodically.

Review:

1. Why composers use the I₆.
2. Where the I₆ is used as a substitute for the fundamental I.
3. Why the fundamental I chord has a feeling of finality.
4. Why the I₆ is more dynamic than the fundamental I.
5. Why the I₆ is not used in a perfect authentic cadence.
6. What chords precede and follow the I₆.
7. What is meant by the word "counterpoint."

For Further Study, Determine:

1. Whether the I chord sounds more final in its fundamental or inverted forms.
2. Which inversion of the I chord is most restricted in use.
3. Whether compositions end on the I₆.
4. Where other examples of counterpoint are to be found.
5. Who was Handel's greatest contemporary in music.
6. What an oratorio is. How the term came to be used in music.

I — Assignment for Writing

1. Scan the following stanzas and write melodies for one or more of them in these different time signatures: $\frac{2}{2}$, $\frac{2}{4}$, $\frac{3}{8}$, $\frac{3}{4}$, $\frac{4}{4}$, $\frac{6}{4}$, or $\frac{6}{8}$. In choosing a metric signature, be sure it is one that will make the phrases four measures in length. (Accompaniment optional.)

(a)   Sunset and evening star,
        And one clear call for me!
    And may there be no moaning of the bar,
        When I put out to sea.

                Crossing the Bar — *Alfred, Lord Tennyson*

(b)   Music, when soft voices die,
        Vibrates in the memory;
        Odours, when sweet violets sicken,
        Live within the sense they quicken.

        Rose leaves, when the rose is dead,
        Are heap'd for the belovèd's bed;
        And so thy thoughts, when thou art gone,
        Love itself shall slumber on.

            Music, When Soft Voices Die —
                    Percy Bysshe Shelley

(c)   There was a little turtle,
        He lived in a box,
        He swam in a puddle,
        He climbed on the rocks.

        He snapped at a mosquito,
        He snapped at a flea,
        He snapped at a minnow,
        He snapped at me.

        He caught the mosquito,
        He caught the flea,
        He caught the minnow,
        But he didn't catch me.[2]

                The Little Turtle — *Vachel Lindsay*[3]

---

[2] If this poem is chosen, set it in three-part form, making the melody of the third stanza the same as that of the first

[3] From *Golden Whales of California*, Copyright 1920, 1948, by The Macmillan Company and used with their permission.

(d)   Merry it is in the good greenwood,
    When the mavis and merle are singing,
    When the deer sweeps by, and the hounds are in cry,
    And the hunter's horn is ringing.
          Merry It Is in the Good Greenwood — Sir Walter Scott[4]

(e)   Soldier, rest! thy warfare o'er,
    Sleep the sleep that knows not breaking;
    Dream of battled fields no more,
    Days of danger, nights of waking.
          Soldier, Rest! — Sir Walter Scott[5]

2. Experiment writing original melodies for instruments other than the piano — either with or without accompaniment. Make them in a definite form: a period, or perhaps a small three-part form consisting of phrases, part III to be an exact or modified repetition of part I.

3. Harmonize at least one of the following melodies for piano, using the accompaniment figure of Example 54, page 79, and those of previous chapters.

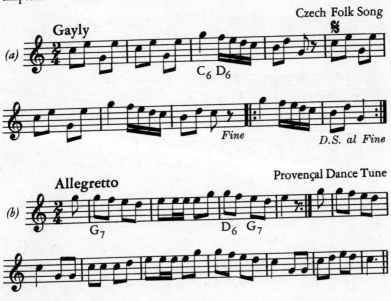

⁴ From *The Poetical Works of Sir Walter Scott*, J. Logie Robertson (Editor), published by Oxford University Press, London.
⁵ *Ibid.*

MOZART, *Don Giovanni,* "Il mio tesoro intanto" [B♭]
Andante grazioso
(h)

Moderato   PAISIELLO
(i)
C₆   D₆

Hornpipe   English Folk Song
(j)

II — Assignment for Playing

1. Harmonize one or more of the melodies in the *Assignment for Writing* (3), or select from the following melodies, using any of the preceding styles of accompaniment:

140 Folk-Songs: Nos. 3, 6, 12, 14, 36, 28, 59 (1-8), 63, 64, 71, 72, 75, 84, 106, 113, 115, 117, 137 (1-8), 140.

Folk Song Sight Singing Series: Book III, No. 100, Book VII, Nos. 61, 82.

2. Improvise melodies in period form as directed in Chapter I.

3. Improvise melodies in period form over this accompaniment figure:

4. Play a number of well-known melodies by ear, both with and without accompaniment.

5. Play the I₆ chord, thus:

6. Play the following chord progression in several different positions. Repeat, inserting the IV or II₆ in place of the I₆, and embellish melody with suspensions.

$$\text{I} \qquad \text{I}_6 \qquad \text{I}_4^6 \qquad \text{V}_7 \qquad \text{I}$$

III — Assignment for Listening

1. *Oral dictation:* harmonic recognition only. Identify chords by letter and Roman numeral.

Schumann, *Piano Concerto,* Op. 54, Finale (1-4).

Brahms, *Symphony II,* Op. 73, First Movement (1-9).

Schubert, *Valses Nobles,* Op. 77, No. 1 (1-8).

Diller, *First Studies in Harmonic Analysis,* No. 39

Mozart, *Piano Sonata,* K332, First Movement (12-22), development section (94-109).

2. *Written dictation (bass, melody, and name of chord).*

Golden Book: "Folk Song" from *Hänsel and Gretel,* p. 84.

Green Book, Twice 55: No. 50, *Vive L'Amour;*
No. 80, *The Strife is O'er* (1-7).

Brahms, *Symphony III,* Op. 90, Andante (1-4).

Mozart, *Piano Sonata,* K332, Allegro, development section (1-8).

Handel, *Israel in Egypt,* No. 10 (3-6).

New Episcopal Hymnal, No. 421, *Retreat.*

IV — Assignment for Analysis

Haydn, *Drumroll Symphony,* Trio (1-8).

Mozart, *Piano Sonata,* K332, Allegro (12-22; 94-109).

Beethoven, *Symphony VII,* Op. 92, Introduction, C Major melody
(23-28);
Bagatelle, Op. 119, No. 4 (1-4);
Sonata, Op. 54, First Movement (1-4).

Schumann, *Träumerie,* Op. 15, No. 7 (1-4);
Papillons, Op. 2, Finale (1-8).

Verdi, *Il Trovatore,* No. 16, Allegro moderato maestoso (1-8).

The following passages for analysis have been selected from the above list. Identify cadences, form, chords, and nonharmonic tones:

HAYDN, *Drumroll Symphony,* Trio [Eb]

MOZART, *Piano Sonata,* K332

Allegro

BEETHOVEN, *Symphony No. 7,* Op. 92 [A]

Poco sostenuto

SCHUMANN, *Scenes from Childhood,* "Träumerei," Op. 15, No. 7 [F]

Lento

(See Chapter XXIX)

Chapter VII

THE VI CHORD

Ex. 58

Poco andante   SCHUBERT (1797 – 1828), *Spring Dreams* [A]

T HIS MELODY, from Schubert's *Winter Journey*, one of his best-known song cycles,[1] develops naturally from its initial figure and simple harmonic background. Much of Schubert's music in this unpretentious vein has a lasting charm that defies time and analysis. And so, when we try to find the secret of such music by examining its technical details, we might discover clues but never the whole truth. This is true of all great art, which, ultimately, rests on feeling, not on technical analysis. On the other hand, a greater understanding of structure, up to a certain point, undoubtedly increases our interest. So let us find some clues in this simple melody without expecting to find the complete answer.

Note the change of the chord in the second measure and also that it would be possible to continue the chord of measure 1 in measure 2. What other form of the I chord is possible in this second measure, and how does it differ in feeling or quality from the chord that Schubert chose?

---

[1] *Winterreise*, written in 1827, about the time of Beethoven's death and only a year before his own death. For practical reasons, the original voice part and piano accompaniment have been condensed in Example 58.

Examine closely measures 1 and 2 and spell each chord upward from its bass tone. Measure 1 contains the chord C–E–G and measure 2, A–C–E or the I and VI chords respectively in the key of C, thus:

Ex. 59

These chords differ in color or quality because of the size of their intervals. In the I, the lowest third is C–E and in the VI, A–C. A comparison of the size of these thirds on the piano shows that C–E contains five black and white keys, whereas A–C has four.

Ex. 60

By the same method of measuring intervals, it will be seen that the fifths of the two chords, C–G and A–E, are equal in size. (See Appendix, page 595.) These equal fifths are called *perfect* because their two tones are similarly related to two different scales. It will be shown later that all "white key" fifths are equal in size and hence perfect except B–F. (See Ex. 104.)

Triads having such equal or *perfect fifths* are named from the size of their lower third built on the root. Since the C chord contains a large (major) third, and the A chord contains a small (minor) third, the C chord is a *major triad* and the A chord is a *minor triad*. Thus, a major triad consists of a major third and a perfect fifth, and a minor triad contains a minor third and a perfect fifth.

Construct a triad on the sixth degree with a major third (A–C sharp), noting the difference in tone color. What other minor triad has been discussed and how was it constructed? Using the method cited above, classify all the thirds in the C major scale as large (major) or small (minor).

To return to Example 58, page 90, listen again to the sound of measures 1 and 2. Although the I or the I_6 could have been used in measure 2, Schubert used the VI in place of the I for variety, in order to get a new harmonic color. Composers often use the VI chord in this way[2] as a substitute for the I.

The substitution of the VI for the I recalls the similar use of the I_6. (Chapter VI, page 76.) Likewise, the cadential V_7 may be preceded by either the IV or the II_6 (Chapter IV, page 46), and the I or the I_4^6 (Chapter V, page 62).

Adding the VI, then, to our list of "substitute chords," we have:

> For I: the I_6 or VI
> For IV: the II_6
> For V: the I_4^6 (at cadence followed by V_7)

There is also a special cadential use for the VI, as shown in measures 2 and 3 of the following excerpt from Handel's *Largo*.[3]

---

[2] Rarely do compositions begin on the VI chord. See Schumann's *Novelletten*, Op. 21, No. 1 and Grieg's *Spring Song*.

[3] This is the ending of a tenor *aria* (air or solo) from Handel's neglected opera, *Xerxes* (London, 1738).

Ex. 61   HANDEL [G]

VI

Substitute the I for the VI chord in measures 2 and 3. This change produces an effect of finality that makes measures 4 and 5 somewhat superfluous. But the VI chord is unexpected and produces an effect of incompleteness because of the use of the VI chord at the point where the final cadence would naturally occur. The surprise and suspense of the VI chord focuses the listener's attention on the final ending much more effectively than the use of the I would have done. It also shows how composers use substitute chords, like colors, to alter the harmonic background.

This temporary substitution of the VI for the I in an ending is called an *evaded* or *deceptive cadence,* a device used for phrase extension. Test its effectiveness by inserting evaded cadences in familiar music. It might almost be termed the *surprise cadence.* It adds suspense and, therefore, interest to the ending. As in the case of the IV–V, contrary motion is usually used in connecting the VI and V₇ chords. The similar motion in Example 61 is exceptional.

The *effect* of an evaded cadence may be obtained by using some other tone than the root in the bass or soprano of the final I chord. Thus the third (I₆) may be used in the bass, or the third or·fifth may be used in the soprano. The latter is known as an *imperfect authentic cadence.* It is used both for evasion at the end of a period and, occasionally, for the ending of either phrase.[4] Note how the perfect authentic cadence is evaded in Schubert's *Spring Dreams,* Example 58, measure 12, page 90.

After an evaded cadence, the composer either repeats the previous cadence material or adds a new ending. How many measures did the evaded cadence add to Example 61, page 93? When a cadence is evaded, obviously at least two measures are added to the phrase and sometimes more, depending on the content.

There are other points of interest in Example 61. Identify all the chords. In measure 1, there are two foreign tones encountered previously. Contrast the C on the second beat of measure 1 with the C at the end of measure 4.

Ex. 62

In measure 1, the C belongs to the preceding chord and is called a suspension. On the other hand, the C at the end of measure 4 belongs to the chord of measure 5. Such a tone that anticipates the chord to which it belongs is called an *anticipation.* Note that, in relation to the chord background, it is the exact opposite of the suspension. Unlike the suspension, however, the anticipation progresses in either direction and, occasionally, may even be introduced by skip.

---

[4] As a matter of fact, any unexpected chord may be substituted for the I, although the VI is the most used. One of the most effective evaded cadences occurs at the end of the Love Duet in the second act of Wagner's music drama, *Tristan,* accompanying the unexpected entrance of King Mark.

Locate the anticipation in this minuet and other familiar music:

Ex. 63   BEETHOVEN, *Sonata,* Op. 49 [G]

Tempo di menuetto

For example, see the opening phrase of *The Last Rose of Summer* or the last phrase of *Annie Laurie.* In the complete *Largo* (Example 61), anticipations will be found in the melody and frequently near the end as a preparation for the final cadence chord.[5] Remember that music is *heard,* not *seen,* and so one's analysis should be primarily aural, not visual. This means that music notation when seen should be heard mentally — an ability that develops gradually and may require considerable practice.

To summarize: the VI chord is a natural substitute for the I, either during the phrase or at the end of the cadence. Thus used in a phrase, the VI chord has the same harmonic setting as the I chord. When used cadentially, it forms an *evaded* or *deceptive* cadence (V–VI), and is followed by a perfect authentic cadence

---

[5] See Schumann's *Album for the Young,* Op. 68, No. 17 for a curious example of an anticipation entered by skip in the bass due to an imitation of the motive in the melody.

to finalize the phrase. The evaded cadence lengthens a phrase by two or more measures. There is also a new nonharmonic tone — the *anticipation,* so called because it anticipates the chord to which it belongs. It occurs most frequently in the melody and often is used, like the VI chord, cadentially.

Apply these new points to the following folk song:

Ex. 64

Sketch the harmonic background (Note an opportunity for an evaded cadence in measure 4.) Work out your own solution before comparing it with the following one.

Ex. 65

as above

Which version is preferable, and why? Note how the accompaniment figure is adapted to fit the melody. Experiment in your own work with the VI chord and the anticipation, but only use them expressively for definite effects 'where they are suggested by the context.

Review:

1. How to use the VI chord.
2. To what chord family the VI belongs.
3. What the quality of the VI chord is.
4. How major and minor triads differ in construction.
5. Three ways of evading a perfect cadence.
6. How an evaded cadence may affect the length of a phrase.
7. What chords may be substituted for the I, the IV, and the V.
8. What an anticipation is.
9. In what voice the anticipation usually occurs.
10. Differences between a suspension and an anticipation.
11. Why analysis of music should be aural, not visual.

For Further Study, Determine:

1. When an imperfect cadence is not deceptive.
2. How many cadences have been studied.
3. How many foreign tones you can identify.

4. Why it is necessary to know the chord background to identify non-harmonic tones.

5. The quality of all the staff (white key) thirds, (Example 60).

6. Why contrary motion is generally used in connecting the VI with the V or V$_7$ chords?

7. Other examples of the evaded cadence.

I — Assignment for Writing

1. Scan the following stanzas and write melodies for one or more of them. Vary the time signatures, choosing any which will make a normal four-measure phrase. It is advisable to use other keys than C major if the student is familiar with them. Experiment by ending the last line of the poem with an evaded cadence and complete it by repeating all or part of the line.

(a)   A cloud outlined in silver,
         Against the purple hill,
         Reflecting blue-green shadows
         Upon the valley still.

                              Color — Larry E. Lawrence

(b)   The gypsy souls of you and me
         Follow the roads together,
         Over the hills and far away
         In fair and stormy weather.

                              Romany — Helena F. Schleich

(c)   I would sleep in fairy beds,
             Under leafy bowers
         Snuggled 'neath a coverlet
             Made by magic showers.
         By day, I'd sing a glad song,
             By night, I'd breathe a prayer,
         If I could be a vagabond
             And wander here and there.

                              Vagabond — Mayme O. Thomson

(d)   Helen, thy beauty is to me
         Like those Nicèan barks of yore
         That gently, o'er a perfumed sea,
             The weary, way-worn wanderer bore
         To his own native shore.

                              To Helen — Edgar Allan Poe

(e)   Give a man a horse he can ride,
      Give a man a boat he can sail;
      And his rank and wealth, his strength and health,
      On sea nor shore shall fail.

Gifts — James Thomson

2. Experiment writing original melodies for instruments other than the piano — either with or without accompaniment; for example, a waltz in a small three-part form consisting of phrases, part III to be an exact or modified repetition of part I extended by an evaded cadence.

3. Harmonize at least one of the following melodies for piano, using any of the accompaniment figures of the preceding lessons.

(d) Andante   German Folk Song (1830)

(e) Andante   MOZART, D Major Piano Sonata, K.284

(f) HAYDN, Symphony, No. 7 (Peters ed.)
Vivace   Theme II

(g) Moderato   English Folk Song

II — Assignment for Playing

1. Harmonize one or more of the melodies in the *Assignment for Writing* (3) or the following melodies, using any of the preceding styles of accompaniment.

> *Folk Song Sight Singing Series:* Book I, Nos. 13-14; Book III, No. 43; Book IV, No. 53.
>
> *140 Folk-Songs.* Concord Series No. 3. Nos. 66, 95.
>
> *Folk Songs of Many Peoples:* Vol. II, Nos. 160-172-199.

2. Improvise melodies in extended period form without accompaniment as directed in Chapter I.

3. Improvise melodies in extended period form over this accompaniment figure:

Repeat the improvisations of other students by ear.

4. Learn the first phrase of *America*, noting the use of the VI chord. Harmonize it, using the VI chord.

5. Play the VI chord, thus:

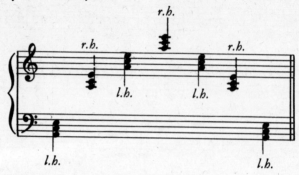

6. Learn also the following chord phrase, and embellish the melody with anticipations:

Change the ending to a *deceptive* cadence and add two measures to complete the phrase. Use contrary motion in all connections of the VI and V₇ chords. Repeat in piano style.

III — *Assignment for Listening*

1. *Oral dictation:* harmonic recognition only.

(*a*) Find the VI chord in the following passages:

Mendelssohn, *At Parting*, Op. 9, No. 6;
> *Songs Without Words*, No. 4 (5-9); No. 7 (2-5);
> No. 42 (2-5).

Schubert, *Songs from First Schubert Vocal Album* (Schirmer Edition):
> *The Hateful Color* (5-8), p. 62;
> *With the Green Lute-Band* (1-3), p. 50;
> *The Question* (1-4), p. 24;
> *The Linden Tree* (3-7), p. 94;
> *Illusion* (1-5), p. 138;
> *Angel of Beauty* (1-8), p. 238;

Romance (1-6), p. 292;
Farewell (5-8), p. 305.

(*b*) Name orally all the chords in the following passages, identifying the chords by quality, letter, and Roman numeral:

Haydn, *B flat Symphony*, VIII (Peters Edition), Adagio (1-4).

Mozart, *F Major Piano Sonata*, K322, Allegro, closing theme;
    A Major Piano Sonata, K331, Variation IV (1-8);
    Violin Sonata, K376, Rondo, Letter C (1-8).

Weber, *Invitation to the Dance*, Op. 65, C Major section (1-25).

Schumann, *Forest Scenes*, Op. 82, No. 1 (1-4).

Brahms, *Violin Sonata*, Op. 78, Adagio (1-5).

Sullivan, *The Lost Chord* (10-13).

2. *Written dictation (quality,[6] bass, melody, and name of chord).*

Golden Book: Home Sweet Home, p. 24;
    Nearer My God to Thee (1-8), p. 61.

Brown Book, Twice 55: No. 37, *Auld Lang Syne;*
    No. 73, *Holy, Holy, Holy* (1-4);
    No. 75, *We Three Kings of Orient Are*, Refrain only.

Home and Community Song Book: Concord Series No. 2.

    O Isis and Osiris, p. 117 (1-12);
    Hail Poetry, p. 147 (1-4).

New Episcopal Hymnal, No. 325 (second tune) *Arlington.*

IV — Assignment for Analysis

Brahms, *Waltz in A flat Major*, Op. 39, No. 15.

Dvořák, *Songs My Mother Taught Me*, Op. 55, No. 4.

Grieg, *Morning Mood*, Op. 64, No. 1.

Wagner, *Lohengrin Prelude*, last three measures;
    Parsifal, Faith Motive.

Mozart, *C Major Piano Sonata*, K545, Rondo (1-8);
    B flat Major Piano Sonata, K281, Andante, second theme;
    Violin Sonata, K379, Adagio (1-4);

    A Major Piano Sonata, K331, Variation IV.

Haydn, *Military Symphony*, Menuetto (1-16).

Beethoven, *Violin Sonata*, Op. 12, No. 3, Rondo (1-8).

The passages for analysis on pages 104, 105, and 106 have been selected from the above list. Identify cadences, form, chords, and nonharmonic tones:

---

[6] From this unit onward, the *quality* (major minor, etc.) may be indicated in addition to the bass, melody, and name of chord.

Moderato   BRAHMS, *Waltz,* Op. 39, No. 15 [A♭]

DVOŘÁK, *Songs My Mother Taught Me,* Op. 55, No. 4 [B]

Andante con moto

GRIEG, *Morning Mood,* Op. 46, No. 1 [E]

WAGNER, *Prelude to Lohengrin* [A]

Lento   WAGNER, *Parsifal* [A♭]

(e)

Faith Motive

Introduction
Adagio   MOZART, *Violin Sonata*, K379 [G]

(f)

Chapter VIII

THE II AND III CHORDS

Ex. 66
Lento

WAGNER, (1813—1883), *Siegfried,** Act III

*From *The Ring of the Nibelungs,* a series of four music dramas based on the old Norse legend of greed and retribution. The complete "Ring" Cycle was first performed in Bayreuth, Germany (August, 1876), in a special theatre built by Wagner for the performance of his works.

BRÜNNHILDE sings this passage as she is awakened by Siegfried from her long sleep. It is suggestive of the joy as well as the uncertainty that she feels on returning to the world. Note that each repetition of the chord in measures 1, 3, and 5 is followed by a higher melody tone leading to the climax in measure 9, a characteristic device of Wagner, after which there is a gradual relaxation in feeling, ending with a questioning uncertainty in measure 12.

Observe the subtle harmonic nuances, the slow rhythm, and the rising melody, all of which contribute to the solemn and mysterious effect. Compare the quality of the chords in measures 1 to 6 which fall naturally into groups of two measures each, 1 and 2, 3 and 4, and 5 and 6. The chords of measures 1 and 2 are different in quality, whereas those of measures 3 and 4 are alike. (Measures 5 and 6 duplicate the quality of measures 1 and 2.) Confirm these differences aurally.

This difference in quality is due, of course, to the size of their respective intervals. Compare the chords in measures 1 and 2, and determine which are major or minor. The triad in measure 4, because of the size of its third (D–F), is a minor triad also.

Sing the chords of Example 66, page 107, measures 1 to 6, listening to the differences in their qualities, thus:

Ex. 67

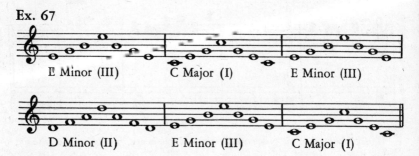

E Minor (III)   C Major (I)   E Minor (III)

D Minor (II)   E Minor (III)   C Major (I)

In the key of C, the E minor chord is numbered III, and the D minor chord, II. These two chords, with the VI (see Chapter VII, page 90), are known as *subordinate triads* in contrast to the *principal triads* I, IV, and V. Note that each group is homogeneous in quality. These two chord groups may be contrasted also in respect to function — the principal triads being *tonal* and the subordinate being *modal,* because of their respective qualities and relationships to the key center. (See Chapter XX, pages 339-340).

Examine the following chorale, which uses both of these chord groups. Note the chord substitutions for repeated melody tones.

Ex. 68

SCHÜLTZ

Soprano
Alto

Tenor
Bass

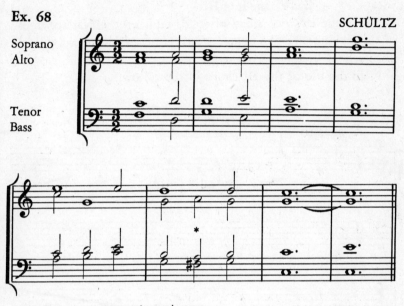

*The F sharp is a color, or chromatic, tone.

These substitutions are especially noticeable in measures 1 and 2. Spell the chords upward from the bass tone. Measure 1 contains F–A–C (IV), and D–F–A (II); measure 2, G–B–D (V), and E–G–B (III). Note that these repeated melody tones suggest a change of chord for variety. Thus the II is substituted for the IV and the III for the V in these measures, since their use changes the chord color without altering the melody. Note, also, the substitution of the VI for the I in measures 3 and 5. From this usage, it may be said that the II chord belongs to the IV group, and the III chord to the V group of chords. (See Chapter III, Example 22.)

Adding the II and III, then, to the list of *substitute chords* previously discussed, we have:

For I, the I_6 or VI

For IV, the II_6 or II

For V_7, the I_4^6 or III

This completes our study of triads built on the first six steps of the major scale. The unique structure of the VII chord will be discussed in Chapter XIII, page 209.

Note the use of the III chord in the following passage:

Ex. 69

SCHUBERT, *Impromptu*, Op. 90, No. 4 [A♭]

Allegretto

This substitution of the III for the V chord to harmonize the descending seventh step of the scale is a useful idiomatic progression. Observe the typical contrary motion required in connecting the III and IV chords. The descending scale may be harmonized as in Example 70.

Ex. 70

In Example 69, page 110, the new accompaniment figure is made by playing the chord tones on the treble staff successively rather than simultaneously. It is a useful accompaniment figure for melodies that require a different chord on each beat.

Example 68, page 109, and Example 69, page 110, also illustrate the use of harmonic and melodic *sequences,* the duplication of a figure or pattern on other scale steps.

Sing this phrase from the Bach Chorale, *My Soul, Now Bless Thy Maker.*

Ex. 71   BACH

Hum a bass for this melody while it is being sung or played. After doing so, test the basses of Example 72 in the same manner, and select the best one.

Note the new figuration 8–7 in Bass 3. Bass 4 is the one that Bach used, although all the others are possible. Is Bach's bass superior, and, if so, why?

Ex. 72

In the complete solution, the simple chord progressions are decorated by a number of foreign tones, thus:

Ex. 73

(Chapter XXIV)

Sing this passage slowly in parts, noting the changes in its harmonic background. Observe that most of the nonharmonic tones are used to fill in the skips between the chord tones.

Hence, judging from previous examples, the II, III, and

VI chords may be substituted for the IV, V, and I chords respectively. Example 74 illustrates the typical use of these substitute chords for melodic repetitions, for the evaded cadence, and for the descending seventh step in a scale line.

Ex. 74

(a) Melodic repetitions   *(b)* Evaded cadence *(c)* Descending scale

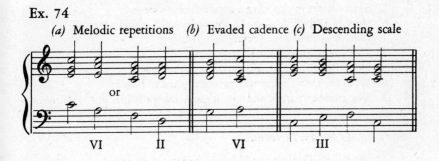

Why is the doubling different in the VI chords in (*a*) and (*b*) above?

Observe, in the above examples, that the II, III, and VI chords seldom progress *directly* to the I, but usually move *through* the V and the IV, thus:

Ex. 75

$$\left.\begin{array}{l} \left.\begin{array}{l} \text{II} \\ \text{VI} \end{array}\right\} \text{ to V} \\[6pt] \left.\begin{array}{l} \text{III} \\ \text{VI} \end{array}\right\} \text{ to IV} \\[6pt] \left.\begin{array}{l} \text{VI} \\ \text{III} \end{array}\right\} \text{ IV V} \end{array}\right\} \text{ to I}$$

However, the use of these new chords will depend largely on your musical taste and discrimination as developed through intelligent listening. Listen carefully to the assignments for hearing and analysis, and base your use of these new harmonic colors largely on *feeling* rather than rules, which are only statements of past experience to be adapted to present usage.

Review:

1. The construction and quality of the II and III chords.
2. To what chord groups the II and III belong.
3. For what chords the II and III may be substituted.
4. One way to harmonize the melodic scale progression 8–7–6.
5. Some factors in choosing a good bass for a melody.
6. How to embellish skips of thirds between chord tones.
7. How to harmonize repeated melody tones.
8. Three uses for substitute triads.
9. How the substitute triads progress to the I chord.
10. What the term "sequence" means applied to music.
11. The number names and qualities of the principal and subordinate triads.

For Further Study, Determine:

1. Whether all substitute triads are similarly constructed.
2. Which triads resolve directly to the I.
3. Which triads are used more frequently: the I–IV–V or the II–III–VI.
4. Several ways of harmonizing the descending scale.
5. The difference between *choral* and *chorale*.
6. The quality of all thirds found on white keys of the piano.
7. Whether sequences may be modified.
8. Why contrary motion is usually used in connecting the III and the IV chords.

I — Assignment for Writing

1. Scan the following stanzas and write melodies for one or more of them. Experiment with any new time signatures that result in four-measure phrases, such as $\frac{2}{2}, \frac{3}{16}, \frac{3}{2}, \frac{4}{8}, \frac{4}{2}$, and $\frac{6}{4}$. Use the evaded cadence as discussed in Chapter VII, page 93. (Accompaniment optional.)

> (*a*)   In mirth he mocks the other birds at noon,
>   Catching the lilt of every easy tune;
>   But when the day departs he sings of love,
>   His own wild song beneath the listening moon.
>
>   *The Mocking Bird* — Henry van Dyke[1]

---

[1] Reprinted from *Music and Other Poems* by Henry van Dyke; copyright 1904 by Charles Scribner's Sons, 1934 by Henry van Dyke; used by permission of the publishers.

(*b*) I think of thee, when golden sunbeams shimmer
        Across the sea;
     And when the waves reflect the moon's pale glimmer
        I think of thee.
                              Love's Nearness — Henry van Dyke[2]

(*c*) The summer's gone — how did it go?
     And where has gone the dogwood's show?
        The air is sharp upon the hill,
        And with a tinkle sharp and chill
     The icy little brooklets flow.
                              September — H. C. Bunner[3]

(*d*) Land of our Birth, our faith, our pride,
     For whose dear sake our fathers died;
     Oh Motherland, we pledge to thee,
     Head, heart, and hand through the years to be!
                        The Children's Song — Rudyard Kipling[4]

(*e*) My true love hath my heart, and I have his,
        By just exchange one for another given;
     I hold his dear, and mine he cannot miss,
        There never was a better bargain driven.
        My true love hath my heart and I have his.
                              The Bargain — Sir Philip Sidney

(*f*) Wait a minute,
     Green bus!
     Slow down!
     Stop!
     I will climb
     Your winding stair
     And ride
     On top.

---

[2] Reprinted from *Music and Other Poems* by Henry van Dyke; copyright 1904 by Charles Scribner's Sons, 1934 by Henry van Dyke; used by permission of the publishers.
[3] From *Rhythm and Harmony in Poetry and Music* by George L. Raymond. Published by G. P. Putnam's Sons, 1894, 1914.
[4] From *Puck of Pook's Hill* by Rudyard Kipling. Copyright 1905, 1906 by Rudyard Kipling. Reprinted by permission of Mrs. George Bambridge and Doubleday & Co., Inc.

> Along
> The busy river,
> Down
> The Avenue.
> Any day
> I like to take
> A trip
> With you.
>
> *The Green Bus* — *James S. Tippett*[5]

(g) How should I your true love know
>   From another one?
>   By his cockle hat and staff,
>   And his sandal shoon.
>   He is dead and gone, lady,
>   He is dead and gone;
>   At his head a grass-green turf,
>   At his heels a stone.
>
> *How Should I Your True Love Know* from *Hamlet* —
> *Shakespeare*

2. Experiment writing melodies for orchestral or band instruments played by members of the class. The phrases may be irregular in length, but the cadences should be clear and definite, ending on the accented beat of the measure. The small three-part form, consisting of one phrase for each part, gives a feeling of unity even though the phrases themselves may be irregular. (Accompaniment optional.)

3. Harmonize at least one of the following melodies for piano, using the accompaniment figure of Example 69 and those from preceding lessons:

Moderato   SCHUMANN, *Little Lullaby*, Op. 124 No. 6*

(a)

IV6   VI   I6 V7   I IV I

(Use Ex. 69)

*This melody has been somewhat condensed.

[5] From *I Go A Traveling* by James S. Tippett, published by Harper & Brothers, New York.

Chorale

(b)

(Use close harmony as in Ex. 70)

Tempo di marcia

Finnish Folk Song

(c)

From Play a Tune *of* The World Music Series, *copyright 1936. Used by permission of Ginn and Company, owners of the copyright.*

GANNE, *La Czarine*

Tempo di mazurka

(d)

III

I_4^6

HUMPERDINCK

Andante

(e)

VI   III

II   V$_9$ VI

(See Chapter XXIX)

(f) Allegretto   Czech Folk Song

(g) Andante con moto   CORON (1806)

(Use Ex. 48)

(h) Moderato   SCHÜLZ

(Use Ex. 28)

II   VI   IV

Used by permission of Harold Flammer, Inc.

(i) Briskly   Hornpipe

G₇

G₇

From Motion Picture Moods, *arranged by Erno Rapée. Reprinted by permission of the copy-right owner, G. Schirmer, Inc.*

II — Assignment for Playing

1. Harmonize one or more of the melodies in the *Assignment for Writing* (3), or select from the following melodies, using any of the preceding styles of accompaniment.

> *140 Folk-Songs.* Concord Series, No. 3. Nos. 35, 60, 103, 120.
>
> *Folk Song Sight Singing Series:* Book II, No. 7; Book III, No. 47; Book V, No. 18.
>
> *Foresman I,* pp. 90, 92; III, p. 62; IV, pp. 52, 75.

2. Improvise melodies without accompaniment in extended period form as directed in Chapter I.

3. Improvise melodies in extended period form using this accompaniment figure:

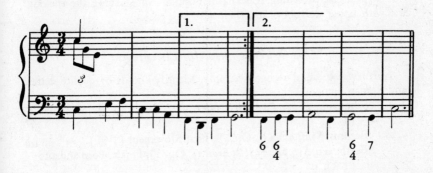

4. Play by ear the melody of the *Doxology* (*Old Hundredth*), and harmonize it in the style of Example 70, page 111, using the II and III chords and chords previously learned.

5. Play the II and III chords thus:

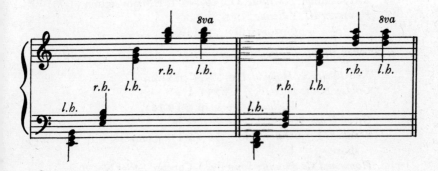

6. Learn to harmonize the descending C major scale beginning I–III–IV–I, or I–V–VI–III, thus:

7. Repeat the preceding scale harmonization embellishing the melody first with upper neighbors and then with suspensions.

III — Assignment for Listening

1. *Harmonic:* aural recognition only. Identify chords by quality, letter, and Roman numeral.

    Schumann, *The Two Grenadiers,* at change to major signature (1-4).

    Brahms, *Symphony II,* Op. 73, First Movement (1-31).

    Beethoven, *Symphony III (Eroica),* Op. 55, Finale, Poco andante (1-8).

    Chopin, *Mazurka,* Op. 24, No. 2 (13-20);
        Nocturne, Op. 48, No. 1, Poco piu lento (1-8).

    Mozart, *Violin Sonata,* K377, Allegro (1-4).

    Schubert, *B flat Piano Sonata,* No. 10, Finale, subordinate theme I, F Major (1-5).

    Rachmaninoff, *Nocturne,* Op. 10, No. 1, F Major section (1-7).

    Foresman III, Yuletide Night, p. 82;
        Christmas Song, p. 130.

2. *Written dictation (quality, bass, melody, and name of chord).*

    New Episcopal Hymnal, No. 577, *Christmas.*

    Golden Book: Doxology, p. 65 (1-4);
        Wedding Chorus, p. 5 (9-16).

    Green Book: No. 80, *The Strife is O'er.*

    Bach, *371 Chorales,* No. 334 (1-4). Compare with *Doxology* above.

    Home and Community Song Book. Concord Series No. 20.

    Glory to God, p. 85 (1-16);

IV — Assignment for Analysis

Chopin, *Mazurka*, Op. 68, No. 3 (last 8 measures).

Wagner, *Parsifal*, Grail Motive, Faith Motive, Bell Motive.

Beethoven, *Violin Sonata*, Op. 24 (Spring), First Movement
(1-10);

    Violin Sonata, Op. 47 (Kreutzer), Andante (1-8);

Finale, subordinate theme.

Haydn, *Gypsy Rondo* (1-8);

    Surprise Symphony, Menuetto (1-8).

Schumann, *Symphony No. 2*, Op. 61, Trio I (1-4).

Schubert, *Knowest Thou the Land* (1-4);

    At Midnight (1-6).

Brahms, *Symphony IV*, Op. 98, scherzo (1-6);

    Romanze, Op. 118, No. 5 (1-4).

Weber, *Invitation to the Dance*, Op. 65, C Major section to the end.

Tchaikovsky, *Symphony VI*, Op. 74 (*Pathétique*), Third Movement (1-2).

Moszkowski, *Spanish Dance*, Op. 12, No. 2, G Major section.

Rimsky-Korsakoff, *Scheherazade*, Op. 35, p. 50 (Schirmer, piano edition).

Mozart, *B flat Major Piano Sonata*, K333, First Movement;

    C Major Piano Sonata, K545, Rondo.

The following passages for analysis have been selected from the above list. Identify cadences, form, chords, and nonharmonic tones, and mark all sequences:

Allegro   CHOPIN, *Mazurka*, Op. 68, No. 3

Lento e solenne   WAGNER, *Parsifal*, Act I

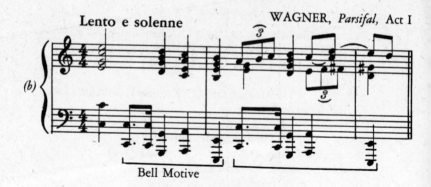

Bell Motive

BEETHOVEN, *Violin Sonata*, Op. 24 (Spring) [F]

Allegro (Principal theme)

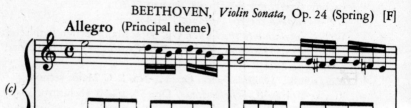

Andante   *Ibid.*

Grail Motive

Presto   HAYDN, *Gypsy Rondo* [G]

(d)

Allegro giocoso   BRAHMS, *Fourth Symphony*, Op. 98 [C]

(e)

MOZART, *B♭ Major Piano Sonata*, K333, First Movement

Allegro

(f)

MOZART, *C Major Piano Sonata*, K545, Rondo

Allegretto grazioso

Summary I

In Part I (Chapters I to VIII) some of the materials used in musical composition have been examined. In the course of the examination, the following facts were established:

(1) The *key* of C major is a group of tones having C (known as the *key tone*) as its point of repose.

The *scale* of C major is composed of the seven staff letters of the key, beginning on C, arranged consecutively in ascending order. These correspond to the white keys on the piano. Music using scale tones predominantly is referred to as *diatonic,* and deviations from diatonic are called *chromatic* changes.

(2) An *interval* is the difference in pitch between two tones, or notes. This difference is named according to the number and size of its staff degrees, counting upward from the lower tone as 1.

It was found that staff thirds, without accidentals, on C, F, and G are major (large), and those on D, E, and A are minor (small); and that all staff fifths are equal in size except B–F which is one half tone smaller than the others. Such equal fifths are termed *perfect.*

(3) A *chord* is a combination of three or more tones either arranged in thirds or reducible to thirds. The types of chords studied were:

A *triad,* represented by three different letters.

A *seventh-chord,* represented by four different letters.

When arranged in thirds, the lowest tone is called the *root* of the chord or triad. The other tones are the third, fifth, or seventh of the chord, counting upward from the root.

(4) A chord may be built on each degree of the scale. The chord is named from the location of its root in the scale: I, V, and so on. The quality of triads having perfect fifths is determined from the size of their lowest third, counting upward from the root. *Major triads* contain a root, a major third, and a perfect fifth; *minor triads* contain a root, a minor third, and a perfect fifth.

In a major key the I, IV, and V are major triads, and the II, III, and VI are minor triads.

(5) A chord or triad is *inverted* when the third, fifth, or seventh is used as the lowest (bass) tone. The physical quality of a chord or triad remains unchanged by inversion.

(6) The I, IV, and V are the basic chords of music. The other chords studied may be used as substitutes for them, thus:

$$
\text{Basic Chords} \left\{
\begin{array}{l}
\text{I} \longrightarrow \text{VI or } \text{I}_6 \\
\text{IV} \longrightarrow \text{II or } \text{II}_6 \\
\text{V} \longrightarrow \text{III, } \text{V}_7 \text{ or } \text{I}_4^6
\end{array}
\right\} \text{Substitute Chords}
$$

Hence, the I, IV, and V are termed *principal* (or *primary*) triads, and the II, III, and VI, *subordinate* (or *secondary*) triads.

(7) Tones that are foreign to the momentary chord are called *nonharmonic*, or *inharmonic*, *tones*. With few exceptions, all these tones are adjacent to the chord tones and are classified by their use as:

Passing tone: stepwise progression between *different* chord tones. (Chapter III, page 32.)

Neighboring tone: stepwise progression returning to the *same* chord tone. (Chapter III, page 32.)

Suspension: tone held over from the preceding beat. (Chapter IV, page 49.)

Anticipation: tone belonging to the following beat. (Chapter VII, page 94.)

8. *Form* in music is the sequence, arrangement, and balance of the tonal material in a composition. The smallest complete unit of form is the phrase. The end of the phrase is called a cadence. Phrases end with these cadences:

Perfect authentic: V_7–I, ending with the chord root in the soprano. (Chapter I, page 8.)

Imperfect authentic:[1] V_7–I, ending with the chord-third

---

[1] The imperfect authentic cadence is sometimes used in place of either the semi-, the evaded, or even the perfect authentic cadence. (Chapter VII, p. 93.)

or fifth in soprano. (Chapter VII, page 93.)

Semi-: V. (Chapter I, page 10.)

Evaded or deceptive: V_7–VI, usually ending with key tone in the soprano. (Chapter VII, page 93.)

Plagal: IV–I, either perfect or imperfect as in the authentic cadences above. (Chapter III, page 30.)

The period consists of two phrases: the first, or *antecedent*, phrase usually ended by a semi-cadence, and the second, or *consequent*, phrase usually ended by a perfect authentic cadence. When the two phrases begin similarly, the period is parallel in construction; otherwise, it is *contrasting*. A phrase may be repeated either singly or as a part of a period.

Suggestions for Study

Find examples in musical literature of the following technical points discussed in Part I.

(1) Chords.

The I, V, V_7, IV, II_6, I_4^6, VI, II, and III chords.

(2) Nonharmonic tones.

Neighboring and passing tones, suspension, retardation, and anticipation.

(3) Form.

(*a*) Period and repeated phrase.

(*b*) Cadences: semi- and authentic (perfect, imperfect, and plagal).

(*c*) The ternary (*A–B–A*) form.

Part II

BASIC INVERTED DISCORDS. THE MAJOR MODE.
MODULATION. TWO- AND THREE-VOICE
WRITING

Chapter IX

MODULATION TO THE DOMINANT KEY

Two-Part Vocal Writing

Ex. 76

BEETHOVEN (1770–1827), *First Piano Concerto*, Op. 15, Rondo

Allegro

THIS SIMPLE, jolly phrase opens the *finale* of Beethoven's *First Piano Concerto*, published in 1801. In music, the term *rondo* refers to a composition whose principal theme recurs (or comes *round* again) periodically. Since *rondos* of this type usually are classified according to the number of returns of the principal theme, the entire movement is a *third rondo* whose

131

over-all thematic design can be expressed in letters as A–B–A–C–A–B–A. Note that the normal four-measure phrase is extended to six measures by the insertion of measures two and five. Such repetition is one of the technical devices by which music grows.

Sing or play the portion of the principal theme quoted above in Example 76. The passage begins in C major, but closes with a feeling for a different tonal center. This change of feeling for the key center is called *modulation*, from the Latin word, *modulari*, to change, fluctuate, or vary.

Precisely why is a change of key center felt in measures 4, 5, and 6? Chiefly because the G in the melody is preceded by F sharp, not F natural, and is harmonized by the G_4^6–D_7 and G chords. The F sharp helps to cancel the feeling for C as a center, since it is not a part of the C major scale. To what scale does it belong? To answer this question, it is necessary to know more about the construction of major scales.

Listen carefully to the different kinds and sizes of seconds (scale steps) which make up the C major scale. Sing each one slowly, thus: C–D, D–E, and so on.

Ex. 77

These seconds obviously are not all the same size, although they appear so on the staff. The two seconds, E–F (3-4) and B–C (7-8), are smaller, and are so because there is no intervening black key. E–F, B–C, and all other adjacent keys on the piano are called *half steps* (half tones). The seconds, separated by an intervening black or white key, are called *whole steps* (whole tones). Half steps are termed *small* or *minor seconds*, and whole steps are termed *large* or *major seconds*. Thus all "white key" (staff) seconds, forming the C major scale, are classified as *major*, except E–F and B–C, which are *minor*.

Listen again to Example 76, page 131, measures 5 and 6. Is the interval F sharp–G a whole or a half step? Between what scale steps does such an interval occur? In this setting, does it sound like 3-4 (mi-fa), or 7-8 (ti-do), and why? What is the new key tone?

We shall better realize why the F sharp suggests a new tonal center, which is G, when we understand the principles underlying these questions. To confirm this, construct a scale similar to the C major scale, but beginning on G, thus:

Ex. 78

Note, also, the new descriptive or functional names that are used for either single tones or chords built upon them as roots. Thus, the I chord may also be called the *tonic* chord; II, the *supertonic,* and similarly for all other chords.

A modulation, then, is the more or less temporary establishment of a new key center or tonal "home." The V₇ chord of the new key often introduces the modulation. Generally, the chord which precedes this V_7 belongs to both keys and is called the "gateway," or *pivotal* chord. That there may be no doubt about the acceptance of the new key, composers usually confirm it by a definite cadence, as Beethoven has done here (Example 76, page 131).

Composers use modulation for key contrasts, as they use chord contrasts within a phrase. Modulation also clarifies the form by emphasizing the difference between various sections or movements of a large composition. Beethoven's modulation to the dominant key (from C, tonic, to G, dominant, in this case) is one of the most frequently used types.

Apply these principles of modulation to the harmonization of the following melody.

Ex. 79

Alla marcia   CORON (1806)

The first phrase of this melody undoubtedly is in the key of C major, but near the beginning of the second phrase, the F sharp suggests the key of G major, confirmed by the cadence in measures 7 and 8. What chords can be used to make this modulation clear? Decide on the general harmonic background and sing a bass while the melody is being played. Compare your solution with the composer's.

Ex. 80

Complete the left hand, using Example 48 (Chapter V, page 67) as a model. Note that the new key (G major) enters in measure 5 through its dominant seventh (V_7) chord D–F sharp–A–C.

Two-Part Vocal Writing

The point has now been reached where a second voice, or part, may be added either to vocal or to instrumental melodies. A second voice (alto) may be written in several ways:

1. By using parallel thirds or sixths as in the opening section of the famous Sextette from Donizetti's opera, *Lucia di Lammermoor*. Sing both parts, then test the second voice alone, thus:

Ex. 81   DONIZETTI, *Lucia,* (1835)

Larghetto

What does this passage show us about two-part writing? Which intervals are most used? This parallel progression of the second voice is satisfactory because it only "reflects" the melody at a different interval (see Chapter IV, *Assignment for Analysis* (*a*), page 59). Using this method, a good second part can be added to many simple melodies. Care must be taken, however, to vary the intervals in order to avoid monotony. In this type of writing, the distance between the voices *should not exceed an octave*. Experiment singing a second part in thirds or sixths to familiar melodies.

2.   Under certain conditions the added voice may repeat the melody of the first voice *exactly*, beginning usually a measure later. Thus, the first melody is "reflected" in the second part by delaying the time of its entrance. This device of strict imitation is called *canon*. A simple type of canon is the *round*, distinguished by the return of the original melody, hence its name. In the

round, the other voice, or voices, repeat the melody only at the unison, or octave, after the completion of the first melodic figure. In other types of canons, the following voice, or voices, may be at any pitch or rhythmic interval. Compare *Three Blind Mice* and the beginning of this two-part Bach Invention in regard to the distinctions just mentioned.

Ex. 82   BACH, *Two-Part Invention*, No. 8

Find other examples of canonic writing in musical literature. (See Chapter III, page 43, *Assignment for Analysis*, (*a*), and Schumann's *Nocturne*, Op. 23, No. 4.) All canons, or rounds, are examples of counterpoint (Chapter VI, page 78). Experiment with this device, using either original or familiar melodies. It is an interesting musical device which will help you to hear and to think music contrapuntally.

3. A voice may be added below the melody by combining the use of parallel thirds and sixths with the contrapuntal idea of a round. Write a second part, melodically interesting, using imitative effects but not following strictly the first part, as in a round, thus:

Ex. 83   SCHUMANN, *Ländlichs Lied*

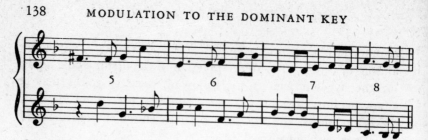

Sing this passage, noting the crossing voices and the dissonant seconds in measures 2, 5, and 6. These dissonant intervals are introduced to avoid monotony and to give more melodic independence to the second part. This freedom is characteristic of the contrapuntal concept of music, which emphasizes the melodic interest of each part more than does the parallel writing in Example 81, page 135. Note, also, that the accidentals only establish a new key center when confirmed by a strong cadence. The cadence in measure 4 (Example 83) is too weak to set up a new key center, and the accidentals in measures 5 and 7 are not cadential. Hence, there are no modulations in this passage.

Your choice of style for the added part will depend on the type of melody used and your own preferences and skill. In any case, make the second voice as interesting as possible, always testing the result by ear.

Review:

1. What modulation is.
2. How a modulation to the dominant key is made.
3. Why composers use modulation.
4. One of the most used modulations.
5. What chord frequently introduces the new key.
6. How the suggestion of the new key is confirmed.
7. The interval construction of the major scale.
8. The difference between a whole and a half step.
9. The quality of the white key (staff) seconds.
10. The descriptive or functional names of the scale steps.
11. Three ways of adding a second voice below a given melody.
12. What a *round*, or *canon*, is.
13. The basic design of a rondo.
14. What is meant by a *pivotal* chord.

For Further Study, Determine:

1. How many major scales are possible beginning on different pitches.

2. Whether compositions begin and end in the same key, and why.

3. How the word "modulation" is used in reference to speech.

4. The meaning of the various descriptive names of the scale steps.

5. To what tones in the scale the prefix *sub-* alludes, and why.

6. Another name for a half step, or minor second.

7. Whether accidentals always produce modulations.

8. How many other piano concertos Beethoven wrote.

9. The difference between a round and a canon and a round and a rondo.

10. The form of Example 76.

11. Where the modulations occur in the following songs:

> *The Star Spangled Banner* (1-4)
> *Columbia, the Gem of the Ocean* (phrase 2)
> *Onward, Christian Soldiers* (phrases 1-2)
> *Sweet and Low* (phrases 1-2)
> *The Blue Bells of Scotland* (middle section)
> *Flow Gently, Sweet Afton* (middle section)
> *O God, Our Help* (phrases 1-2)

I — Assignment for Writing

1. Scan the following stanzas and set one or more of them to music for one or two voices. (Accompaniment optional.) Experiment modulating to the dominant key for one of the cadences at the end:

(*a*) Wind that shakes and rattles my window,
    What strange sights have you seen tonight?
How many miles have you swept with your roaring
    Since you woke me up in the dawn's cold light?
Wind that whistles and sings in the darkness,
    Where have you been this whole day through?
I long for your freedom of mad, wild roaming —
    Wind, how I envy you!

Winter Wind — E. A. Fordon[1]

(*b*) O lead me by the hand,
And let my heart have rest,
And bring me back to childhood land,
To find again the long-lost band
Of playmates blithe and blest.

Play Song — Henry van Dyke[2]

---

[1] Originally published in *New York State Education*, December, 1937.

[2] Reprinted from *Music and Other Poems* by Henry van Dyke; copyright 1904 by Charles Scribner's Sons, 1934 by Henry van Dyke; used by permission of the publishers.

(c)   Forget, forget!
    The tide of life is turning;
    The waves of light ebb slowly down the west:
    Along the edge of dark some stars are burning
    To guide thy spirit safely to an isle of rest.

Sleep Song — Henry van Dyke[3]

(d)   A soft veil dims the tender skies,
        And half conceals from pensive eyes
    The bronzing tokens of the fall;
    A calmness broods upon the hills,
        And summer's parting dream distills
    A charm of silence over all.

Indian Summer — Henry van Dyke[4]

(e)   Up the airy mountain,
        Down the rushy glen,
    We daren't go a-hunting
        For fear of little men;
    Wee folk, good folk,
        Trooping all together;
    Green jacket, red cap,
        And white owl's feather.

The Fairy Folk — William Allingham

(f)   Who would be
    A mermaid fair,
    Singing alone,
    Combing her hair
    Under the sea,
    In a golden curl
    With a comb of pearl,
    On a throne?

    Who would be
    A merman bold,
    Sitting alone,
    Singing alone

---

[3] Reprinted from *Music and Other Poems* by Henry van Dyke; copyright 1904 by Charles Scribner's Sons, 1934 by Henry van Dyke; used by permission of the publishers.
[4] Reprinted from *Music and Other Poems* by Henry van Dyke; copyright 1904 by Charles Scribner's Sons, 1934 by Henry van Dyke; used by permission of the publishers.

Under the sea,
With a crown of gold,
On a throne?

The Mermaid — Alfred, Lord Tennyson

2. Write an "echo song" or some type of "work song," for three voices, using canonic imitations. (Optional.)

3. Write some duets for band or orchestral instruments in repeated period form. For example, for two violins or two saxophones. Make the cadences clear and definite by ending each phrase on the accented beat of the measure. (Optional.) Play these duets in class.

4. Add a second voice to at least one of the following melodies. Write out on two staves any melody which may be treated as a round, the second voice beginning a measure later than the first voice. From this point, all vocal melodies may be treated *instrumentally*. See (3).

Reprinted by permission from 140 Folk-Songs, Concord Series No. 3. Published and copyrighted by the E. C. Schirmer Music Company.

*Two composers have written variations on this theme. See Mozart, *Twelve Variations on "Ah Vous Dirais-je, Maman* for piano, K265, and Dohnanyi's *Variations on a Nursery Tune* for orchestra. The latter is recorded.

5. Harmonize at least one of the following melodies for piano, using the accompaniment figures from the preceding lessons:

II — Assignment for Playing

1. Harmonize one or more of the melodies in the *Assignment for Writing* (5) above, or select from the following melodies, using any of the preceding accompaniment figures:

     Folk Song Sight Singing Series: Book VI, Nos. 65, 67

2. Improvise melodies without accompaniment in repeated period form as directed in Chapter I.

3. Improvise a repeated period form over this accompaniment figure:

Allegro

MOZART, *Variation* (Adapted)

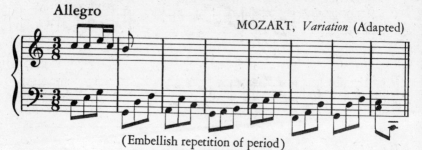

(Embellish repetition of period)

4. Play by ear the melody of the *Blue Bells of Scotland* (C major); then fill in the chords in the right hand over this bass:

(See Chapter XXV)

(See Chapter XXII)

5. Memorize these chord patterns which modulate to the dominant key, and repeat each in piano style with nonharmonic embellishments.

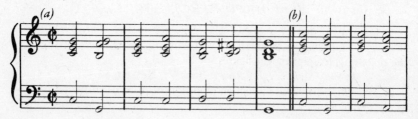

III — Assignment for Listening

1. *Oral dictation:* harmonic recognition only.

   Strauss, *Vienna Life Waltzes,* No. 3.
   Clementi, *Sonatina,* Op. 36, No. 1, Allegro (1-8).
   Kuhlau, *Sonatina,* Op. 55, No. 3, Allegretto (1-8).
   Haydn, *C Major Symphony* (Peters Edition), Finale (1-16).
   Chopin, *Mazurka,* Op. 50, No. 3, B Major theme.

2. *Written dictation (quality, bass, melody, and name of chord).*

   Golden Book: The Old Oaken Bucket, p. 106;
              Hail Columbia, p. 9.
   Sing!: Silver Threads Among the Gold (8-12), p. 46.
   Green Book, Twice 55: No. 133, *Fine Knacks for Ladies* (1-4).
   Home and Community Song Book: Concord Series No. 2. *Lo, How a Rose,* p. 87.
   New Episcopal Hymnal, No. 289, *St. Anne;*
              No. 64, *Winchester;*
              No. 336, *Rathbun.*

IV — Assignment for Analysis

Schumann, *Symphony III,* Op. 97, Scherzo (1-8).
Schubert, *German Dances,* Op. 33, Scherzando (1-8).
Beethoven, *Symphony I,* Op. 21, Finale (1-8);
        Symphony IV, Op. 60, First Movement, subordinate theme.
Mozart, Minuet from *Don Giovanni.*
Beethoven, *Sonata,* Op. 26, Scherzo (1-8);
        Sonata, Op. 27, No. 2, Allegretto (1-8).
Chopin, *Waltz in A flat Major,* Op. 34, No. 1, principal theme (1-8);
        Mazurka in F Minor, Op. 7, No. 3 (41-48).
Moszkowski, *Spanish Dances,* Op. 12, No. 1, principal theme.

The passages for analysis on the following pages have been selected from the above list. Identify cadences, form, chords, and nonharmonic tones.

Tempo di minuetto   MOZART, *Don Giovanni*

Vivace   CHOPIN, *Valse*, Op. 34, No. 1

Allegro   CHOPIN, *Mazurka*, Op. 7, No. 3

MOSKOWSKI, *Spanish Dance*, Op. 12, No. 1

Allegro brioso

Chapter X

THE V$_5^6$ CHORD

Ex. 84

THIS CHARMING old French dance was written in 1727 by
Jacques Aubert, who was a member of Louis XV's special band
of 24 violinists. It is easy to imagine the scene of its first performance with the players in ornate court dress, playing by candlelight.
Aside from its charm and gaiety, the dance contains several points
of interest. It is made of very simple material, the melodic and
rhythmic figures of measures 1 and 3 heard against a repeated
chord background. Yet it gives the impression of a developed
and well-balanced whole. How is this accomplished?

Listen first to the harmonic background. Since the excerpt begins
and ends on the G chord, the prevailing tonality must be that of
G major. Note the accidental after the clef sign. When a composition is in the key of G major, the required accidental (F sharp)
is written after each clef throughout the piece,[1] thus:

Ex. 85

This means that each F on the staff is to be changed to F sharp,
unless canceled by a natural (♮), thus saving the trouble of
writing the sharp (♯) each time the F occurs. This accidental (or
group of accidentals) after the clef is called the *key signature.*
It identifies the key as its name indicates.

---

[1] Note that, though key signatures are repeated on each successive staff, time
signatures are given *only once,* at the beginning of the composition.

In Example 84, page 148, note that the strong cadence on the D major chord in measure 7 temporarily establishes D as a new key tone.[2] As was stated in Chapter IX, page 132, this change of tonality is called a modulation. Note that key signatures are not changed for modulations except in long compositions in which the new key is used for entire sections.

In the second phrase the key of D major enters at the C sharp in measure 5. Spell this chord upward from the bass, C sharp–A–G. What is the root of the chord? Rewrite the chord in fundamental position, thus:

Ex. 86

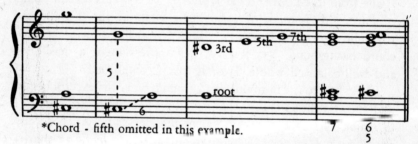

*Chord - fifth omitted in this example.

It is the first inversion of the A$_7$ chord, having the chord third (C sharp) in the bass. As in previous cases of chord inversion, the inverted chord is named from the number of staff degrees (interval) between the bass and the other tones of the chord — 6 (C sharp to A), 5 (C sharp to G), and 3 (C sharp to E), in this case. Hence, this is an A$^6_5$ chord usually written as such, or, in the key of D major, the dominant six-five (V$^6_5$). It will be well to remember that the first inversion of *any* seventh-chord is symbolized $^6_5$, just as the inversion of any triad is symbolized 6.

Observe that the V$^6_5$ chord is a dissonant chord (Chapter II, page 19) whose bass, being the seventh degree of the scale,

[2] Using the pattern of the major scale (Chapter IX), construct a scale beginning on D. Note that the new sharp (#) is always the seventh of the scale, C sharp in this case, in addition to the F sharp carried over from the key of G major.

has a strong tendency to resolve up to the key tone. The V$^6_5$ is used as a substitute for the V$_7$ except, of course, in the perfect authentic cadence.

Identify aurally the other chords in Example 84, page 148, consulting the music only when necessary. If in doubt, follow the chord indicated by the left hand. How many other V$^6_5$ chords occur in this passage? Listen for dissonant chords on the leading tone resolving to the I chord. Try using the V$_7$ in place of the V$^6_5$. How do they differ in effect? Which is more active? Which makes the more melodic bass line?

The composer does not rely entirely on harmonic, melodic, and rhythmic variety to hold our interest, but he also utilizes formal structure. Note that there is a perfect authentic cadence in measure 8, which divides the composition exactly in half. This division creates a new form (consisting of two contrasting sections, each ending with a perfect authentic cadence), which is called an A–B, or two-part (binary), form. It is distinguished from the A–B–A form chiefly by the nonrepetition of A after B, although parts A and B frequently have similar endings, as in Example 84, page 148.[8] Although the A–B form is comparatively rare, we will find it useful in setting two-stanza poems to music.

Without doubt, though, the melody is the most interesting feature of this dance. It achieves unity through repetition. For example, compare the approach to the cadences of phrases 1 and 2 (first and second endings), and note the similarity of measures 12 and 13 to measure 1. Such repetitions always give the effect of unity and coherence. All these devices are interesting and important musically only because they contribute to the natural, spontaneous, and artless effect of the composition. The composer himself may have been entirely unaware of them when writing, but he probably was conscious of such devices while learning his craft.

---

[8] See Percy Goetschius; Masters of the Symphony (Boston: Oliver Ditson Co., 1929), pages 24-30, for a discussion of the relationship of the primitive A–B form to the A–B–A form. For further examples, see Mozart's Minuet (Chapter IX), Brahm's Lullaby, and the folk song, Robin Adair.

Consider the following melody (Example 87) by the old
Italian master Corelli. Sing the tune several times, noting the
chord skips and also the sequences in the second part. Compare
its similarity, in mood and construction, with Example 84, page
148. Sing one of these basses while the melody is being played or
sung. Is Corelli's bass (No. 3) preferable? How does his bass
compare with the others? Note the harmonic sequence in the
second part suggested by the melody.

Ex. 87

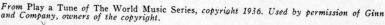

It is also interesting to experiment with a more independent contrapuntal bass for the last phrase, which brings out new harmonic combinations to be discussed later, thus:

Ex. 88

To summarize: it was found that the V$_7$ chord may be used in its first inversion as a V$^6_5$ chord, built on the leading tone of the scale and resolving to the I chord, and that it is used as a substitute for the fundamental V$_7$ except in the perfect authentic cadence. Hence, it can be used for modulation, as its bass is then the leading tone of the new tonality. It also provides an opportunity for a more melodic bass line.

It was noted that keys are identified by key signatures — a group of required accidentals written immediately after each clef. Since F sharp is required in the scale of G major, its signature, or key identification, is one sharp.

Finally, a new form was examined: the A–B (two-part, or binary) form, consisting of two contrasting sections, each ended by a perfect authentic cadence.

Use the V$^6_5$ and the A–B form in your writing, but only where they occur naturally for musical reasons, not artificially for their own sake.

Review:

1. What a V$^6_5$ chord is.
2. What is the bass of a V$^6_5$ chord.
3. Why the first inversion of a seventh chord is called $^6_5$.
4. Some uses of the V$^6_5$ chord.
5. What chord most frequently follows the V$^6_5$.
6. What a key signature is.
7. What the signature for G major is.
8. Why key signatures are used.
9. The pitches in the D major scale.
10. What scale step is always altered to make the next sharp scale.
11. What is meant by the A–B form.
12. Two other names for the A–B form.
13. The difference between the A–B and the A–B–A forms.
14. What parts of an A–B form may be similar.
15. One way of giving greater organic unity to a melody.

For Further Study, Determine:

1. Why the V$^6_5$ is not used in the perfect authentic cadence.
2. The complete figuration for the V$^6_5$.

3. Why the V$^6_5$ is dissonant.

4. The form of *The Star Spangled Banner, America, Juanita,* and *Home, Sweet Home.*

5. What a *gigue* is and other ways of spelling the word.

6. How a sequence differs from a repetition.

7. Whether the idea of sequence can be used for chords as well as for melody.

8. Whether sequence and repetition must be exact.

9. Examples of sequence and repetition in this chapter and elsewhere.

10. Whether the first perfect cadence in an *A–B* form may be in the dominant key.

11. What the word "binary" means and why it is applied to the *A–B* form.

I — Assignment for Writing

1. Scan the following stanzas and set one or more of them to music in the key of G major, or in others if preferred, for both one and two voices (accompaniment optional). Experiment modulating to the dominant key and returning to the tonic key at the end. Two-stanza poems may be set in *A–B* form.

(*a*) The lark will make her hymn to God,
  The partridge call her brood,
  While I forget the heath I trod,
  The fields wherein I stood.

  'Tis dule to know not night from morn,
  But greater dule to know
  I can but hear the hunter's horn
  That once I used to blow.
       The Lark — Rudyard Kipling[*]

(*b*) Summer eve is gone and past,
  Summer dew is falling fast;
  I have wandered all the day,
  Do not bid me farther stray!
  Gentle hearts, of gentle kin,
  Take the wandering harper in!

---

[*] From *The Light that Failed* by Rudyard Kipling. Copyright 1897, 1899, 1903 by Rudyard Kipling. Reprinted by permission of Mrs. George Bambridge and Doubleday & Company, Inc.

I have song of war for knight,
Lay of love for lady bright,
Fairy tale to lull the heir,
Goblin grim the maids to scare;
Dark the night, and long till day,
Do not bid me farther stray!

Song from Rokeby — Sir Walter Scott[5]

(c)   I must down to the seas again, to the
           lonely sea and the sky,
       And all I ask is a tall ship and a star to
           steer her by,
       And the wheel's kick and the wind's song
           and the white sail's shaking,
       And a gray mist on the sea's face and a
           gray dawn breaking.

Sea Fever — John Masefield[6]

Sequence or repetition may be used in setting the following poems:

(d)   Waken, lords and ladies gay,
       On the mountain dawns the day,
       All the jolly chase is here,
       With hawk, and horse, and hunting spear!
       Hounds are in their couples yelling,
       Hawks are whistling, horns are knelling,
       Merrily, merrily, mingle they,
       'Waken, lords and ladies gay!

Hunting Song — Sir Walter Scott[7]

(e)   Hie away, hie away,
       Over bank and over brae,
       Where the copsewood is the greenest,
       Where the fountains glisten sheenest, . . .
       Over bank and over brae,
       Hie away, hie away.

Gallatley's Song to Deerhounds — Sir Walter Scott[8]

---

[5] From *The Poetical Works of Sir Walter Scott*, J. Logie Robertson (Editor), published by The Oxford University Press, London.

[6] From John Masefield, *Story of a Round House and Other Poems.* Copyright 1912, by The Macmillan Company.

[7] From *The Poetical Works of Sir Walter Scott*, J. Logie Robertson (Editor), published by The Oxford University Press, London.

[8] *Ibid.*

(*f*)   As the dawn was breaking the Wolf Pack yelled
Once, twice, and again!
Feet in the jungle that leave no mark!
Eyes that can see in the dark — the dark!
Once, twice, and again!
Hunting Song of the Seeonee Pack — Rudyard Kipling[9]

2. Write a song of three stanzas for two voice parts, each voice singing one stanza alone and both singing the last stanza.

3. Write a *gigue* in two-part form (G major, ⁶⁄₈ or ¹²⁄₈ as in Example 87) for two violins, modulating to the dominant key at the end of Part I. Part II of this dance often begins in the dominant key with an inversion of the melody of Part I. Make the cadences clear and definite by ending on the accented beat of each cadence measure. (Optional.)

4. Add a second voice, either alto or bass, to at least one of the following melodies. Can any of them be treated as a canon or a round, the second voice entering one measure later?

MOZART, *Marriage of Figaro*, No. 21, "Ricevete, o padroncina"

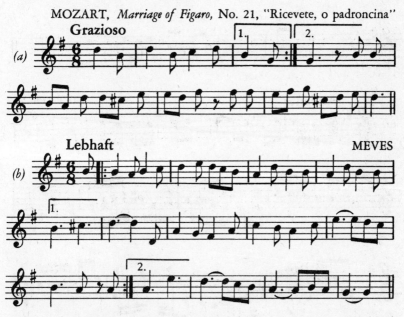

From *Thirty Vocal Duets, published by Breitkopf and Hartel. Reprinted by permission of Associated Music Publishers, Inc.*

[9] From *The Jungle Book* by Rudyard Kipling. Copyright 1893 by Rudyard Kipling. Reprinted by permission of Doubleday & Co., Inc.

(Arrange for two voices or two violins)

Allegretto poco mosso   FRANCK, *Violin Sonata*, Finale

Andante   METHFESEL

From Thirty Vocal Duets, *published by Breitkopf and Hartel. Reprinted by permission of Associated Music Publishers, Inc.*

Moderato — HANDEL, *Judas Maccabaeus*

(e)

Fine

D.C. al Fine

Alla marcia — Old Song

(f)

Reprinted by permission from A Book of Songs, *Concord Series No. 14.* Published and copyrighted by the E. C. Schirmer Music Company.

See also *140 Folk-Songs.* Concord Series No. 3. Nos. 111, 119, 129.

5. Harmonize at least one of the following melodies for piano, using the accompaniment figures in the preceding lessons. Analyze the form of each melody used.

Allegretto — French Folk Song

(a)

From Play a Tune of The World Music Series, *copyright 1936. Used by permission of Ginn and Company, owners of the copyright.*

English Folk Song

Allegro

(b)

V VI III IV

Fine

D.C. al Fine

From Play a Tune of The World Music Series, copyright 1936. Used by permission of Ginn and Company, owners of the copyright.

Gayly

Danish Folk Song

(c)

V$_5^6$

1.

2.

IV I$_4^6$

GLUCK, Armide

Andantino

(d)

V$_5^6$

1.

2.

Fine

V$_7$

D.C. al Fine

German Folk Song (Adapted)

Giocoso

(e)

Fine

DI   V⁶₅

D.C. al Fine

Used by permission of Harold Flammer, Inc.

CLEMENTI, *Sonatina,* Op. 36, No. 2

Allegretto

(f)

D⁶₄

KUHLAU, *Sonatina,* Op. 20, No. 1

Allegro

(g)

V⁶₅

Chorale

II — Assignment for Playing

1. Harmonize one or more of the melodies in the *Assignment for Writing* (5), or select from the following melodies, using any of the preceding accompaniment figures:

> *Play a Tune: Shepherds' Dance,* German, p. 15;
> *Gavotte,* Gillet, p. 27;
> *Dance it Merrily,* Folk Tune, p. 62.

2. Improvise melodies without accompaniment in the *A–B* form.

3. Improvise an *A–B* form using this accompaniment figure and melodic sequence in part II:

After MARTINI

4. Learn *America* in the key of G major. What is its form?

5. Play the V⁶₅ chord, thus:

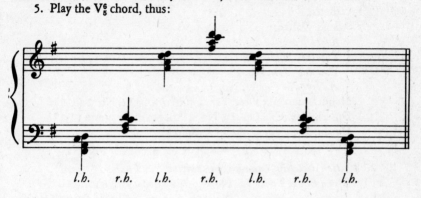

6. Memorize the following chord patterns which modulate to the dominant key, and repeat each in piano style, with nonharmonic embellishments:

(a)

(b)

III — *Assignment for Listening*

1. *Oral dictation:* harmonic recognition only. Identify chords by quality, letter and Roman numeral.

    Beethoven, *Sonata,* Op. 22, Andante (1-12);

                 Sonata, Op. 49, No. 2, Rondo (1-16).

Schumann, *Papillons,* Op. 2, No. 10 (1-8).
Brahms, *Violin Sonata,* No. 1, Op. 78, First Movement, subordinate theme.
Strauss Waltzes:
> *Roses from the South;*
> *Treasure Waltz,* No. 1;
> *You and You,* No. 2;
> *A Night in Venice,* No. 3.

Mendelssohn, *Six Pieces for Children,* Op. 72, No. 2 (1-4).
Dussek, *Sonatina,* Op. 20, No.3, Allegro quasi presto (1-14).
Haydn, *Sonata in C Major,* Adagio (1-5).
Kuhlau, *Sonatina,* Op. 88, No. 2, Allegro con brio (1-8).

2. *Written dictation (quality, bass, melody, and name of chord).*
> *Green Book, Twice 55:* No. 8, *Isle of Beauty* (1-8);
> 　　　　No. 147, *Chorus of Blessed Spirits* (1-5).
> *Brown Book, Twice 55:* No. 78, *Deck the Halls* (1-4);
> 　　　　No. 84, *The Heavens Resound* (1-4).
> *Play a Tune:* Theme from *Don Juan* (Mozart), p. 69.

Gluck, Chorus from *Alceste,* No. 20 (1-8).
Haydn, *The Creation,* No. 3, "A New Created World" (24-16 from end).
Schubert, *Pax Vobiscum* (1-9);
> *The Crusaders* (5-8).

IV — Assignment for Analysis

Bach, *Third Cello Suite,* Bourrée.
Haydn, *Military Symphony (G),* Finale (1-8).
Mozart, *Piano Concerto D Minor,* K466, Romanza (1-8);
> *Piano Concerto E Major,* K482, Rondo (1-8);
> *Marriage of Figaro,* No. 11, No. 12 (1-36), No. 14 (1-11);
> *Don Giovanni,* No. 12, "Batti, Batti," (1-16);
> *Viennese Sonatinas,* No. I, Menuetto and Finale, No. V, Menuetto and Polonaise;
> *Divertimento,* No. 13, Allegro;
> *Piano Sonata A Minor,* K310, Presto (A Major section);
> *Violin Sonata,* K301, Allegro (1-16).

Beethoven, *Sonata,* Op. 10, No. 1, Adagio Molto (1-8);
> *String Quartette,* Op. 18, No. 1, Allegro con brio (1-8).

Verdi, *Il Trovatore,* No. 21, "Home to Our Mountains" (1-12).
Schubert, *Piano Sonata,* Op. 143, Andante (1-4);
> *Litany;*
> *The Quail.*

Chopin, *Waltz*, Op. 69, No. 2, B Major section.

Mendelssohn, *Song Without Words*, No. 25 (1-4).

The following passages for analysis have been selected from the above list. Identify cadences, form, chords, and nonharmonic tones, and note pivotal chords:

BACH, *Third Cello Suite*, (1720), "Bourrée"

Allegro moderato

MOZART, *Marriage of Figaro*, "Voi, che sapete"

Andante con moto

BEETHOVEN, *Piano Sonata,* Op. 10, No. 1 [A♭]

Adagio molto

IV₆

BEETHOVEN, *String Quartet,* Op. 18, No. 1 [F]

Allegro con brio

IV₆

CHOPIN, *Waltz*, Op. 69, No. 2

VERDI, *Il Trovatore*, No. 21,"Home to Our Mountains"

Chapter XI

THE V⁶₅ CHORD (*Continued*)

Three-Part Vocal Writing

Ex. 89

J. S. BACH (1685—1750), *Sixth Violoncello Suite*, Gavotte (Adapted)

T HE VIGOROUS dance[1] quoted on the preceding page was written by Bach while he was instrumental director (*Kapell-meister*) for the Duke of Cothen (1717-1722), during which period nearly all of his chamber music was composed. Listen to the sturdy, square-cut rhythm and the consistent use of melodic figure. Identify the cadences and name the form.

Note the key signature of D major (F sharp and C sharp) after the clef. Obviously, the strong cadence on the A major chord in measure 8 establishes A as a new tonal center,[2] entered through the G sharp in measure 7. Spell this chord upward from the bass tone, G sharp–E–D, noting that its root is E. Rewrite the chord in fundamental position, thus:

Ex. 90

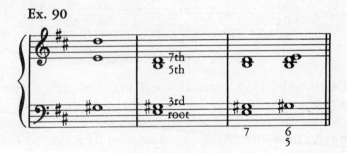

This E$_7$ chord is the V$_7$ of the key of A major. In the first inversion, with the chord third (G sharp) in the bass, it becomes the V$_5^6$. This is another example of the new key being entered through its V$_5^6$. Determine whether it is consonant or dissonant, and why.

---

[1] The *gavotte* is a French dance, so called because it was danced by the Gavots, or Gap-men, who lived in the town of Gap in the Haute-Alpes. The gavotte is usually written in *A–B* form with similar endings for Parts I and II. It begins on the third pulse of the measure ($\frac{4}{4}$) in contrast with the *bourrée* (*Assignment for Analysis,* (*a*), page 165), which begins on the last half of the second beat in $\frac{2}{2}$. The tempo of the gavotte is also somewhat slower than the bourrée.

[2] Using the pattern of the major scale (Chapter IX), construct a major scale beginning on A. Note that the new sharp (G sharp) is the seventh of the scale and is added to the two sharps (F sharp and C sharp) of D major. See Example 89.

The consonance or dissonance of any chord naturally depends upon its intervals. The interval E–D in measure 7 is a seventh since it is one letter less than an octave. As in the case of seconds and thirds, there are two kinds of staff, or white key, sevenths: major (large) and minor (small). The major sevenths are only one half tone less than the octave, whereas the minor sevenths are a whole tone smaller. *Consequently, all staff sevenths are minor (small) except C–B and F–E.* Compare the seconds and sevenths on the staff, thus:

Ex. 91

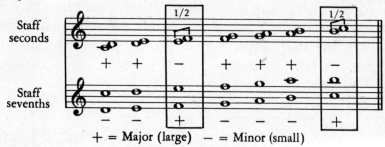

Staff seconds

Staff sevenths

+ = Major (large)   − = Minor (small)

Test all these intervals by ear. Hence all major and minor sevenths involving accidentals may be named by comparing them with the octave. What kind of a seventh does the V₇ chord contain? Remember that all sevenths are dissonant. The only consonant intervals are the perfect intervals,[3] and the major and minor thirds and sixths. All others are dissonant and demand resolution or completion.

Example 91, above, also shows that major intervals *when inverted* become minor in quality, and that, by the same process, minor intervals become major. Classify the inversions of major and minor thirds in a chart similar to that in Example 91.

Identify the other chords in Example 89, page 168. In measure 2, the first melody tone (D) does not belong to the chord (A major), although it is a neighbor of the chord tone C sharp. Note that it is preceded by the skip G–D. Such a non-chord tone, entered by skip and resolved stepwise, is called an *appoggiatura,*[4]

---

[3] See Chapters VII and XIII, pages 91 and 209.

[4] For historical reasons, some theorists also classify accented passing tones as *appoggiaturas.*

or, if very brief, an *acciaccatura*. Many examples of this nonharmonic tone can be found in passages already cited, or in this opening theme of Beethoven's *Piano Sonata*, Op. 14, No. 2:

Note that the lower *appoggiatura*, like the lower neighboring tone, is usually chromatic.

Consider the use of the V⁶₅ in the following Bach melody, which is quite similar to Example 89, page 168, singing the bass while the melody is being played, thus:

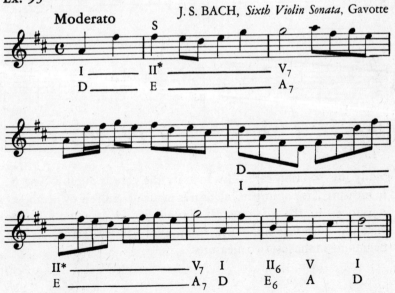

*The II is used here as a substitute for the IV (see Chapter V).

The first half of measure 1 sounds like the tonic chord unless the
F sharp is treated as a suspension. Note also the long extension
of the V_7 in measures 2 and 3. Bach harmonized it rather elab-
orately, thus:

Ex. 94

J. S. BACH, *Sixth Violin Sonata*, Gavotte

Study this solution carefully. Identify the chords aurally. The B_7
in measure 2 is not important, as it is made up entirely of neighboring tones to the adjacent V^6_5. Locate an *appoggiatura* in the
example and determine the form. Note the reference to the
beginning in the last two measures.

Three-Part Vocal Writing

Since Chapter IX, page 131, we have been experimenting with two-voice writing. Now observe how a third voice may be added by singing in parts the following passage, "See the Conquering Hero Comes," from Handel's oratorio, *Judas Maccabaeus:*

Ex. 95

Note how the effectiveness of this passage is enhanced by the close position of the chords (Example 31), and the predominance of thirds and sixths. In choosing chords, first decide upon the simplest harmonic background; that is, decide where the I, IV, and V chords may be used. Then add or substitute other fundamental or inverted chords to enrich the harmony. Experiment in rearranging for three voices some two-voice harmonizations that you have made previously. Contrast instrumental and vocal three-part writing as shown in Examples 89 and 95.

The principle of the round or canon can be used for three as well as for two voices, although the technical difficulties naturally increase with each added voice. Try singing the well-known round, *Three Blind Mice,* in three parts, then write it out to observe how the three voices fit together.

To summarize:

1. The next sharp key after D major is A major, whose three sharps are F sharp, C sharp, and G sharp, the new sharp (G sharp) being, as usual, the seventh of the scale.

2. The staff sevenths are all minor (small) except C–B and F–E. Consequently, the seventh (G–F) of the V$_7$ chord in C major is a minor (small) seventh, and sets the pattern for the V$_7$ in all keys.

3. The nonchord tone, preceded by a skip, is called an *appoggiatura*.

4. Finally, when writing for three women's voices, parallel thirds and sixths are as effective in three- as in two-voice writing, and the voices should be spaced as closely together as possible. When specially constructed, a melody may also be used as a three-voice canon or round. The term "voice" is applied also to the individual lines of instrumental writing.

Facility in using this material will come gradually with practice. Test all written work aurally.

Review:

1. The pitches in the A major scale.
2. The V$_7$ and the V$^6_5$ chords in the key of A major.
3. How inversion affects the quality of major and minor intervals.
4. The quality of the staff, or white key, sevenths.
5. The quality of the seventh in the V$_7$ chord.
6. How to name major and minor sevenths involving accidentals.
7. Which are the only consonant intervals.
8. What an *appoggiatura* is.
9. Some general principles of three-part vocal writing.
10. Why the gavotte was so named.
11. The usual form of the gavotte.
12. Some rhythmic differences between the gavotte and the bourrée.

For Further Study, Determine:

1. The construction of the V$_7$ in terms of its triad and seventh.
2. A simple way to find the name of the key from a sharp key signature.
3. Whether the inversion of a chord affects its consonance, dissonance, or major-minor quality.

4. How many black keys are always enclosed by a large and a small staff, or "white key," seventh. (See Example 91, page 170.)

5. Why three women's voices are most effective in close position.

6. Some differences between instrumental and vocal three-part writing as shown in Examples 89 and 95.

7. How an *appoggiatura* differs from a neighboring tone.

8. The form of Examples 89, 93, and 95.

9. What dances were included in the Bach suite.

I — Assignment for Writing

1. Scan the following stanzas and set at least one of them to music in the keys of D or G major for one, two, or three voices (accompaniment optional). Experiment modulating to the dominant key. The form will depend on the number of stanzas in the poem: two stanzas suggesting the *A–B,* and three stanzas the *A–B–A* form.

(*a*)   Pound, pound, pound,
       Is the blacksmith's work.
       He sits on a little stool all day
       And passes his time
       By pounding away.

       Pound, pound, pound,
       As he soles the horses' hoofs.
       Taking his time, taking his time,
       He goes around to every hoof,
       Picking it up, putting it down,
       Pound, pound, pound, pound.

The Blacksmith[5]

(*b*)   Very
       Merry we go
       Around on the merry-go-round,
       Up and down
       Music we hear
       Tunes that cheer
       As we go round and round
       And round and round.

The Merry-go-round[6]

---

[5] From *Creative Power,* by Hughes Mearns, copyright, 1929, reprinted by permission of Doubleday & Co., Inc.

[6] From *Creative Power,* by Hughes Mearns, copyright 1929, reprinted by permission of Doubleday & Co., Inc.

(c) Onward I speed,
I'm swift, I'm free!
The hounds are following, following me!
Up and over the boulder I spring,
Over and up, like a bird on the wing.

Onward I speed,
I'm swift, I'm free!
The hounds have stopped at the foot of the tree.
The hounds are baffled!
Baffled by me!

Fox Thoughts[7]

(d) Tink-a-tink, tink-a-tink,
By the light of the star,
On the blue river's brink,
I heard a guitar.

I heard a guitar,
On the blue waters clear,
And knew by its music
That Selim was near!

Tink-a-tink, tink-a-tink,
How the soft music swells,
And I hear the soft clink
Of the minaret bells!

Tink-a-tink — William Makepeace Thackeray

(e) Whenever the moon and stars are set,
Whenever the wind is high,
All night long in the dark and wet,
A man goes riding by.
Late in the night when the fires are out,
Why does he gallop and gallop about?

Whenever the trees are crying aloud,
And ships are tossed at sea,
By, on the highway, low and loud,
By at the gallop goes he.
By at the gallop he goes, and then
By he comes back at the gallop again.

Windy Nights — Robert Louis Stevenson

---

[7] From *Creative Power*, by Hughes Mearns, copyright 1929, reprinted by permission of Doubleday & Co., Inc.

(f)   My heart leaps up when I behold
       A rainbow in the sky:
       So was it when my life began;
       So is it now I am a man;
       So be it when I shall grow old,
         Or let me die!
                 The Rainbow — William Wordsworth

(g)   Strephon kissed me in the spring,
         Robin in the fall,
       But Colin only looked at me
       And never kissed at all.

       Strephon's kiss was lost in jest,
         Robin's lost in play,
       But the kiss in Colin's eyes
         Haunts me night and day.
                 The Look — Sara Teasdale[8]

2. Write a gavotte in *A–B* form (D major) for piano, or an instrumental group of three violins or two violins and a cello. Modulate to the dominant key at the end of part I. Follow Example 89 or 94 as models of three-voice writing which may be much more free for instruments than for voices. Begin each phrase of both parts on the third beat of the measure. Experiment using *appoggiaturas*. (Optional.)

3. Add a second voice, either alto or bass, to some of the following melodies. Can any of them be treated as a round?

Czech Folk Song

Allegro

(a)

SCHLETTERER

Moderato

(b)

---

[8] From Sara Teasdale, *Rivers to the Sea*. Copyright, 1915 by the Macmillan Company and used with their permission.

From Thirty Vocal Duets, *published by Breitkopf and Hartel. Reprinted by permission of* Associated Music Publishers, *Inc.*

Allegretto Folk Song

(c)

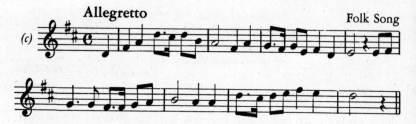

(Arrange for two voices or violin and violoncello)

Allegro vivace BEETHOVEN, *Fourth Symphony, Op. 60*

(d)

etc.

4. Harmonize some of the following melodies for three women's voices. Can any of them be treated as a round?

Moderato WEBBE

(a)

etc.

5. Harmonize some of the following melodies for piano, using any of the previous accompaniment figures. Analyze the form of each melody.

SCHUBERT, from *C Minor Sonata* (Adapted)

DUSSEK, *Sonatina*, Op. 20, No. 3

Allegro

GOUNOD, Waltz from *Faust*

(c)

1.

D V$^6_5$ V$_7$

2.

Chorale

(d)

GLUCK, Gavotte

Grazioso

(e)

1.

2.

D I$^6_4$ V$_7$

Allegro   MOZART, *Marrige of Figaro*

II — Assignment for Playing

1. Harmonize one or more of the melodies in the *Assignment for Writing* (5), or select one of the following melodies, using any of the preceding styles of accompaniment. Use V$_5^6$ whenever effective.

    140 Folk-Songs. Concord Series No. 3. Nos. 9, 34, 38, 74, 82, 105, 118, 119.

    Silver Book: Nos. 13, 42, 51, 73, 86.

2. Improvise melodies without accompaniment in the *A–B* form.

3. Improvise a gavotte in the *A–B* form, using this harmonic background. Note the use of sequences.

Moderato   After BACH, *Fifth French Suite*, Gavotte

4. Play by ear in the key of D major *Oh, Susanna,* and *Massa's in the Cold Ground.* Add a harmonic background.

5. Modulate from D major to A major, using the chord pattern in Chapter X, *Assignment for Playing* (3), embellished by *appoggiaturas.*

6. Transpose simple melodies and passages for analysis in this chapter down a major (large) second, from the key of D major to C major.

Note on transposition. The process of transposition is dependent upon the student's ability to think in the new tonality, that is, to be able to transfer the music from the original key to the new key by recognition of patterns and relationships, rather than by transposing single pitches. In doing so, his attention should be focused upon such salient features as use of scale-line, skips, common tones, and the relationship of the outer voices. Think horizontally rather than vertically. Thus, in transposing, for example, from C major to D major, the pitches should be read one letter higher *in the key of D major* rather than by transposing each pitch upward a major second. The use of specific intervals, such as a major second, is necessary only when accidentals differing from the key signature occur.

III — Assignment for Listening

1. *Oral dictation:* harmonic recognition only. Identify chords by quality, letter, and Roman numeral.

> *First Lessons,* Book I (Carroll), Bach, *March,* No. 9.
> Haydn, *C Minor Symphony* (Peters Edition), No. 9, Finale (1-8).
> Mozart, *Coronation Concerto,* K537 (D), Larghetto (1-2).
> > *A Major Piano Sonata,* K331, Menuetto (1-18); Trio (1-16).
> Schubert, *A Major Piano Sonata,* Op. 120, Andante (1-8);
> > *D Major Piano Sonata,* Op. 53, Scherzo (1-8).

2. *Written dictation (quality, bass, melody, and name of chord).*
> *Golden Book: Abide With Me,* p. 49 (1-4);
> > *Now Thank We All Our God.* p. 65 (1-7);
> > *Hark the Herald Angels Sing,* p. 68 (1-12);
> > *From Every Spire on Christmas Eve,* p. 70;
> > *Away in a Manger,* p. 72 (1-4).

New Episcopal Hymnal, No. 402, *Munich* (1-4),
No. 558, *University College*,
No. 449, *Olivet*,
No. 598, *Homeland* (1-4),
No. 120, *Angelica* (1-8).

IV — Assignment for Analysis

Beethoven, *Piano Sonata*, Op. 7, Allegro (1-8);
Violin Sonata, Op. 12, No. 2, Allegro vivace (1-16);
Pastoral Symphony, Op. 68, First Movement,
subordinate theme.
Chopin, *Waltz*, Op. 34, No. 3 (48-56).
Mendelssohn, *Six Pieces for Children*, Op. 72, No. 4 (1-5).
Schubert, *Piano Sonata*, D Major, Op. 53, con moto (1-8);
Piano Sonata, A Major, Op. 120, Andante (1-15).
Schumann, *Scenes from Childhood*, Op. 68, No. 33, Part III;
Papillons, Op. 2, No. 11, (4-7);
Novelletten, Op. 21, No. 8, Trio I.
Strauss, *A Night in Venice* (Universal Edition), p. 60.
   The following passages for analysis have been selected from the above list. Identify cadences, form, chords, nonharmonic tones, and note pivotal chords.

BEETHOVEN, *Piano Sonata*, Op. 7 [E♭]

Vivace   CHOPIN, *Waltz*, Op. 34, No. 4

(b)

IV₆

Allegro vivace   SCHUBERT, *Piano Sonata*, Op. 53

(c)

etc.

Allegro   SCHUMANN, *Papillons*, Op. 2, No. 11

(d)

Trio I

SCHUMANN, *Novelletten*, Op. 21, No. 8 [D♭]

Allegro

(e)

Chapter XII

THE V$^4_3$ CHORD

Ex. 96

BEETHOVEN (1770 – 1827), *Violin and Piano Sonata*, Op. 12, No. 2

Andante con moto

chromatic
chord

LISTEN TO this melody which Beethoven uses as the theme for a series of variations in his first sonata[1] for violin and piano.

---

[1] The classic and romantic sonata is an instrumental composition of three or four contrasted movements, one of which is in the so-called *sonata-allegro* form, a large, basically *A–B–A* design. A *symphony* is a sonata written for orchestra. The word *"sonata"* is Italian, meaning an instrumental "sound-piece" as contrasted with a *"cantata,"* a "singing-piece" or vocal composition.

It shows the young composer of twenty-nine in a serious and reflective mood. Observe how naturally the melody unfolds, constantly increasing in intensity to the climax in measure 7. Since there is a cadential break in measure 4, followed by a new second phrase, the form of the excerpt is a contrasting period.

The chords of the measures 1 to 4 establish the prevailing tonality of A major, whose key signature is used. Learn the position of the three sharps on the staff; note that each additional sharp is placed to the right of the previous one, as high on the staff as possible. The new key center of E is established by the cadence in measures 7 and 8, first suggested by the D sharp in measure 5.[2]

Spell the chord in measure 5 upward from the bass tone, F sharp–A–B–D sharp. Its root may be found by arranging these tones in thirds, thus:

Ex. 97

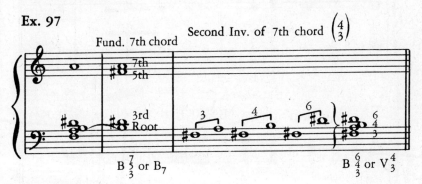

In the original order (F sharp–A–B–D sharp), it is clearly the second inversion of the B$_7$ chord, having the chord fifth (F sharp) in the bass. This second inversion is called a $\frac{6}{3}$, or simply $\frac{4}{3}$, chord from the number of staff degrees between its bass tone (F sharp) and the other tones of the chord, thus: F sharp to D sharp — 6; F sharp to B — 4; F sharp to A — 3 (see Example

---

[2] Write the E major scale, first with accidentals only, then with the correct key signature. Note that the new sharp (D sharp) is the seventh of the scale and, when added to the signature of A major, makes a four sharp signature: F sharp, C sharp, G sharp, and D sharp.

97). Since its root is B in the key of E major, it is called a dominant ⁴₃, or V⁴₃. (See footnote 3.) It is used here as a means of modulation from A major to E major. Spell the V₇, V⁶₅, and V⁴₃ chords in the keys of C, G, D, A, and E major.

Play Example 96, page 188, again. How many other ⁴₃ chords can be found? Note that they resolve in several different ways. The bass tone of the V⁴₃, the second scale step, may move up or down one degree — either down to the tonic, or up to the third degree of the scale. In both of these resolutions the chord seventh follows the direction of the bass, thus:

Ex. 98   SCHUBERT, *Moment Musical*, Op. 94, No. 2 [A♭]

Compare the variations of these resolutions in Example 96, page 188, and in the *Assignment for Analysis*. In listening, note that the V⁴₃ is a discord whose bass usually resolves *down* to the I chord, in contrast to the progression of the V⁶₅ bass tone *up* to the I chord.

---

³ Note that the figuration ⁴₃, although applied here to a dominant seventh, may indicate the second inversion of *any* seventh chord. Spell ⁴₃ chords from any pitch on the staff.

Listen to these two inversions of the V$_7$ until their differences in sound and resolution are apparent:

Ex. 99

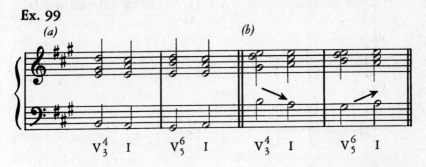

In analysis, inversions of seventh chords are easily identified by their adjacent tones, for example, the seconds, D–E, in Example 99 (*b*). In such clusters, the upper tone is always the chord root and the lower tone the chord seventh.

In harmonizing a melody, use the V$_3^4$ anywhere for the fundamental V$_7$ (except at a cadence) to improve the bass line or for harmonic color. First, decide on the general harmonic background (I–IV–V$_7$), using fundamental chords. Then develop this harmonic background by employing inversions to improve the bass line. For example, this melody naturally suggests the following simple harmonic background:

Ex. 100   *Adeste Fideles* (Cantus Diversi, 1751)

Yet how much more effective is the use of the inversions in Example 101. Notice the $_3^4$ chord at the end of measure 1, which is similar in use to that in Example 96, page 188, measure 6.

Ex. 101

*A chromatic chord of dominant seventh quality. Note the indication of the raised tone (D sharp) six letters above the bass. There are also some suggested chromatic alterations in bass 2. The harmonization of bass 1 is from the *Episcopal Hymnal* (1940 Edition).

Make the same use of the V⁴₃ and inversions in your own work, experimenting with various possibilities until a satisfactory solution is found.

Review:

1. What part of the chord is in the bass in a V⁴₃ chord.
2. What scale step is the bass of the V⁴₃.
3. Why the second inversion of a seventh chord is called a ⁴₃.
4. How the V⁴₃ chord is used and resolved.
5. Whether the V⁴₃ may be used for modulation.
6. The V₇, V⁶₅, and V⁴₃ chords in C, G, D, A, and E major.
7. How to recognize inverted seventh chords by the progression of their bass.
8. How to identify inverted seventh chords when the chord contains adjacent tones (seconds).
9. The key signatures of G, D, A, and E major.
10. The pitches in the E major scale.

For Further Study, Determine:

1. Why the V$^4_3$ is rarely used in cadences.
2. Whether the V$^4_3$ is dissonant, and why.
3. Why no modulation is made by using the $^4_3$ chords in Example 96, measure 6; Example 91, measure 1.
4. Uses of the V$^4_3$ chord in familiar music.

I — Assignment for Writing

1. Scan the following stanzas and set one or more of them to music in the key of A major (or other familiar keys) for one, two, or three voices (accompaniment optional). Experiment modulating to the dominant key through the V$^4_3$, returning to the tonic key at the end. Keep within reasonable vocal range. Set two-stanza poems in the *A–B*, and three-stanza poems in the *A–B–A* form.

(*a*) Whisky frisky,
Hippety hop,
Up he goes
To the tree top!

Whirly, twirly,
Round and round,
Down he scampers
To the ground.

The Squirrel — Author Unknown

(*b*) Our Lord Who did the Ox command
To kneel to Judah's King,
He binds His frost upon the land
To ripen it for Spring —
To ripen it for Spring, good sirs,
According to His Word.
Which well must be as ye can see —
And who shall judge the Lord?

God bless the master of this house,
And all who sleep therein!
And guard the fens from pirate folk,
And keep us all from sin,
To walk in honesty, good sirs,

Of thought and deed and word!
Which shall befriend our latter end . . .
And who shall judge the Lord?

A Carol — Rudyard Kipling[4]

(*c*)   My heart's in the Highlands, my heart is not here;
My heart's in the Highlands a-chasing the deer;
A-chasing the wild deer, and following the roe,
My heart's in the Highlands wherever I go.

Farewell to the Highlands, farewell to the North,
The birthplace of valor, the country of worth:
Wherever I wander, wherever I rove,
   The hills of the Highlands forever I love.

My Heart's in the Highlands — Robert Burns

(*d*)   Hush! the waves are rolling in,
   White with foam, white with foam;
Father toils amid the din;
   But baby sleeps at home.

Hush! the winds roar hoarse and deep,
   On they come, on they come!
Brother seeks the wandering sheep:
   But baby sleeps at home.

Hush! the rain sweeps over the knowes,
   Where they roam, where they roam;
Sister goes to seek the cows;
   But baby sleeps at home.

Gaelic Lullaby — Author Unknown[5]

(*e*)   Winds through the olive trees
   Softly did blow,
Round little Bethlehem
   Long, long ago.

---

[4] From *Rewards and Fairies* by Rudyard Kipling. Copyright 1910 by Rudyard Kipling. Reprinted by permission of Mrs. George Bambridge and Doubleday & Co., Inc.

[5] From *The Golden Flute*, Alice L. Hubbard (Editor), published by John Day Co., Inc., 1932.

Sheep on the hillside lay
  Whiter than snow;
Shepherds were watching them,
  Long, long ago.

Then from the happy sky,
  Angels bent low,
Singing their songs of joy,
  Long, long ago.

For in a manger bed,
  Cradled we know,
Christ came to Bethlehem,
  Long, long ago.
                        Long, Long Ago — Author Unknown[6]

(*f*)   The stormy March is come at last,
          With wind, and cloud, and changing skies;
        I hear the rushing of the blast
          That through the snowy valley flies.

        Then sing aloud the gushing rills
          In joy that they again are free,
        And brightly leaping down the hills,
          Renew their journey to the sea.
                        March — William Cullen Bryant

(*g*)   In the hush of the autumn night
        I hear the voice of the sea.
        In the hush of the autumn night
        It seems to say to me —
        Mine are the winds above,
        Mine are the caves below,
        Mine are the dead of yesterday
        And the dead of long ago.
                        The Voice of the Sea — T. B. Aldrich

---

[6] From *The Golden Flute*, Alice L. Hubbard (Editor), published by John Day
Co., Inc., 1932.

2. Experiment writing rounds for either two voices or two instruments. Either voice may begin first. Let the second voice enter a measure later. The ending may be free. Make them short and simple — four measures or so — using only half and quarter notes. Make some preliminary study of rounds.[7] The first poem given above would make a good vocal round. (Optional.)

3. Harmonize some of the following melodies for three women's voices. Can any of them be treated as a round?

_____

[7] See the *Brown* and *Green Books* (Boston: C. C. Birchard and Company), and *Rounds and Canons* (Hall and McCreary).

CALVISIUS, Chorale (1597)

4. Harmonize at least one of the following melodies for piano, using any of the accompaniment figures used in preceding chapters. Analyze the form of the melody harmonized.

GOUNOD, *Faust* (Ballet Music)

Allegro energico   WAGNER, March from *Rienzi*

(b)

V₇

1.   2.

Allegretto   English Folk Song

(c)

Allegretto   English Folk Song

(d)

(e) Chorale

(f) Chorale

II — Assignment for Playing

1. Harmonize one or more of the melodies in the *Assignment for Writing* (5) or select one of the following melodies, using any of the preceding accompaniment figures and the V⁴₃ wherever it would be effective.

    140 Folk-Songs. Concord Series No. 3. Nos. 21, 30, 61, 119, 134.

    Oxford Sight Singing Series: Book VI, Nos. 67, 69; Book VII, Nos. 83, 84, 86.

    Play a Tune: Mountain Dance, p. 60.

2. Improvise melodies without accompaniment in *A–B* form.

3. Improvise a minuet in *A–B* form, using this harmonic background. Develop the melody from the figure used at the beginning of each phrase.

Moderato   After MOZART

E V₇

4. Play by ear in the key of A major the melody of *Flow Gently, Sweet Afton*. Repeat with a simple harmonic background.

5. Play the V$^4_3$ chord, thus:

6. Use the following chord patterns to modulate from A major to E major, and repeat each in piano style. Use also the chord pattern from Chapters IX and X. Devise original modulatory patterns with embellishments.

7. Transpose simple melodies and passages for analysis in this lesson up a large (major) second from the keys of D major to E major, and G major to A major. Review note on transposition (Chapter XI, *Assignment for Playing*).

III — Assignment for Listening

1. *Oral dictation:* harmonic recognition only. Identify chords by quality, letter, and Roman numeral.

Handel, *Largo* from *Xerxes* (1-15).

Mozart, *Marriage of Figaro,* "Deh Vieni"; "Via resti serviata."

Schubert, *Violin Sonata,* Op. 137, No. 3, Andante (18)-;
  Impromptu, Op. 90, No. 2 (1-8);
  C Major Fantasie, Op. 15, Presto (79-86);
  Who is Sylvia? (1-5);
  The Quail (1-4);
  The Stars (17-29).

Haydn, *C Major Sonata,* No. 5, Schirmer ed., Allegro con brio, (9-16).

Schumann, *Papillons,* Op. 2, No. 6, A Major section.

Weber, *Invitation to the Dance,* Op. 65, Wiegend.

Moszkowski, *Serenata,* Op. 15, No. 1 (1-10).

Tchaikovsky, *Nutcracker Suite,* Op. 71a, Waltz, Part II.

2. *Written dictation (quality, bass, melody, and name of chord):*
Sing!: Passing By, p. 19.
Golden Book: Onward, Christian Soldiers, chorus (1-4).
Brown Book, Twice 55: No. 117, *In the Time of Roses* (1-4);
    No. 136, *A Capital Ship,* chorus (1-8).
Green Book, Twice 55: No. 7, *Harvest Home* (1-8);
    No. 84, *Landing of the Pilgrims* (1-8).
Play a Tune: Italian Folk Tune, p. 33;
    Seventeenth Century Dance, p. 66;
    Country Dance, p. 66.
Schubert, *A Major Piano Sonata (Grand),* No. 2, Allegro, subordinate theme (1-4);
    A Major Piano Sonata, Op. 120, Allegro moderato, principle theme (1-4).
New Episcopal Hymnal, No. 577, *Christmas,*
    No. 388, *St. Thomas (Williams),*
    No. 306, *Carey,*
    No. 430 (Second tune), *Lux Benigna,*
    No. 119, *Wareham.*

IV — Assignment for Analysis

Boccherini, *Minuet* (1-8).
Handel, *Largo* from *Xerxes* (1-9).
Mozart, *G Major Piano Sonata*, K283, Allegro (1-10).
Beethoven, *String Quartet*, Op. 135, Lento (3-6);

> *Ninth Symphony*, Op. 125, Adagio, second theme;
> *Piano Sonatas:* Op. 10, No. 3, Minuetto (1-8),
> > Op. 14, No. 2, Andante (1-8),
> > Op. 26, Theme (1-6),
> > Op. 31, No. 2, Adagio (1-5),
> > Op. 31, No. 3, Scherzo (1-8),
> > Op. 31, No. 3, Menuetto (1-4),
> > Op. 49, No. 2, Menuetto (1-8),
> > Op. 111, Arietta (1-9);

> *Rondo*, Op. 51, No. 1 (1-8);
> *Rondo*, Op. 51, No. 2 (1-8);
> *Rondo a Capriccio*, Op. 129, E Major section (1-8).

Chopin, *Waltz*, Op. 64, No. 3 (1-9);

> *Sonata*, Op. 35, First Movement, second theme;
> *Nocturne*, Op. 48, No. 2, Molto più lento.

Schumann, *Carnival*, Op. 9, Waltz Allemande.
Brahms, *Wie Bist Du* (1-4).
Strauss, *Blue Danube Waltzes*, Nos. 1, 2, 3;

> *Tales from the Vienna Woods*, Nos. 1, 4;
> *Vienna Life*, Nos. 1, 3, 4;
> *Voices of Spring;*
> *Artist's Life*, Nos. 2, 5;
> *Wine, Women, and Song*, Nos. 1, 2, 3;
> *You and You*, Nos. 1, 2, 3;
> *Roses From the South*, Nos. 1, 2, 3;
> *Treasure Waltzes*, Nos. 2, 3;
> *A Night in Venice*, Nos. 1, 2, 3.

(All these Strauss waltzes could be used for aural analysis.)

The following passages for analysis have been selected from the above list. Identify cadences, form, chords, nonharmonic tones, and pivotal chords.

Tempo di minuetto

BOCCHERINI

(a)

HANDEL, Largo (Xerxes)

Largo

(b)

Allegro   BEETHOVEN, *Piano Sonata*, Op. 10, No. 3

(c)

(chromatic $\frac{4}{3}$)

CHOPIN, *Sonata*, Op. 35 [D♭]

Moderato

(d)

(Left hand simplified)

Molto vivace   SCHUMANN, *Carnival*, Op. 9

(e)

(Chromatic
embellishment)

BRAHMS, *How Art Thou Verily my Queen,* Op. 32, No. 9

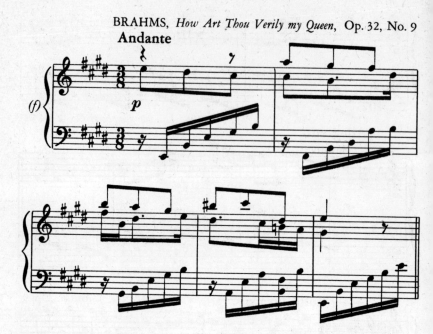

Chapter XIII

THE VII$_6$ CHORD

Ex. 102

HAYDN (1732 – 1809), *London Symphony No. 2* (1791)

Allegretto

HAYDN'S GAIETY is evident here. The excerpt quoted begins with a simple pattern or *motive* of three notes repeated on various pitch levels. During this motive development, the key center changes and, at the end, a new tonality is established.

Determine how this change of tonality occurred by an aural analysis of the harmonic background. At the beginning of Example 102, the tonal center (key tone) is F, and, consequently, the composition is in the key, or tonality, of F major,[1] as shown by the new key signature of one flat.

It is obvious that, at the end, C has been established as a new key center through the consistent use of B natural, beginning in measure 5. Therefore, the passage modulates from F major to C major.

Listen again to measure 5, which contains the first B natural. Examine the chord to which it belongs. Spell the chord upward from its bass tone, and then arrange it in thirds, thus:

Ex. 103

(1) As in Ex. 102　　(2) Arranged in 3rds

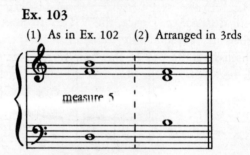

The chord then becomes B–D–F, which makes the original form of the chord (D–F–B) the first inversion of the B triad, notated B₆. Since the root, B, is the seventh scale step of C major, the chord is the VII₆ in this key.

This indicates that a new key may be entered through the first inversion of its leading-tone triad. Spell this VII chord in fundamental and inverted form in the other keys studied: G, D, A, E, and F major.

---

[1] Write the F major scale, first using accidentals only, then with the correct key signature (one flat — B flat). Note that the new accidental in flat keys is always the fourth of the scale.

What is the quality of this VII chord? (Example 103.) Recall that B–D is a small, or minor, third, and that all staff, or "white key," fifths are equal in size and quality except B–F, which is one half tone smaller, thus:

Ex. 104

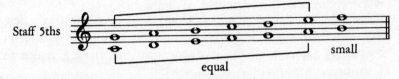

This small fifth (B–F) is called *diminished*. Since the VII chord (B–D–F) contains this fifth, it is a *diminished triad*. It is also a dissonant triad, because diminished intervals create that desire for movement and resolution which was associated in Chapter II, page 19, with dissonance. Hence, the VII chord in all major keys is a diminished and, consequently, a dissonant triad.

Before discussing the use of the VII chord, note the interval, F–B, which occurs when the chord is inverted. It can be named by comparing it with the other staff or "white key" fourths and fifths, thus:

Ex. 105

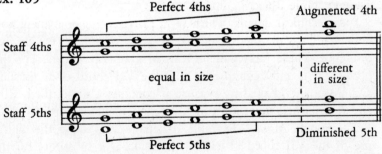

These equal fifths (and their inversions, the fourths) are called *perfect,* because each tone belongs in the major scale of the other tone. Staff primes and octaves also belong to this group of perfect intervals. The small fifth (B–F) is called *diminished,* and the large fourth (F–B), is called *augmented.*

These new terms (*perfect, augmented,* and *diminished*) provide the needed vocabulary to complete the naming of all staff, or "white key," intervals, thus:

1. Primes (unisons), fourths, fifths, and eighths (octaves) are classified as perfect, augmented, or diminished.

2. Seconds, thirds, sixths, and sevenths are classified as major or minor.[2]

Perfect intervals and major and minor thirds and sixths are *consonant.* All other intervals are *dissonant.* By experiment, prove that inversion reverses the quality of all except perfect intervals.[3]

The relative size of intervals may be clarified by this diagram in which each level represents one half step:

Ex. 106

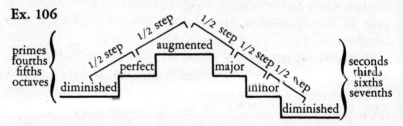

Name every possible interval built from C as the lower tone, using Example 106 as a guide.

Such technical details, which seem far from the enjoyment and understanding of the music itself, are given here chiefly for reference. These facts will be learned gradually *by use.* For the present, it is sufficient to note that the VII chord is diminished and dissonant in quality, because it contains a diminished fifth, and that its first inversion contains an augmented fourth.

The Haydn *Minuet,* Example 102, page 207, shows the typical use of the VII chord in its first inversion as a substitute for the V⁴₃ chord. This will be more evident by comparing the sound and

---

[2] Seconds, thirds, sixths, and sevenths are occasionally made augmented or diminished by the use of accidentals. Such chromatic intervals may be now named (if necessary) by comparison with the staff intervals whose qualities are known. Thus, to name G sharp–C, compare it with G–C, and so on.

[3] When the two tones of an interval are sounded simultaneously, the result is a *harmonic* interval, but if sounded consecutively, the two tones are called a *melodic* interval.

construction of the two chords, thus:

Ex. 107   The VII₆   The V$\frac{4}{3}$

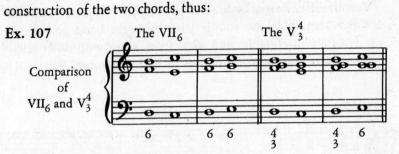

Comparison
of
VII₆ and V$_3^4$

Like the V$_3^4$, the VII₆ may resolve either down to the I or up to the I₆. It is especially useful in harmonizing the ascending leading tone in the melodic progression 5–6–7–8, although it also harmonizes the second and fourth scale steps. In general, its use is similar to that of the V$_3^4$, and, consequently, it is very rarely found in any position except the first inversion. Since the root of the VII₆ is the leading tone of the scale, it is seldom, if ever, doubled.

Consider the use of the VII₆ chord in the following melody:

Ex. 108*   BACH, *371 Chorales,* No. 234

*See Chapter XXI for an explanation of new figurations below basses.

Test these different solutions by singing the bass with the melody. Then play the chords with the right hand and decide which bass is preferable, and why. Experiment with other possibilities. Note the recurring figures in Bach's solution, thus:

Ex. 109

Bass No. 1

Although four-part vocal writing is not discussed until Chapter XXI, page 360, the passage is pertinent now since it illustrates the use of the VII₆ to harmonize the ascending leading tone of the scale. Furthermore, for present purposes the VII₆ is useful especially in three-part writing, as the V_3^4 is impossible in fewer than four voices. The VII₆ also is useful in instrumental writing. The aural difference between the two chords is so slight that long practice is required to distinguish them. Try using one for the other until this difference is apparent. Such recognition is the difference between mere hearing and intelligent listening to music. Remember that the ear is to the musician what the eye is to the painter, and that intelligent listening makes one aware of tonal color as the painter is aware of physical color.

Review:

1. What part of the chord is the bass tone of the VII₆.
2. What scale step is the bass tone of the VII₆.
3. How the VII₆ is used.
4. Whether the new key may be entered through its VII₆ chord.
5. What special melodic progression is harmonized by the VII₆.
6. How the VII₆ differs from the V_3^4.
7. What the VII₆ is in the keys of C, G, D, A, E, and F major.

8. What choice of doubling there is in the VII$_6$.
9. Why it is particularly useful in three-voice writing.
10. The pitches and signature of the F major scale.
11. Which intervals are called perfect, major, minor, augmented, and diminished.
12. Which staff fourth and fifth are not perfect.
13. What is meant by the inversion of an interval.
14. Which intervals are consonant and which are dissonant, and why.
15. The quality of staff intervals having C as the lower tone.

For Further Study, Determine:

1. Whether the VII$_6$ may be used in a final cadence.
2. Why the VII$_6$ is a dissonant chord.
3. Whether you can find examples of the VII$_6$ in familiar music.
4. What the dissonant staff intervals are.
5. How the dissonant staff fourth and fifth resolve.
6. What the interval F–B was called in medieval music, and why.
7. Between what scale steps the dissonant staff intervals occur.

I — Assignment for Writing

1. Scan the following poems and set at least one of them to music in the key of F major (or other familiar keys) for one, two, or three voices. Work as directed in Chapter XII, page 193.

(*a*)   Flow down, cold rivulet, to the sea,
          Thy tribute wave deliver;
     No more by thee my steps shall be,
          For ever and for ever.

     Flow, softly flow, by lawn and lea,
          A rivulet, then a river:
     Nowhere by thee my steps shall be,
          For ever and for ever.

     But here will sigh thine alder tree,
          And here thine aspen shiver;
     And here by thee will hum the bee,
          For ever and for ever.
               A Farewell — Alfred, Lord Tennyson

(*b*)   A mist of memory broods and floats,
          The border waters flow;
     The air is full of ballad notes,
          Borne out of long ago.

Old songs that sung themselves to me,
Sweet through a boy's day-dream,
While trout below the blossom'd tree
Plashed in the golden stream.
Twilight on the Tweed — Andrew Lang

(*c*) In a branch of willow hid
Sings the evening katy-did:
From the lofty locust bough
Feeding on a drop of dew,
In her suit of green array'd
Hear her singing in the shade
Katy-did, Katy-did, Katy-did!
To a Katy-did — Philip Freneau

(*d*) When all the world is young, lad,
And all the trees are green,
And every goose a swan, lad,
And every lass a queen:
Then hey for boot and horse, lad,
And round the world away!
Young blood must have its course, lad,
And every dog its day.

When all the world is old, lad,
And all the trees are brown;
And all the sport is stale, lad,
And all the wheel run down;
Creep home and take your place there
The spent and maimed among;
Pray God you find one face there,
You loved when you were young.
When All the World is Young — Charles Kingsley

(*e*) Sailing over the emerald sea,
The ship of my dreams is waiting for me;
Riding about on the sparkling crest,
Like an albatross wandering, never at rest.

The gray gulls are calling,
The wild waves swaying,
Now they are rising and now they are falling,

Waving, beckoning, calling to me.
My heart's on the shore, but my soul's on the sea.
The Ship of My Dreams — William Kimball Flaccus[4]

(f)   Give a man a horse he can ride,
            Give a man a boat he can sail;
        And his rank and wealth, his strength and health,
            On sea nor shore shall fail.

        Give a man a pipe he can smoke,
            Give a man a book he can read:
        And his home is bright with a calm delight,
            Though the room be poor indeed.

        Give a man a girl he can love,
            As I, O my love, love thee;
        And his heart is great with the pulse of Fate,
            At home, on land, on sea.

                                Gifts — James Thomson

2. Experiment writing short rounds for two or three voices or instruments. Work as directed in Chapter XII, page 196. For example, write words for an echo song to be set as a canon, or write a humorous piece in which the two voices or instruments never succeed in beginning together, although they try several times. (Optional.)

3. Harmonize at least one of the following melodies for three women' voices. Can any of them be treated as a round?

ARNOUD

Allegretto

(a)

⁴From *Singing Youth*, Mabel Mountsier (Editor), published by Harper & Brothers, 1927.

See also:

140 Folk-Songs. Concord Series No. 3. Nos. 115, 120, 130.

Wagner: *Rheingold* and *Götterdammerung,* the Rhine Maidens' Music.

Sullivan, *The Mikado,* "Three Little Maids from School."

4. Harmonize at least one of the following melodies for piano, using any of the preceding accompaniment figures. Analyze the form of each melody.

Welsh Folk Song

Fine

D.C. al Fine

Moderato

Russian Folk Song

(e)

KUHLAU, *Sonatina,* Op. 55, No. 4

Allegro

(f)

(Use broken chord triplet accompaniment figure)

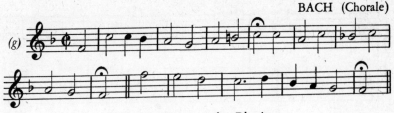

BACH (Chorale)

II — Assignment for Playing

1. Harmonize one or more of the melodies in the *Assignment for Writing* (4) above, or select one of the following melodies, using any of the preceding accompaniment figures. Use the V_3^4 or the VII_6 whenever possible.

> *Folk Song Sight Singing Series:* Book III, Nos. 24, 45;
> Book IV, No. 27;
> Book V, Nos. 22, 49.

> *140 Folk-Songs.* Concord Series No. 3. Nos. 16, 31, 114, 129, 131, 132, 135.

> *Foresman IV, Sailor Chantey,* p. 103.

2. Improvise melodies without accompaniment in the *A–B–A* form, each part a phrase in length.

3. Improvise a march in *A–B–A* form, using this harmonic background. Develop the melody from the initial figure of each part.

After HANDEL, *Joshua* (March)

4. Play by ear, in the key of F major, the melody of Brahms' *Lullaby*. Repeat with suitable accompaniment.

5. Use the following chord patterns in the keys of C, G, D, A, E, and F major. Repeat (*a*), (*b*), and (*c*) in piano style. Repeat with embellishments.

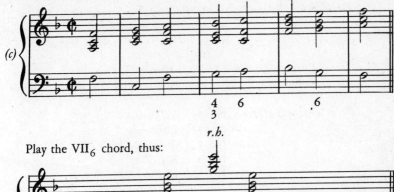

Play the VII₆ chord, thus:

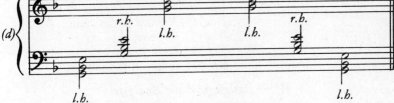

6. Transpose simple melodies and passages for analysis in this chapter down a major or a minor second to keys already studied. Review note on transposition, Chapter XI, *Assignment for Playing*, page 183.

III — Assignment for Listening

1. *Oral dictation:* harmonic recognition only. Identify chords by quality, letter, and Roman numeral.

Handel, *Messiah*, No. 2, "Comfort Ye" (1-4).
Mozart, *D Major Symphony*, K250, Trio I;
       Haffner Symphony, K385, Minuetto.
Schubert, *Moment Musical*, Op. 49, No. 6, Trio.
Schumann, *Album for the Young*, Op. 68, Nos. 2, 4, 10.
Mendelssohn, *On Wings of Song*, Op. 34, No. 2 (1-8).
Kuhlau, *Sonatina*, Op. 55, No. 4, Alla Polacca, No. 5, Andante.
Play a Tune: English Folk Tune, p. 10;
       Czech Folk Tune, p. 61;
       Serenade (Widor), p. 49.

2. *Written dictation (quality, bass, melody, and name of chord).*
Golden Book: Oh God, Beneath Whose Guiding Hand, p. 22.

Green Book, Twice 55: No. 87, *Faith of Our Fathers* (1-4) ;
                    No. 89, *Good King Wenceslas;*
                    No. 117, *Now Is the Time of Maying*
                        (1-8).
Sing!: Thou'rt Like Unto a Flower (Rubinstein), p. 25.
Mendelssohn, *Elijah,* No. 35, "Holy is God the Lord," chorus
    (5-8).
New Episcopal Hymnal, No. 399, *Ravenshaw,*
                    No. 111, *Melcombe,*
                    No. 151, *Morning Hymn,*
                    No. 153, *Ratisbon,*
                    No. 116, *Bedford,*
                    No. 165, *Tallis' Canon,*
                    No. 169, *Nutfield* (second tune),
                    No. 455, *St. Peter,*
                    No. 542, *Duke Street,*
                    No. 292, *Innocents* (second tune).

IV — Assignment for Analysis

Bach, *371 Chorales,* Chorale No. 188;
    Fifth French Suite, Gavotte (1-8) ;
    Sixth Violincello Sonata, Sarabande (1-8) ;
    B Minor Mass, "Et in Spiritum Sanctum";
    English Suite I, Bourrée I (Canon).
Beethoven, *Piano Sonata,* Op. 14, No. 1, Rondo (1-8) ;
        Violin Sonata, Op. 24, Scherzo and Rondo themes;
        Bagatelle, Op. 126, No. 1 (1-8).
Schumann, *Novelletten,* Op. 21, (1-4).
Handel, *Messiah,* "The Kingdoms of This World" from the
    "Hallelujah Chorus."
Wagner, *Die Meistersinger,* Eva's Motive.
Brahms, *Violin Sonata,* Op. 100, principal theme;
        Requiem, "Behold All Flesh," G flat major section (1-8).
Tchaikovsky, *Symphony IV,* Op. 36, Second Movement, second
            theme;
            Symphony VI, Op. 74, Third Movement, second
            theme.
Mozart, *Viennese Sonata,* No. 2, Rondo.

The passages for analysis on the following pages have been selected
from the above list. Identify cadences, form, chords, and nonharmonic
tones. Note pivotal chords.

BACH, *371 Chorales*, No. 188

II$_7$

II$_5^6$

BACH, *Sixth Violoncello Sonata*, "Sarabande"

Lento

p

RONDO   BEETHOVEN, *Violin and Piano Sonata*, Op. 24 (Spring)

Allegro non troppo

(c)

VII₆

Allegro   HANDEL *Messiah*, "Hallelujah Chorus"

(d)

BRAHMS, *Violin and Piano Sonata*, Op. 100

Allegro amabile

MOZART, *Viennese Sonatinas II*, Rondo

Allegro

WAGNER, *Die Meistersinger*, Eva's Motive

Moderato

Chapter XIV

THE V$\frac{4}{2}$ CHORD

Ex. 110

MOZART (1756–1791), *Don Giovanni,* "Il mio tesoro intanto" (1787)

Andante grazioso

*Note the embellished resolution of the chord-seventh (E flat) at measure 3.

Mᴏʀᴇ ᴛʜᴀɴ 150 years ago in Prague, Mozart conducted the first performance of his opera, *Don Giovanni,* one of the oldest works in the operatic repertoire. The passage quoted above is typical of the graceful, flowing melodic line for which Mozart is famous. Note its rhythmic variety and how the repetition of measure 3 gives a feeling of balance and unity. Could measure 4 be omitted, since it is only repetition? Experiment with this repetitive device in original melodies.

226

Listen again to determine the tonality. Observe the new key signature of two flats (B flat and E flat) which confirms our impression of B flat as the key center at the beginning. This means that the passage begins in the key of B flat major.

However, the ending indicates that there has been a change of tonality (modulation) from B flat major[1] to F major, in measure 5, through the chord containing E natural. Name this chord by spelling it upward from the bass tone, and then arranging it in thirds, thus:

Ex. 111

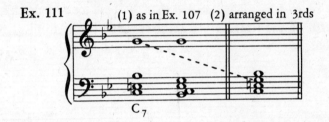

Hence, it is clear that the chords in measure 5 are only two different forms of the C_7 chord (C–E–G–B flat), first having the root C, then the chord-seventh, B flat, in the bass. Since it is a C_7 chord and introduces the key of F major, it can also be called a V_7 chord in F major.

Write the inversions of the V_7 chord that are already known, and add this new one having the chord-seventh in the bass, thus:

Ex. 112

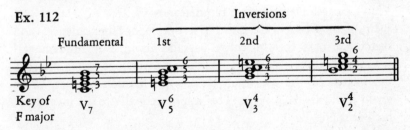

---

[1] Write the B flat major scale, first using accidentals only, then with its own key signature of two flats (B flat and E flat). Note that the new accidental in flat keys is always the fourth of the scale. Since this is true, the name of flat keys corresponds to the next to the last flat in the signature.

The third inversion ($^4_2$) is also named from the intervals it contains, counting upward from the bass tone. The complete figuration $^6_4_2$ is usually abbreviated to $^4_2$, or even 2. These figurations represent the third inversion of any seventh chord, although, for the present, they apply only to the V$^4_2$.

What is the quality of the V$^4_2$? Play it alone and sing the resolution — first of the bass, then of the soprano. Is it the same as in Example 110? Because of the active chord-seventh in the bass, the tendency of the V$^4_2$ to resolve down to the I$_6$ is very strong. Test this in the other keys, including B flat major. It is easy to do so when it is recalled that the bass tone of the V$^4_2$ is the fourth of the scale, which resolves down to the third of the scale, thus:

Ex. 113

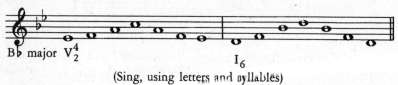

B♭ major V$^4_2$ I$_6$

(Sing, using letters and syllables)

The V$^4_2$ is used as a substitute for the other forms of the V$_7$, except in the perfect authentic cadence where the fundamental position is essential. As a substitute for the V$_7$, the V$^4_2$ is one of the means we have for entering a new key. Check the uses of the V$_7$ in Example 110 and other familiar music.

In harmonizing a melody, first decide on the cadences and sketch the bass for the entire passage, using only fundamental I, IV, and V chords before considering inversions. Then improve this sketch by the use of inversions for harmonic variety or to avoid awkward bass skips. This applies equally to all inversions, including the V$^4_2$.

With these suggestions in mind, plan a chord background for this melody, thus:

Ex. 114
TRIO   MOZART, *G Major Symphony**

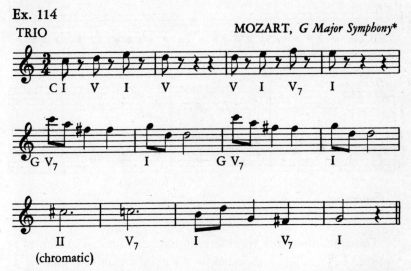

C I   V   I   V   V   I   V$_7$ I

G V$_7$ I   G V$_7$ I

II   V$_7$ I   V$_7$ I
(chromatic)

*This symphony is usually attributed to Leopold Mozart, the father of the famous composer, Wolfgang Amadeus Mozart, but the minuet and this trio are probably by the son. (See Einstein, new Köchel catalog, page 905.)

Test it by singing the bass while the melody is being played. Work out a number of solutions and compare them with the original:

Ex. 115
TRIO   MOZART, *G Major Symphony*

II

(chromatic)

Thus far, three-part vocal writing has been limited to women's voices. In arranging melodies to be sung by mixed groups, a single baritone part may be written for the men. This is easily done by rewriting the lowest alto part in the bass clef for convenience in reading, thus:

Ex. 116

Chorale (1715)

Make this change in some previous arrangements written for three women's voices which have an alto whose range lies between:

Ex. 117

Try singing both versions in class. How do they differ in effect? When the three voices are evenly spaced, the alto or baritone may be as much as a tenth or twelfth below the melody.

Review:

1. What part of the chord is the bass tone of the V$_2^4$.
2. What scale step is the bass tone of the V$_2^4$.
3. How the V$_2^4$ is used.
4. Whether the V$_2^4$ is used for modulation.
5. The V$_2^4$ in the keys of C, G, D, A, E, F, and B flat major.
6. How to recognize the V$_2^4$ by its resolution.
7. The pitches and signature of the B flat major scale.
8. Whether the V$_2^4$ is used in a perfect authentic cadence.
9. How to rewrite a low alto part for baritone.

For Further Study, Determine:

1. Why the V$_2^4$ is a dissonant chord.
2. Why the V$_2^4$ is not used in a perfect authentic cadence.
3. The difference in effect between the inversions of the V$_7$.

4. How many inversions of the V$_7$ are possible.
5. How many examples of the V$\frac{4}{2}$ occur in familiar music.
6. What the time signature ¢ means (Example 110).

I — Assignment for Writing

1. Scan the following poems and set at least one of them to music in the key of B flat major (or other familiar keys) for one, two, or three voices. Work as directed in Chapter XII, page 193. (Accompaniment optional.)

(a)   O, inexpressible as sweet,
         Love takes my voice away;
      I cannot tell thee when we meet
         What most I long to say.

      But hadst thou hearing in thy heart
         To know what beats in mine,
      Then shouldst thou walk, where'er thou art
         To melodies divine.

      So warbling birds lift higher notes
         Than to our ears belong;
      The music fills their throbbing throats,
         But silence steals the song.

     O, Inexpressible as Sweet — George Edward Woodberry[2]

(b)   Those evening bells! those evening bells!
         How many a tale their music tells,
         Of youth and home, and that sweet time
      When last I heard their soothing chime!

      Those joyous hours are passed away;
      And many a heart that then was gay,
      Within the tomb now darkly dwells,
      And hears no more those evening bells.

      And so 'twill be when I am gone —
      That tuneful peal will still ring on;
      While other bards shall walk these dells,
      And sing your praise, sweet evening bells.
           Those Evening Bells — Thomas Moore

---

[2] Reprinted by permission of Mrs. Charles D. Woodberry.

(c) As I was going to St. Ives,
     I met a man with seven wives,
     Every wife had seven sacks,
     Every sack had seven cats,
     Every cat had seven kits.
     Kits, cats, sacks, and wives,
     How many were going to St. Ives?

     Riddles — Nursery Rhyme

(d) On gossamer nights when the moon is low,
         And stars in the mist are hiding,
     Over the hill where the foxgloves grow
     You may see the fairies riding.
         Kling! Klang! Kling!
         Their stirrups and their bridles ring,
     And their horns are loud and their bugles blow,
     When the moon is low.

     The Fairy Thrall — Mary C. G. Byron

(e) Bees! Bees! Hark to your bees!
     "Hide from your neighbours as much as you please,
     But all that has happened, to us you must tell,
     Or else we will give you no honey to sell."

     The Bee Boys' Song — Rudyard Kipling[3]

(f) Give to me the life I love,
         Let the lave go by me,
     Give the jolly heaven above
         And the byway nigh me.
     Bed in the bush with stars to see,
         Bread I dip in the river —
     There's the life for a man like me,
         There's the life for ever.

     The Vagabond — Robert Louis Stevenson

2. Continue writing two- or three-part vocal and instrumental rounds and canons. Strict imitation at the close may be abandoned in order to make a good final cadence. (Optional.)

---

[3] From *Puck of Pook's Hill* by Rudyard Kipling. Copyright 1905, 1906 by Rudyard Kipling. Reprinted by permission of Mrs. George Bambridge and Doubleday & Co., Inc.

3. Harmonize at least one of the following melodies for three women's voices. Use three staves and, on the lower staff, rewrite the alto as a baritone part using the bass clef (see Example 116). Which one may be treated as a round?

German Chorale (1738)

(a)

German Chorale (1704)

(b)

DYKES

(c)

Moderato   WAGNER, *Lohengrin*

(d)

Andante   HANES

(e)

4. Harmonize at least one of the following melodies for piano, using any of the preceding accompaniment figures. Analyze the form of each melody used.

Andante   German Folk Song

(a)

II$_6$

Andante   German Folk Song

(b)

Andante   HIMMEL (1765), *Mignon*

(c)

I_6 V_3^4

(A) V_2^4

Allegro con brio   English Folk Song

(d)

Allegro   KUHLAU, Rondo, Op. 40, No. 2

(e)

V_5^6

German Chorale

II — Assignment for Playing

1. Harmonize one or more of the melodies in the *Assignment for Writing* (4) above, or select one from the following melodies, using any of the preceding styles of accompaniment. Where can you use the V$^4_2$?

   Folk Song Sight Singing Series: Book V, Nos. 23, 28, 36.

   140 Folk-Songs: Concord Series No. 3. Nos. 25, 78, 91, 94.

2. Improvise melodies without accompaniment in *A–B* form.

3. Improvise a march in *A–B* form, using this harmonic background. Develop the melody from the initial figure of each part.

(Continue chords, using this bass)

4. Play by ear, in the key of B flat major, the melody of *The Star Spangled Banner* and repeat, supplying as many chords as possible.

5. Learn and play the following chord patterns in C, G, D, A, E, F, and B flat major, then repeat (*a*) and (*b*) in piano style. Play patterns of preceding chapters in B flat major. Devise original patterns, using the V$_2^4$ for modulation to the dominant key. Repeat with embellishments.

6. Transpose simple melodies in passages for analysis in this chapter up a major or minor second. Review note on transposition, Chapter XI, page 183, *Assignment for Playing.*

III — *Assignment for Listening*

1. *Oral dictation:* harmonic recognition only. Identify chords by quality, letter, and Roman numeral.

Haydn, *London Symphony No. 4* (B flat Major), Adagio (1-10);
   Minuetto (1-20); Finale (1-8); Trio (1-12);
   Symphony in B flat Major (Peters Edition), No. 12,
   Minuet (9-20).
Mendelssohn, *The Question,* Op. 9, No. 1 (1-12);
   In Maytime, Op. 8, No. 11 (5-13).
Beethoven, *Violin Sonata,* Op. 12, No. 1, Rondo (1-8).
Weber, *Invitation to the Dance,* Op. 65, Wiegand.
Moszkowski, *Melodie,* Op. 18, No. 1 (1-16).

2. *Written dictation* (*quality, bass, melody, and name of chord*).
Golden Book: American Hymn (Keller) (1-8).
Sing!: Cradle Song (Brahms);
   Finlandia (Sibelius) (1-8).
New Episcopal Hymnal, No. 352, *Diademata,*
     No. 52, *Dix,*
     No. 28, *Regent Square.*
Haydn, *Symphony in C Major* (Peters Edition), No. 7, Minuet.
Kuhlau, *Sonatina,* Op. 55, No. 4, Andante (1-8),
    Op. 88, No. 3, Andantino (1-8),
    Op. 88, No. 2, Andante (1-8).

IV — *Assignment for Analysis*

Haydn, *London Symphony in C Minor,* No. 5, Trio (1-8);
   The Creation, "With Verdure Clad" (1-4).
Mozart, *The Violet* (1-7);
   Violin Sonata, K547, Andante, theme,
      K306, Allegretto, principal theme,
      K376, Rondo, principal theme;
   Piano Sonata, K333, B flat Major, Rondo, second theme,
      K280, F Major, Presto (1-16),
      K284, D Major, Rondeau en Polonaise
      (1-8),
      K282, E flat Major, Minuet I (1-12).

Beethoven, *Ninth Symphony,* Op. 125, Adagio, theme I (3-10) ;
    Bagatelles, Op. 119, No. 11 ;
    Piano Sonata, Op. 2, No. 1, Adagio (1-8),
        Op. 2, No. 2, Largo (1-8),
        Op. 2, No. 3, Adagio (1-4),
        Op. 2, No. 3, Rondo, second theme,
        Op. 22, Rondo, principal theme;
    Minuet in G, Trio;
    Piano Sonata, Op. 27, No. 2, Allegretto (1-16),
        Op. 49, No. 1, Rondo, second theme,
        B flat Major (1-9).
Schubert, *Impromptu in G flat Major,* Op. 90, No. 3 (1-8).
Mendelssohn, *Songs Without Words,* No. 44, (1-4) ;
    Piano Concerto, G Minor, Op. 25, Andante (13-17).
Wagner, *Tannhauser,* "Pilgrims' Chorus" (1-8).
Tchaikovsky, *Symphony V,* Op. 64, Andante, principle theme;
    Finale, subordinate theme;
    String Quartet, Op. 11, Andante cantabile (1-8).

The following passages for analysis have been selected from the above list. Identify cadences, form, chords, nonharmonic tones, and pivotal chords.

TRIO   HAYDN, *C Minor Symphony* (London, No. 5)

HAYDN, *The Creation*, "With Verdure Clad"

BEETHOVEN, *Ninth Symphony*, Op. 125

WAGNER, *Tannhauser*, "Pilgrim's Chorus"

II
(chromatic embellishment)

TCHAIKOVSKY, *Fifth Symphony,** Op. 64

Andante cantabile

(e)

*See also Finale, subordinate theme (piano score).

TCHAIKOVSKY, *String Quartet,* Op. 11

Andante cantabile

(f)

Chapter XV

THE V$_2^4$ CHORD (*Continued*)

Ex. 118

MOZART (1756—1791), *String Quartet*, K428, Finale

Allegro vivace

T HE THEME quoted on the preceding page is found in one of the six string quartets dedicated to Haydn from whom Mozart learned much about this difficult medium. In fact, the passage is somewhat reminiscent of Haydn's style. Observe the two contrasting secticons: the questioning eighth note figure, and the bustling sixteenth notes that serve as a basis for each part.

What key center is set up in measure 1 and confirmed by the cadence in measure 6? Note the new key signature of E flat major[1] at the beginning. What tone is the key center at the end — E flat or B flat? This change of key center (modulation) is suggested by the A natural in measure 12, and established by the cadence in measure 14. Spell the last chord in measure 12 upward from its bass tone, rearrange it in thirds, and sing the chord and its resolution in *arpeggio* form, thus:

Ex. 119*

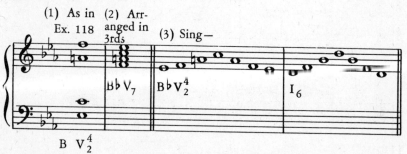

*When singing these measures, note the strong tendency of the chord-seventh (E flat) to move down to the third of the B flat chord (D).

Therefore, it is an F$_7$ with its seventh (E flat) in the bass or, in other words, an F$_2^4$, or V$_2^4$, in the key of B flat major. In the same way, show why the principal chord in measure 3 is a B flat$_2^4$, or V$_2^4$, in the key of E flat major.

To what chord does this V$_2^4$ resolve in measure 4 of Example 118, page 243. Compare the progression of the bass and melody tones in the $_2^4$ chords of measures 4 and 12 in Example 120.

---

[1] Write the E flat major scale, first using accidentals only, then with its own key signature of three flats (B flat, E flat, and A flat).

Ex. 120

(Measure 4)

(Measure 12)

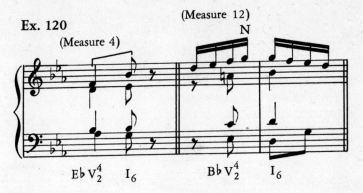

Eb V$^4_2$ I$_6$ Bb V$^4_2$ I$_6$

Note that both V$^4_2$ chords resolve downward in the bass, but that the melody tone in measure 4 skips upward a fourth.

This skip of a fourth in the melody (measure 4) is a common variation of the usual stepwise or stationary melody tones in a V$^4_2$ resolution. It occurs again in this passage from the music drama, *Siegfried:*

Ex. 121

Moderato   WAGNER, *Sigfried*, Act 3, Scene 3

G   V   V$^4_2$ I$_6$

*Chromatic chord.

Which part of the V$^4_2$ chord (root third, fifth, or seventh) skips upward a fourth in Example 118, measure 4, and Example 120, measure 3? Occasionally, the melody tone of the V$^4_2$ skips upward even further than a fourth, as in the second theme of Beethoven's *Coriolanus Overture*[2]:

Ex. 122

BEETHOVEN, *Coriolanus Overture,* Op. 62 (Theme II)

Allegro con brio

It is evident, then, that the melody tone of the V$^4_2$ chord often skips upward a fourth or more instead of remaining stationary or moving stepwise. Since these skips are from the fifth, or root, of the chord, this exceptional resolution may be used to harmonize the melodic skips from 2 to 5, or from 5 to 8 in the scale, as in the following chorale:

Ex. 123

---

[2] These exceptional skips of the V$^4_2$ occur only in the melody, while the bass progresses down normally one-half tone to the I$_6$ in all these examples. The bass of the V$^4_2$ only skips downward to other inversions of the V$_7$ chord. See Example 121.

In arranging melodies for mixed voices, it is often desirable to write a single baritone part which has a lower range than the usual low alto part (see Chapter XIV, page 230). The average range of this baritone part is an octave lower than the alto, as may be seen by comparing the range of the two voices, thus:

Ex. 124

In your arrangements, use the middle rather than the extreme register of each voice. For example, the first phrase of *America* might be arranged thus for soprano, alto, and baritone:

Ex. 125

Work out the rest of the melody for this vocal combination, using the accepted harmonization, and test the result by singing it in class. This type of writing requires considerable skill. Do not be satisfied until you have found *by experiment* and *strict*

self-criticism which spacing of the chord tones sounds most satisfactory. In general, these voices sound best when spaced fairly close together, especially the soprano and alto. However, in order to give the baritone a good melodic part, it is often necessary for it to be more than an octave from the soprano.

Review:

1. The pitches and signature of the E flat major scale.
2. The V^4_2 in all major keys through four sharps and three flats.
3. How the chord-seventh of the V^4_2 resolves.
4. How the bass of the V^4_2 moves when the melody skips a fourth upward.
5. A new way to harmonize the melodic skips 2-5 and 5-8.
6. The average range of the baritone voice.
7. How to harmonize melodies for soprano, alto, and baritone.
8. What a string quartet is (the form and instruments used).
9. Through what chord the modulation is made in Example 118.

For Further Study, Determine:

1. The chords and form of Examples 118, 121, and 122.
2. Whether the melodic skip in the V^4_2 resolution can be found in familiar music.
3. The best spacing for chord tones using soprano, alto, and baritone.
4. Some characteristics of string quartet style in contrast to that of piano or voices.

I — Assignment for Writing

1. Scan the following poems and set them to music in the key of E flat major, or other familiar keys, for two or three voices. Work as directed in Chapter XII, page 193. (Accompaniment optional.)

> (*a*) Let it be forgotten, as a flower is forgotten,
>   Forgotten as a fire that once was singing gold.
> Let it be forgotten for ever and ever,
>   Time is a kind friend, he will make us old.
>
> If anyone asks, say it was forgotten
>   Long and long ago,
> As a flower, as a fire, as a hushed footfall
>   In a long-forgotten snow.
>
> *Song — Sara Teasdale*[3]

---

[3] From Sara Teasdale, *Rivers to the Sea*, Copyright 1915 by The Macmillan Company and used with their permission.

(*b*) Bird of the wilderness,
      Blithesome and cumberless,
      Sweet be thy matin o'er moorland and lea!
      Emblem of happiness,
      Blest is thy dwelling-place —
      O to abide in the desert with thee!

                    The Skylark — James Hogg

(*c*) "Summer is coming, summer is coming,
          I know it, I know it, I know it.
      Light again, leaf again, life again, love again,"
          Yes, my wild little Poet.

      "Love again, song again, nest again, young again,"
          Never a prophet so crazy!
      And hardly a daisy as yet, little friend,
          See, there is hardly a daisy.

              The Throstle — Alfred, Lord Tennyson

(*d*) The sun is ever full and bright,
      The pale moon waneth night by night.
          Why should this be?

      My heart that once was full of light
      Is but a dying moon to-night.

      But when I dream of thee apart,
      I would the dawn might lift my heart,
          O sun, to thee.

          Sadness — The Odes of Confucius[4]

(*e*) High o'er the hill the moon barque steers.
          The lantern lights depart.
      Dead springs are stirring in my heart;
          And there are tears . . .
      But that which makes my grief more deep
      Is that you know not when I weep.

                    Tears — Wang Seng-Ju[5]

---

[4] Taken from *Lute of Jade*, rendered by L. Cranmer-Byng, published by E. P. Dutton & Co., Inc., New York.
[5] *Ibid.*

(f)   The Lady Moon is my lover,
          My friends are the oceans four,
       The heavens have roofed me over,
          And the dawn is my golden door.
       I would liefer follow the condor
          Or the seagull, soaring from ken,
       Than bury my godhead yonder
          In the dust of the whirl of men.

                              A World Apart — *Chang Chin-Ho*[6]

2. Harmonize at least one of the following melodies for soprano, alto, and baritone. Experiment treating them as rounds, the second voice entering one measure later. Add baritone parts to melodies previously arranged for soprano and alto.

[6] Taken from *Lute of Jade,* rendered by L. Cranmer-Byng, published by E. P. Dutton & Co., Inc., New York.

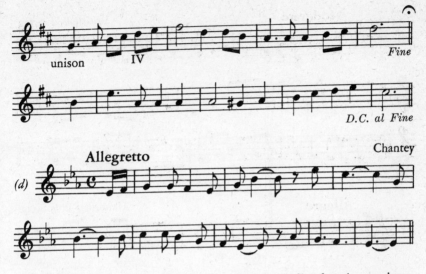

unison   IV   *Fine*

D.C. al Fine

Allegretto   Chantey

(d)

3. Harmonize at least one of the following melodies for piano, using any of the preceding accompaniment figures, except (*a*) and (*b*) which should be in close harmony. Analyze the form of each melody used.

Chorale

(a)

Chorale (1675)

(b)

Moderato   British Folk Song

(c)

Allegro   Ukrainian Folk Song

(d)

D$_3^4$ G$_6$ D$_2^4$

Allegretto   MOZART, *The Violet*

(e)

D$_2^4$ D$_2^4$

Allegretto   German Folk Song

(f)

D$_2^4$

Moderato   English Folk Song

Fine

D.S. al Fine

Reprinted by permission from 140 Folk-Songs, Concord Series No. 3. Published and copyrighted by the E. C. Schirmer Music Company.

II — Assignment for Playing

1. Harmonize one or more of the melodies in the *Assignment for Writing* (3).

2. Improvise melodies without accompaniment in the *A–B–A* form. Experiment with phrases of unusual length (three or five measures) and some modulation.

3. Improvise a three-part form, using the following period for part I. Make part II a phrase in the same style, modulating to B flat major through its V$\frac{4}{2}$ chord. Instead of repeating all of part I for part III, use only its consequent (last) phrase.

Finnish Folk Song

Moderato

From Play a Tune of The World Music Series, *copyright 1936. Used by permission of Ginn and Company, owners of the copyright.*

4. Play by ear in the key of E flat major the melody of *Believe Me If All Those Endearing Young Charms*. Repeat with a suitable accompaniment.

5. Play the following chord patterns in the keys of C, G, D, A, E, F, B flat, and E flat major, and repeat in piano style. Play the chord patterns of preceding lessons in E flat major. Devise original patterns using the V$\frac{4}{2}$ chord for modulating to the dominant key. Repeat with embellishments.

6. Transpose simple melodies and passages in this lesson down a major or minor second. Review the note on transposition, Chapter XI, page 183, *Assignment for Playing*.

III — *Assignment for Listening*

1. *Oral dictation:* harmonic recognition only. Identify chords by quality, letter, and Roman numeral.

        Beethoven, *Ecossaises* (1-64);

             Sonata, Op. 10, No. 1, Finale (16-28);

             Eroica Symphony, Op. 55, Finale, Poco andante (1-8).

        Bach, *Fourth French Suite*, Gavotte, Sarabande (1-8);

           Sixth French Suite, Minuet (complete).

        Mozart, *Violin Sonata*, K547, Andante, theme;

           String Quartet, K575, D Major, Minuet (1-16).

        Kuhlau, *Sonatina*, Op. 55, No. 5, Tempo di Marcia (1-23); Vivace assai (1-16).

Brahms, *Violin Sonata,* Op. 78, Adagio (1-9).

Gabriel-Marie, *Serenade Badine,* C Major section.

Cui, *Bagatelle Italienne* (1-8).

Tchaikovsky, *Nocturne in F Major,* Op. 10, No. 1 (1-17);
   Romance, Op. 5, Allegro energico (1-4).

Schubert, *Impromptu,* Op. 90, No. 2 (1-8).

2. *Written dictation (quality, bass, melody, and name of chord).*
   Sing!: The Keys of Heaven.
   Brown Book, Twice 55: No. 89, *Cantique de Noël* (16-23).
   Green Book, Twice 55: No. 148, *Raise the Strain* (1-2).
   Home and Community Song Book. Concord Series No. 2. *No, John*
      (1-4).
   Haydn, *The Creation,* "The Heavens are Telling."
   Mendelssohn, *Lieder,* No. 5, *A Pilgrim's Song,* Op. 8 (1-15);
      No. 3, *Spring Song,* Op. 34 (6-18).
   Schumann, *Lieder,* No. 22, *Sunday* (1-12).
   New Episcopal Hymnal, No. 94, *St. Kevin* (second tune),
      No. 515, *Albano.*

IV — Assignment for Analysis

Schubert, *Piano Sonata,* Op. 122, Allegro moderato (1-4).

Tchaikovsky, *Romance,* Op. 5, Allegro energico (1-4).

Schumann, *Piano Sonata,* Op. 22, Rondo, subordinate theme;
   Album for the Young, Op. 68, No. 22 (1-8).

Boccherini, *Minuet in A,* Trio.

Thomas, Gavotte from *Mignon.*

Mozart, *Violin Sonata,* K305, Andante;
   Jupiter Symphony, K551, Andante (1-4);
   E flat Major Symphony, K543, Menuetto (1-16);
   G Minor Symphony, K183, Trio, (1-8).

Beethoven, *String Quartet,* Op. 18, No. 6, Adagio (1-8);
   String Quartet, Op. 130, Cavatine (1-9);
   Sonata, Op. 27, No. 2, Allegretto;
   Sonata, Op. 49, No. 2, Rondo (32-48).

Wagner, *Parsifal,* Parsifal Motive.

Play a Tune: Rondo from *Sextette,* Op. 71 (Beethoven), p. 30;
   No. 1, *Bagatelle,* Op. 33 (Beethoven), p. 69.

The passages for analysis on the following pages have been selected from the above list. Identify cadences, form, chords, nonharmonic tones, and pivotal chords.

Allegro moderato   SCHUBERT, *Sonata*, Op. 122, Finale

(a)

Allegro energico   TCHAIKOVSKY, *Romance*, Op. 5

(b)

SCHUMANN, *Piano Sonata*, Op. 22, Scherzo

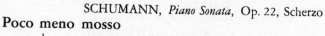

Poco meno mosso

(c)   Theme II

TRIO   BOCCHERINI, *Minuet in A Major*

THOMAS, "Gavotte" from *Mignon*

Allegro   MOZART, *G Minor Symphony*, Trio, K183

(f)

Allegretto   BEETHOVEN, *Sonata*, Op. 27, No. 2

(g)

BEETHOVEN, *Rondo,* Op. 71

WAGNER, *Parsifal Motive*

Chapter XVI

IMPLIED MODULATION TO
THE DOMINANT KEY

Ex. 126

DONIZETTI, Adapted from *Il Nome*

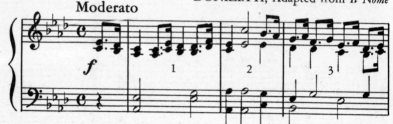

Donizetti, as an opera composer, wrote many popular melodies in the traditional theatrical style of his day. However, Example 126, though typical in style, is an independent song not taken from any of his larger works. Are there any prevailing rhythmic or melodic figures? Observe the new key signature of A flat major.[1] Sing the passage, noting the cadences in measures 4 and 8.

---

[1] Write the A flat major scale in treble and bass, first with accidentals only, then with its own key signature of four flats — B flat, E flat, A flat, and D flat. Learn this new signature, noting that the name of the key corresponds to the next to the last flat in the signature.

These cadences are on different chords and belong to different key centers. Test by singing the key tone after each cadence. The first is an imperfect authentic cadence in A flat major, whereas the second is a perfect authentic cadence in E flat major, the dominant key.

The first chord in measure 7 suggests the new tonality of E flat major. Spell this chord upward from the bass tone, and sing the chord and its resolution, thus:

Ex. 127

(a) As in
    Ex. 126   (b) Sing

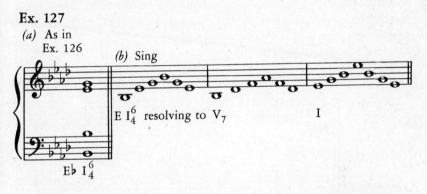

The new key (E flat) is entered through its I_4^6 chord without the use of definitive accidental (D natural) *in the melody* to suggest the modulation. The setting up of a new key without a melodic accidental to indicate the change of tonality is a new and important type of modulation. In Example 126, page 260, the change is merely *implied* and the I_4^6 is used as a substitute for the V_7 to initiate the modulation. Hence, an *implied modulation* is one without indicative accidentals in the melody, as for example, the following theme from Beethoven's *Symphony No. 2 in D Major,* Op. 36:

Ex. 128

Recall other melodies that modulate without using accidentals, for example, Schumann's *Traümerei,* or Dvořák's *Humoresque.*

Name all the chords and nonharmonic tones in Example 126, page 260. Note especially the sixteenth notes in measure 3 which do not belong to the chords. Such a nonharmonic tone, whose resolution skips down a third, is an *échappée.* It occasionally skips up a third also. Larger skips than a third in both directions may be found, but they are rare.

Sing the following melody harmonized for soprano, alto, and baritone or bass, first with the two upper voices and baritone, then with the two upper voices and bass:

Ex. 129   Moderato   SULLIVAN

*Note the use of the fundamental VII and VII $^{0}_{7}$ in the baritone version.

Compare these two versions carefully in regard to the vocal range, the doubling, and the general effect. Observe that the harmonic background is not altered by the difference in register. The average bass voice has a range approximately a third below the baritone, thus:

Ex. 130

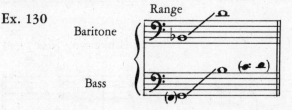

It is best to use the middle register of each voice. How could the baritone part of Example 125, page 247, be altered to make it suitable for bass? Make these changes and test the results by singing the new version.

In arranging for soprano, alto, and bass, note that the two upper voices are written fairly close together (not more than an octave apart), whereas the bass is sometimes rather widely separated from them. However, such wide spacing should not be frequent or extreme, particularly between the upper voices.

The melodic interest of the three voices will vary according to the character of the music. Example 129 is average in its use of nonharmonic tones to avoid wide skips and to give melodic interest to each voice. (See measure 1, in which passing tones are used in the lower voices.) On the other hand, the part writing may be simple or elaborate, depending on the melody, tempo, and effect desired, thus:

Ex. 131   Allegro   SULLIVAN, *The Pirates of Penzance*

Chorale (Unknown, *circa* 1558)

Soprano
Alto

(b)

Bass

Experiment with this vocal three-part combination. Make each part as interesting and independent as possible. To do so, it will sometimes be necessary to double either the third or the root of the chord, thus omitting the fifth. Less frequently, the third is omitted,[2] especially in the V, or I chords at a cadence, thus:

Ex. 132

Soprano
Alto ·

·Baritone

Though good part writing requires skill, it is based on comparatively few general principles. Some of the most important of these principles have to do with *parallel motion between voices,* and may be summarized as shown on page 265.

---

[2] See Chapter II, Example 17, page 22.

1. Between any two voices, parallel thirds and sixths sound well in moderation.

2. Parallel fourths are good except between the bass and the soprano.

3. Parallel fifths and octaves are usually avoided because they weaken the melodic flow and independence of the parts in this style of writing.

Composers sometimes use parallel fifths for special effects. Parallel octaves resulting from the continuous doubling of one voice have always been used. Instrumental music is much more free in the use of parallel fifths and octaves than is vocal music. The use of parallel fifths and octaves is dependent upon stylistic considerations and, for this reason, they should be avoided for the present. By keeping these general principles in mind, the freedom and interest of your writing will be increased.

Review:

1. The pitches and signature of the A flat major scale.
2. How a melody may modulate without using accidentals (implied modulation).
3. Through what chord or chords the new key is often introduced.
4. The rhythmic location of the cadential I⁶₄ in Example 126.
5. The average range of the bass voice.
6. How to harmonize melodies for soprano, alto, and bass.
7. How these voices are usually spaced.
8. Unusual doublings that are sometimes necessary.
9. Some guiding principles pertaining to parallel part writing.
10. The characteristics of an *échappée.*

For Further Study, Determine:

1. The form of Example 126.
2. Whether an implied melodic modulation (that is, without accidentals) may be ignored in harmonization.
3. Which of the two, bass or baritone, sounds better with soprano and alto.
4. Why the bass is sometimes used instead of the baritone.
5. What an aria is.

I — Assignment for Writing

1. Scan the following poems and set at least one of them to music in
the key of A flat major (or other familiar keys) for one, two, or three
voices — (soprano, alto, and bass). (Accompaniment optional.)

(*a*) O Mistress mine! where are you roaming?
O! stay and hear; your true love's coming,
    That can sing both high and low.
Trip no further, pretty sweeting;
Journeys end in lovers' meeting,
    Every wise man's son doth know.

What is love? 'tis not hereafter;
Present mirth hath present laughter;
    What's to come is still unsure:
In delay there lies no plenty;
Then come kiss me, sweet and twenty,
    Youth's a stuff will not endure.
O Mistress Mine from *Twelfth Night* — *Shakespeare*

(*b*) The singers of serenades
    Whisper their faded vows
Unto fair listening maids
    Under the singing boughs.

And the mandolines and they,
    Faintlier breathing, swoon
Into the rose and gray
    Ecstasy of the moon.
Mandoline from *Fêtes Galantes* — *Verlaine*[3]

(*c*) The old dream comes again to me:
    With May-night stars above,
We two sat under the linden-tree
    And swore eternal love.

Again and again we plighted troth,
    We chattered, and laughed, and kissed;
To make me well remember my oath
    You gave me a bite in the wrist.
O darling with the eyes serene,
    And with the teeth so white!
The vows were proper to the scene,
    Superfluous was the bite.
The Old Dream Comes to Me Again — *Heinrich Heine*
(*Translated by James Thomson*)

---

[3] Reprinted by permission of Dodd, Mead & Company.

(d) My true love hath my heart, and I have his,
By just exchange one for another given:
I hold his dear, and mine he cannot miss,
There never was a better bargain driven:
    My true love hath my heart, and I have his.

His heart in me keeps him and me in one,
My heart in him his thoughts and senses guides:
He loves my heart, for once it was his own,
I cherish his because in me it bides:
    My true love hath my heart, and I have his.
                   The Bargain — Sir Philip Sidney

(e) Under the greenwood tree
Who loves to lie with me,
And turn his merry note
Unto the sweet bird's throat,
Come hither, come hither, come hither:
    Here shall he see
    No enemy
But winter and rough weather.
Under the Greenwood Tree from *As You Like It* —
                               Shakespeare

(f) The night will never stay,
The night will still go by,
Though with a million stars
You pin it to the sky,
Though you bind it with the blowing wind
And buckle it with the moon,
The night will slip away
Like sorrow or a tune.
      The Night Will Never Stay — Eleanor Farjeon[4]

2. Using the given harmonization of familiar songs, arrange them for soprano, alto, and bass, or add a bass part to melodies which have been previously arranged for soprano and alto alone.

3. Experiment with arrangements or original compositions for instrumental trios, for example, two violins and cello, two cornets and trombone, three saxophones, or two clarinets and English horn (bass clarinet or bassoon may be substituted for the latter). Play these arrangements or original compositions in class.

---

[4] From *Gipsy and Ginger,* published by E. P. Dutton & Co., Inc., New York.

4. Harmonize at least one of the following melodies for soprano, alto, and bass. Can any of them be treated as a three-part round?

SULLIVAN, *The Pirates of Penzance,* No. 12

Allegro marziale

Add the soprano and alto to this bass melody:

Moderato

German Folk Song

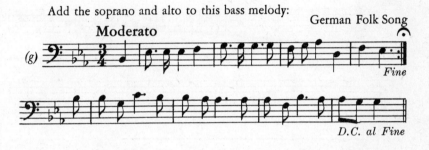

5. Harmonize at least one of the following melodies for piano, using any of the preceding accompaniment figures. Analyze the form of each melody used.

SULLIVAN, *Patience*

Allegretto

Bach, *371 Chorales,* Nos. 84, 217

Folk Song Sight Singing Series: Book VI, No. 90; Book VII, Nos. 29, 77

II — *Assignment for Playing*

1. Harmonize any of the melodies in the *Assignment for Writing* (5).

2. Improvise a tango in two- or three-part form, using the following motive for part 1 (a period modulating to the dominant key). Part 2 is to be a phrase ending on the V_7 chord of the tonic key. Part 3 will also be a phrase in the tonic key beginning like part 1.

Moderato   Tango Argentino

3. Improvise melodies in two- or three-part form, details optional. Repeat from memory and harmonize. (Optional.)

4. Play by ear in the key of A flat major (first alone, then with accompaniment) the melody of *Columbia, The Gem of the Ocean,* and *Comin' Thro' the Rye.*

5. Play the following chord pattern in all the major keys studied, and repeat in piano style. Devise original patterns, modulating to the dominant key through its I_4^6 chord. Embellish these patterns with *échappées.*

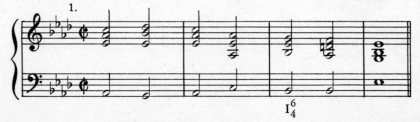

I_4^6

2.

I_4^6

6. Transpose simple melodies and passages from this unit up a major or minor second. Review the note on transposition, Chapter XI, page 183, *Assignment for Playing.*

III — *Assignment for Listening*

1. *Oral dictation:* harmonic recognition only. Name chords by quality, letter, and Roman numeral.

Handel, *Harmonious Blacksmith* (1-4).

Haydn, *Symphony V* (Peters Edition), Largo (1-6);
  Piano Sonata in D, No. 7, Schirmer ed., Finale (1-8) ;
  Piano Sonata in A flat, No. 8, Schirmer ed., Finale (entire
    exposition).

Mozart, *Piano Concerto in E flat Major,* K365, Menuetto (1-12).

Beethoven, *Symphony I,* Op. 21, First Movement, subordinate
    theme (53-60); Trio;
      Sonata, Op. 31, No. 1, First Movement (1-11),
          Op. 31, No. 3, Scherzo (1-8),
          Op. 110, Moderato cantabile (1-12),
          Op. 2, No. 2, Largo (1-19),
          Op. 2, No. 3, Allegro con brio, second theme;
            Adagio (1-11) ;
      Sonata, Op. 26, Andante, theme (1-16).

Schumann, *Album for the Young,* Op. 68, Nos. 1, 2, 7, 10, 17.

Schubert, *The Trout* (7-14).

Moszkowski, *Serenata,* Op. 15, No. 1 (1-10).

Chopin, *Waltz,* Op. 34, No. 1 (17-24).

Smetana, *String Quartet,* "From My Life," Largo (7-22).

Strauss, *Night in Venice,* D Major Section (Universal Edition),
    page 62.

Diller, *First Studies in Harmonic Analysis:*
        Ein Scheckiges Pford (Schumann), page 37;
        Sleep Little Son (Weber), page 34;
        When the Moon Shone Bright (Klaass), page 35.

2. *Written dictation (quality, bass, melody, and name of chord)*.
> *Brown Book, Twice 55:* No. 71, *Lead Kindly Light* (9-12);
> > No. 72, *I Need Thee Every Hour* (1-8).
> *Golden Book: My Faith Looks Up to Thee*, p. 59 (1-8).
> Beethoven, *Symphony II*, Op. 36, Larghetto (1-8).
> Schubert, *Ecossaises* (1-8).

IV — Assignment for Analysis

> Beethoven, *Six Easy Variations in G,* theme;
> > *Minuet in G* (1-8);
> > *Sonata Pathetique,* Op. 13, Adagio (1-8).
> Schumann, *Carnival,* Op. 9, Preamble (1-8);
> > *Vienna Carnival-Scene,* Op. 26, Scherzino (1-8).
> Schubert, *Piano Sonata,* Op. 122, Trio (1-10);
> > *Piano Sonata in C Minor,* Adagio (1-8);
> > *Moment Musical,* Op. 94, No. 1 (1-6);
> > *Impromptu,* Op. 142, No. 1 (1-8).
> Mozart, *Symphony in E flat,* K543, Andante (1-8).
> Chopin, *Ballade,* Op. 23, second theme;
> > *Ballade,* Op. 47 (1-8); second theme (53-61).
> Verdi, March from *Aida,* Part II.
> Sibelius, *Finlandia,* second theme.
> Sullivan, *Patience,* No. 15 (1-8).

The following passages for analysis have been selected from the above list. Identify cadences, form, chords, nonharmonic tones, and pivotal chords used in modulations.

THEME   BEETHOVEN, *Six Easy Variations*

D.C. al Fine   Fine

BEETHOVEN, *Sonata Pathétique*, Op. 13

SCHUMANN, *Vienna Carnival-Scene*, Op. 26, Scherzino

SCHUBERT, *Impromptu*, Op. 142, No. 2 (Adapted)

MOZART, E♭ Major Symphony, K543

Andante con moto

(e)

CHOPIN, G Minor Ballade, Op. 23

Meno mosso

(f)

CHOPIN, *Ab Major Ballade*, Op. 47

VERDI, *Aida*, "Grand March"

SIBELIUS, *Finlandia*, (2nd theme)

Allegro espressivo

(Sing this passage in four parts)

Published by Breitkopf and Hartel and reprinted by permission of Associated Music Publishers, Inc.

Andante   SULLIVAN, *Patience*

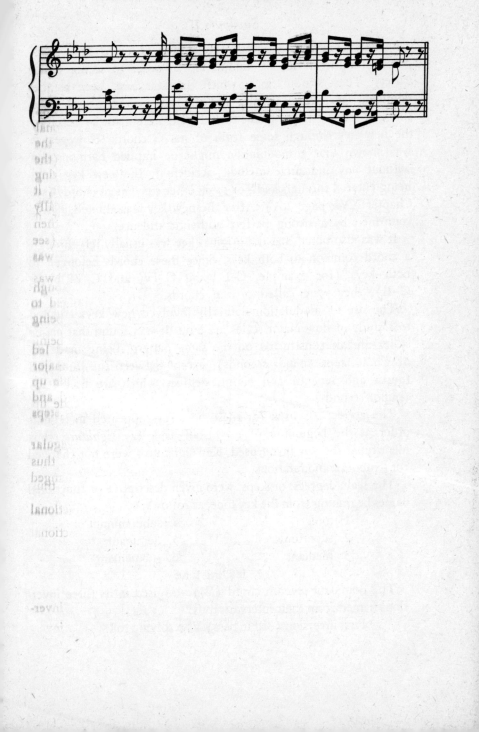

Summary II

In Part II (Chapters IX-XVI), it was observed how composers use the device of modulation in order to secure tonal variety. These modulations, which thus far have been to the dominant key, were usually indicated by an accidental (the changed leading tone) in the melody and were made by entering the new key through some form of its V_7 chord. However, it was shown that a modulation might be implied harmonically without any indicative melodic accidental; the new key then being entered through its I^6_4, or some other convenient chords (see Chapter XVI, page 261). After the new key was entered, it was confirmed by a strong perfect authentic cadence.

It was also noted that the original key was usually left through a chord common to both keys. Since these chords belonged to both keys (for example, C–I being G–IV, and C–VI being G–II), they were called *pivotal* chords.

The use of modulation naturally involved new keys and led to a study of how major scales are built. It was found that major scales are all constructed on the same pattern, being made up of whole steps (major seconds), except between the third and fourth and seventh and eighth degrees which are half steps (minor seconds).

The accidentals used for these new keys appeared in regular order at the beginning of each staff as a *key signature,* thus identifying the key being used. Key signatures were not changed for temporary modulations.

The scale degrees, or steps, were given descriptive or functional names beginning from the key tone, as follows:

1. tonic	4. subdominant
2. supertonic	5. dominant
3. mediant	6. submediant

7. leading tone

The dominant-seventh chord (V_7) was used in its three inversions named from their intervals, thus:

First inversion (3rd in bass) V^6_5 resolving to I.

Second inversion (5th in bass) V$^4_3$ resolving to I (or I$_6$).

Third inversion (7th in bass) V$^4_2$ resolving to I$_6$.

In the inversions of the dominant seventh, no tone of the chord was omitted or doubled. It was found that these inversions were useful as substitutes for the V$_7$ in entering the new dominant key smoothly without skips.

It was noted that there were two special resolutions of the inverted V$_7$ chord:

(1) The V$^6_5$ could resolve upward to the I$_6$, in which case the chord seventh also moved upward in parallel thirds with the bass.

(2) The melody tone of the V$^4_2$ sometimes skipped upward from two to five, or five to eight of the scale.

It was also found that the diminished triad (VII), containing a minor third and a diminished fifth, could be used in its first inversion (VII$_6$) as a substitute for the V$^6_5$ which it resembles. Either its third or fifth could be doubled and its voices resolved stepwise to the I or I$_6$. Neither the fundamental position nor the second inversion was found in the music examined.

The study of staff intervals in previous chapters was completed by identifying those in the V$_7$ chord. Consequently, the facts regarding all staff intervals may be conclusively summarized, thus:

Chapter IX, page 132: major seconds: all, except
                        minor seconds: E—F'and'B—C.

Chapter VII, page 91: major thirds: C—E, F—A, G—B.

Chapter VIII, page 108: minor thirds: all others.

Chapter XIII, page 209: perfect fourths: all, except
                        augmented fourths: F—B.

The quality of the remaining intervals was found by inverting these known ones, since inversion reverses the quality of all except perfect intervals, thus:

Chapter XIII, page 209: perfect fifths: all except
                        diminished fifth: B—F.

By inversion of thirds: minor sixths: E–C, A–F, B–G
                        major sixths: all others.

Chapetr XI, page 170: minor sevenths: all except
major sevenths: C—B, F—E.

The staff prime and octave are, of course, perfect.

Rearranging this table of white key, or staff, intervals, it was found that primes (unisons), fourths, fifths, and octaves were classified as perfect, augmented, or diminished; and seconds, thirds, sixths, and sevenths were classified as major or minor. All perfect intervals and major and minor thirds and sixths were *consonant;* all other intervals were *dissonant.*

Three new nonharmonic tones were added:

(1) The *appoggiatura* (Chapter XI), a neighboring tone entered by a skip.

(2) The *accacciatura* (Chapter XI), a very short neighboring tone entered by a skip.

(3) The *échappée* (Chapter XVI), a neighboring tone left by a skip.

A study was made of vocal harmonization for three women's voices, or two women's and one man's voice (baritone or bass). Also, it was found possible at times to harmonize a melody contrapuntally by repeating the melody itself in the other voices, beginning in successive measures after the first voice. This exact repetition of the melody by other voices formed either a *canon* or a *round.*

The writing and improvisation of small two-part (*A–B*) and three-part (*A–B–A*) forms was continued, as well as the analysis of the chords and forms of the selected passages from musical literature.

Suggestions for Study

Find examples in musical literature of the following technical points discussed in Part II:

(1) Intervals.

Each type of interval listed in Chapter XIII, Example 106, p. 210.

(2) Chords.

(*a*) V_5^6, V_3^4, V_2^4, and VII_6.

(*b*) Modulations to the dominant key, either with or without melodic accidental.

(3) Nonharmonic tones.

The *appoggiatura* and *échappée*.

(4) Form.

  (*a*) The binary (*A–B*) form.

  (*b*) The canon and round.

Part III
BASIC INVERSIONS. THE MINOR MODE.
FOUR-VOICE WRITING

Chapter XVII

THE MINOR MODE:
PARALLEL AND RELATIVE SCALES

Ex. 133

MOZART, *C Minor Piano Fantasia*, K475

MOZART composed this *Fantasia* on May 20, 1785 and dedicated it to Teresa von Trattner, his pupil, who was also his landlord's wife. The year before, he had written the *C Minor*

287

Sonata, K457, for her, and in 1786 both works were published together as they appear today. This passage leads from the *allegro* section of the first movement directly into the second movement.

Play or hear this entire C minor *Fantasia*. Even its beginning is strange:

Ex. 134

Adagio

As the music continues, it reveals a new Mozart, who suggests the romanticism of the 19th century rather than the formalism of his own. (Compare Example 134 above with Example 118 and 117.)

Returning to Example 133, page 287, play measures 1 to 4 and sing the key tone. Evidently this passage is not in the key of C, as the lack of signature would indicate, but in the key of F. Play measures 5 to 8. How many are similar to measures 1 to 4? This comparison shows that the first three measures of each phrase are identical except for the substitution of A flat for A, and D flat for D. Do these changes alter the feeling of F as the key tone?

These two phrases, then, sound fundamentally alike yet somewhat different, because of the use of the altered A flat and D flat. The tonality of measures 1 to 4 is readily recognized as F major, although the signature is missing. Measures 5 to 7 are in *F minor* and represent the *same tonality* (key center), but a *different mode* (from the Latin *modus*, meaning style or manner). The Latin word, *minor*, as applied previously to intervals, means *lesser*.

Which scale degrees have been altered in changing the second phrase of Example 133, page 287, from the major to the minor mode? Arrange the tones of measures 1 to 4, and measures 5 to 8 into scale sequences, thus:

Ex. 135

measures 1 — 4

1	2	3	4	5	6	7	8
do	re	mi	fa	sol	la	ti	do

measures 5 — 8

1	2	3	4	5	6	7	8
do	re	*me*	fa	sol	*le*	ti	do

In F major, A is the third step and D is the sixth step. Therefore, since this minor mode is formed by lowering by one half step the third and sixth degrees of the corresponding major scale, *all major scales can be thus altered to minor.*

Sing F major, then F minor (Example 135) by making these changes. Remember that F major and F minor are two forms of the *same tonality,* differing in mode but *not in key.* Note the change in syllables for the minor mode. Experiment in the same manner with other familiar major scales.

Although the major and minor scales are not the only ones used, the bulk of music in the classic and romantic periods is based on these two patterns. Learn the minor scale as a variation of its corresponding major scale without regard to its individual whole- and half-tone construction.

Since the tonality of this *Fantasia* as a whole is C, Mozart uses no signature for the short transitional passage quoted in Example 133. Normally, the signature of one flat would be used for F major, but what of F minor? In Example 136, the F minor scale is written with the flat signatures already known.

Ex. 136

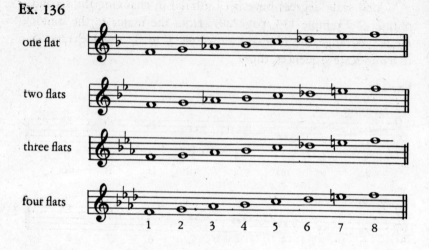

one flat

two flats

three flats

four flats

The signature of four flats (A flat) requires only *one* accidental (for E), whereas the others require two or more. The signature of A flat (four flats) is therefore the one usually used for F minor.

Test the effect of the lowered third and sixth scale steps, especially in the I, IV, and V chords already used, by playing and singing each chord in the major, then in the minor mode, thus:

Ex. 137

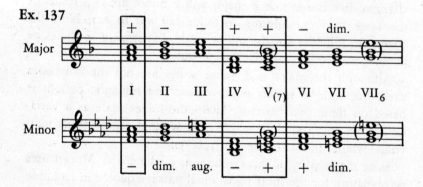

Major

I   II   III   IV   V(7)   VI   VII   VII6

Minor

In minor, the III chord requires special treatment, which will be discussed later. The II and VII, being diminished in quality, are used only in the first inversion.

To summarize: two modes (the major and the minor) are commonly used in music. The familiar major scale can be altered to minor by lowering its third and sixth degrees one half tone. For convenience, the minor scale usually "borrows" the signature of the major scale beginning on its third step. But this signature alone fails to keep the the leading tone (seventh step) in the normal half-step relationship to the tonic. Consequently, it must be altered by an accidental, which raises the seventh step one half tone, thus preserving the half-step relationship between the leading tone and its tonic.

Major and minor scales having the same key tone, or letter-name, are called *parallel* scales; those using the same key signature are termed *relative* scales. Parallel scales are more closely related *aurally* than relative scales are.

Comparing the quality of the chords in the two modes, it is evident that the I and IV chords become minor in the minor mode, while the V chord remains major in both modes. Of the other fundamental triads, the VI becomes major in the minor mode, the III becomes augmented, and the II and the VII are diminished. For this reason, it will be recalled that the II and the VII are not used in minor except in the first inversion. The augmented III is more logically treated as an embellishing chord in the area of chromatic harmony, and, consequently, will not be discussed in this work.

Review:

1. What the word "mode" means when applied to music.
2. How many modes are in general use today.
3. The difference between the major and minor modes or scales.
4. How the major scale may be changed to minor.
5. The syllables used for the minor scale.
6. The signature "borrowed" by the minor scale.
7. What alteration must be made in using this "borrowed" signature.
8. Relative and parallel scale relationships.
9. Which relationship is the closer aurally.
10. Which triads agree in quality with the prevailing mode.
11. Why F major and F minor are not different tonalities.

For Further Study, Determine:

1. Other scales sometimes used in addition to the major and minor.
2. Why the minor scale "borrows" a major signature.
3. What chords remain the same in quality in both modes.
4. The chords used in Example 133.
5. The tonality of Example 134.
6. Where Mozart lived when he wrote the *Fantasia*.
7. Why a composition is called "classic" or "romantic."
8. To which type this *Fantasia* belongs.
9. Whether the change from F major to F minor is a modulation.

I — Assignment for Writing

1. Scan the following poems and set at least one of them to music for one, two, or three voices. Experiment with the minor mode. (Accompaniment optional.)

> (a)   The moon in the heavens
>   Was silent and cold;
> The clouds that blew by it,
>   Like galleons of old,
> Moved slowly, sedately,
>   As onward they rolled.
>
> The stars of the evening
>   So far, yet close by,
> Stared hard at the city
>   In silence, and I
> Mused on the quiet
>   That reigns in the sky.
>
> *Nocturne — James Flexner*[1]

> (b)   The North Wind shakes the shivering moon
> And rattles the windows with a banging tune
> Hurling his message at the earth
> And hugging the trees with a shout of mirth.
>
> Howling his challenge to the night
> With all his blustering windy might
> The North Wind clings to his hard-won prize
> With a mist-wreath'd brow and starlit eyes.
>
> *North Wind — Lincoln Reis*[2]

---

[1] From *Creative Youth,* by Hughes Mearns, copyright 1925 by Doubleday & Company, Inc.
[2] *Ibid.*

(c)   A soldier of fortune was I, was I,
       As carefree as ever a lark in the sky,
       The older and wiser in scorn passed me by,
           For I was a soldier of fortune.

       I roamed through each village and town, every town,
       But my purse remained empty — I won no renown,
       And the fates laughed in triumph to see me cast down,
           For I was a soldier of fortune.

       But a richer reward than mere gold did I earn,
       And a maid taught me that which I yet had to learn,
       So that now I've a haven to which I can turn,
           For I'm no more a soldier of fortune.

                         Cavalier Ditty — Aline Wechsler[3]

(d)   The autumn comes, a maiden fair
           In slenderness and grace,
       With nodding rice-stems in her hair
           And lilies in her face.
       In flowers of grasses she is clad;
           And as she moves along,
       Birds greet her with their cooing glad
           Like bracelets' tinkling song.
                         The Seasons — Kalidasa[4]

(e)   On the mountain, in the valley,
       Singing birds again do rally;
       Now is seen
       Clover green;
       Winter, take away thy teen!
           Trees that erst were gray to view
       Now their verdant robes renew;
       In their shade
       Nests are made;
       Thence the toil of May is paid.
                On the Mountain — Sir Neidhart von Reuenthal
                    (*Translated by Jethro Bithell.*)

---

[3] From *Creative Youth,* by Hughes Mearns, copyright 1925 by Doubleday & Company, Inc.
[4] From *Panchatantra* by Arthur W. Ryder, used by permission of The University of Chicago Press.

(f)   A howling storm is brewing,
    The wind and rain are wild;
    And what can my love be doing,
    That pale and frightened child?

There at the window dreaming,
    I see her, worn and white;
    With eyes no longer beaming,
    She stares into the night.

The Storm — Heinrich Heine[5]

2. Harmonize one or more of the following melodies for soprano, alto, and bass. If some of them can be treated as rounds, do so. Experiment adding a bass part to melodies previously arranged for soprano and alto. (Optional.)

Moderato

Spanish Folk Song

(a)

[5] Translated by Louis Untermeyer. From *Heinrich Heine, Paradox and Poet*, by Louis Untermeyer, copyright 1937 by Harcourt, Brace and Company, Inc.

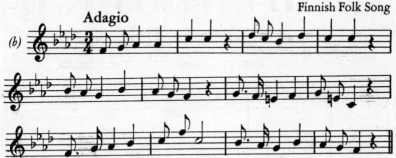

Adagio

Finnish Folk Song

(b)

Moderato

Russian Folk Song

(c)

Allegro

CHERUBINÍ

(d)

Chorale

(e)

3. Harmonize at least one of the following melodies for piano, using any of the preceding accompaniment figures, or new ones that are effective. Identify the form of each melody used.

Andante con moto   Russian Folk Song

(a)

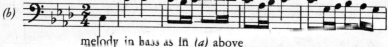

Moderato   Cuban Tune

(b)

melody in bass as in (a) above

Moderato   Polish Folk Song

(c)

(c♯)   (f♯)   (B)

II — *Assignment for Playing*

1. Harmonize any of the melodies in the *Assignment for Writing* (3).
2. Improvise melodies (period form) in F-minor. Repeat from memory.
3. Improvise a chorale in F minor in period form.
4. In the keys of A and F major, play by ear the melody of the *Marseillaise,* and repeat with suitable harmonic background. Note change of mode.
5. Learn the chord patterns on page 298, and repeat each in piano style. Experiment playing them in other keys with embellishments.

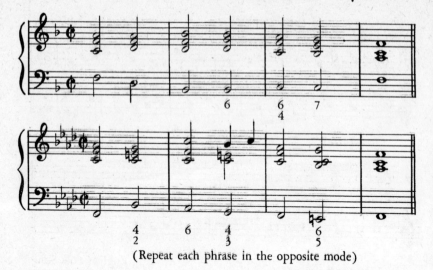

(Repeat each phrase in the opposite mode)

6. Transpose simple melodies and chord passages in this chapter down a minor third to keys already studied. Review note on transposition, Chapter XI, page 183, *Assignment for Playing.*

III — *Assignment for Listening*

1. *Oral dictation:* harmonic recognition only. (Name chords by quality, letter, and Roman numeral.)

(*a*) For contrast of mode:

    Schubert, *Moment Musical,* Op. 94, No. 4, Trio, D flat;

        Impromptu, Op. 142, No. 2, Trio, D flat,

                No. 4, Più Mosso.

    Chopin, *Waltz,* Op. 34, No. 2, Sostenuto,

             Op. 69, No. 2, B Major section;

        Mazurka, Op. 50, No. 2, A flat Major.

    Grieg, *Anitra's Dance* (58-69).

    Beethoven, *Violin Concerto,* Op. 61, Finale, second theme.

(*b*) Minor mode only:

    Beethoven, *Piano Sonata,* Op. 2, No. 1, First Movement (1-8).

    Haydn, *Symphony in C Major,* No. VII (Peters Edition), Adagio, Minore (1-8), p. 115 (piano score).

2. *Written dictation* (*quality, bass, melody, and name of chord*).

    Green Book, Twice 55: No. 83, *Watchman Tell Us of the Night*

(Parry) (1-4); No. 69, *Go Down Moses.*

Golden Book: Go Down Moses, page 97.

IV — Assignment for Analysis

Haydn, *Symphony in E flat Major* (Peters Edition), No. VIII,
Introduction;
Symphony in C Major, No. VII (Peters Edition), Adagio
(1-4); Minore (1-3);
Surprise Symphony, Andante, Theme and Minor Variation.

Beethoven, *Egmont Overture,* Op. 84, Introduction (1-4);
Symphony II, Op. 36, Largetto (33-34); First Move-
ment, development section, p. 30;
Symphony IV, Op. 60, Introduction;
Symphony VIII, Op. 93, Trio;
Piano Sonata, Op. 7, Third Movement (43-54),
Op. 13, Adagio (37-40); Rondo (25-33).

Schubert, *Thanks to the Brook,* cf. (5-10) with (22-26);
Impromptu, Op. 90, No. 4 (1-12),
Op. 142, No. 4, Più Mosso (1-17).

Tchaikovsky, *Symphony V,* Op. 64, Motive, Introduction to First
and Fourth Movements.

Mozart, *Piano Sonata, F Major,* K322, Adagio (1-8);
Symphony in E flat Major, K543, Andante (25-28).

Brahms, *To an Aeolian Harp,* Op. 19, No. 5 (1-6).

The following passages for analysis have been selected from the above
list. Identify cadences, chords, nonharmonic tones; note especially the
pivotal and modulatory chords and the contrast between the major and
minor modes.

BEETHOVEN, *Fourth Symphony,* Op. 60

(measures 33–40)   BEETHOVEN, *Second Symphony*, Op. 36

Larghetto

(measures 43–54)   BEETHOVEN, *Piano Sonata*, Op. 7

Allegro

BEETHOVEN, *Egmont Overture,* Op. 84 (Adapted)

INTRODUCTION
Sostenuto, ma non troppo

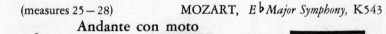

(measures 25—28)   MOZART, *E♭ Major Symphony,* K543

Andante con moto

BRAHMS, *To an Aeolian Harp,* Op. 19, No. 5

Poco lento

Chapter XVIII

THE HARMONIC MINOR SCALE:
DOMINANT MODULATIONS

Ex. 138

CHOPIN, (1810–1849), *Mazurka*, Op. 7, No. 3 (1832)

CHOPIN wrote the above passage shortly after he had left his native Warsaw and settled permanently in Paris. As a patriot, he loved his country's dances and immortalized two of them, the *mazurka* and the *polonaise*,[1] by many compositions in these forms. This passage, from one of his early mazurkas, illustrates his idealization of the original dance rhythm. It is based on a recurrent two-measure rhythmic figure over a very simple harmonic background.

---

[1] The *mazurka* is a Polish dance which originated in national songs accompanied by dancing. It was named for the ancient province of Masovia and was known as early as the 16th century. (Grove, *Dictionary*, Vol. III, pp. 356-357. New York: The Macmillan Company, 1935.)

The *polonaise* (Fr.) was first used late in the 16th century as a stately processional march or walking rhythm for the opening ceremonies of the Polish court. (Grove, *op. cit.*, Vol. IV, pp. 218-219.)

Play or listen to the passage, noting the mode, cadences, and form. Observe that the first phrase (measures 1 to 4) is in F minor, and that the second phrase (measures 5 to 8) ends in the tonality of C, whose mode is not established.

Modulation to the dominant key from the major mode was discussed in Chapters IX-XVI. This type of modulation also frequently occurs in the minor mode. In fact, modulation to the dominant key from either mode is probably the most common type found in music.[2] Through what chord is it made here? Is there any *pivotal* or "gateway" chord? Note the effect of the minor mode on the quality of the chords used.

Although the major scale has only one pattern, the minor scale has several, according to the context or the whim of the composer. The third and sixth degrees of the minor scale we found in Examples 133, 135, and 136 (Chapter XVII) were one half tone lower than those of the parallel major scale, thus:

Ex. 139

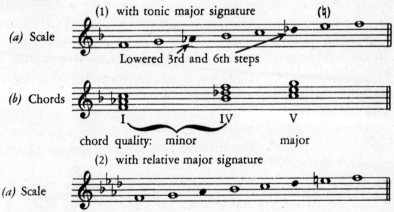

---

[2] Note that the dominant *key* of F minor is C *minor*. While the dominant *chord* of a minor key is major in quality, the dominant key remains minor. Thus, in this example, the modulation from F minor to C major is equally possible but not as frequently used.

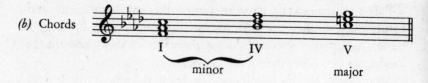

(b) Chords

This form is known as the *harmonic minor scale* because it is best adapted for harmonic purposes, especially at cadences. It is important to note that the quality of the I and IV chords agrees with the prevailing mode, while the V chord remains major in both modes. (For the quality of all chords, refer back to Example 137, page 290.)

Compare the sound of the interval between the sixth and seventh steps of the major scale and harmonic minor scale beginning on F. Since they are consecutive scale steps, they both use the same letters (D–E), but the pitches differ owing to the use of D flat in the minor mode. From the construction of the C major scale, we know that D–E is a major second; D flat–E, being half a tone larger, is called an *augmented second*. (See Example 106, page 210.) From this example, work out a statement defining augmented and diminished intervals. How many of each are found in the major and harmonic minor scales? Experiment singing and playing their resolutions. The following passage from Schumann shows the melodic use of the augmented second, which is comparatively rare:

Ex. 140

SCHUMANN, *First Symphony,* (Spring), Op. 38

Allegro animato

The minor mode puts at the student's disposal many new and interesting resources. Other factors being equal, the minor mode usually suggests sadness, but occasionally it may convey gaiety, as in the old Scottish folk song, *Charlie Is My Darling*:

Ex. 141

On the other hand, some of the most somber or tragic music may be found in the major mode, as for example, the "Dead March" from Handel's oratorio *Saul*.

Ex. 142

Can you recall similar examples of solemn major or gay minor tunes?

If you have not already done so, identify the mode of music heard or remembered as major or minor. Experiment reversing the mode of familiar melodies, observing how the whole character and color of the music is altered by a change of mode.

Review:

1. The construction of the harmonic minor scale.
2. The difference in quality between the dominant key and the dominant chord usually used in the minor mode.
3. The quality of each principal triad in the minor mode.
4. The type of modulation most used in both modes.
5. The construction of an augmented second.
6. Where the augmented second occurs in the harmonic minor scale.
7. The origin of the *mazurka* and the *polonaise*.

For Further Study, Determine:

1. Why the harmonic scale is so named.
2. Which is the pivotal melodic tone in Example 138.
3. Why the quality of the V chord remains major in the harmonic minor scale.
4. What interval would result from the inversion of an augmented second.

I — Assignment for Writing

1. Scan the following stanzas and set at least one of them to music for one, two, or three voices, preferably soprano, alto, baritone, or bass.

Experiment with the minor mode and modulation to the dominant key.
(Accompaniment optional.)

(*a*) The moon, like a round device
On a shadowy shield of war,
Hangs white in a heaven of ice
With a solitary star.

The wind has sunk to a sigh,
And the waters are stern with frost;
And gray, in the eastern sky,
The last snow-cloud is lost.

White fields, that are winter-starved,
Black woods, that are winter-fraught,
Cold, harsh as a face death-carved
With the iron of some black thought.

Snow — Madison Cawein[3]

(*b*) Dark hills at evening in the west,
Where sunset hovers like a sound
Of golden horns that sang to rest
Old bones of warriors under ground,
Far now from all the bannered ways
Where flash the legions of the sun,
You fade — as if the last of days
Were fading and all wars were done.

The Dark Hills — E. A. Robinson[4]

(*c*) Nature's first green is gold,
Her hardest hue to hold.
Her early leaf's a flower;
But only so an hour.
Then leaf subsides to leaf.
So Eden sank to grief,
So dawn goes down to day.
Nothing gold can stay.

Nothing Gold Can Stay — Robert Frost[5]

---

[3] From *The Vale of Tempe* by Madison Cawein, published and copyrighted by
E. P. Dutton & Co., Inc.
[4] From E. A. Robinson, *Three Taverns*. Copyright, 1920, by Edwin Arlington
Robinson. Used by permission of The Macmillan Company, publisher.
[5] From *Complete Poems of Robert Frost, 1949*, by Robert Frost. Copyright 1923,
1949 by Henry Holt & Company, Inc.

(d)   My songs to sell, good sir!
        I pray you buy.
      Here's one will win a lady's tears,
        Here's one will make her gay,
      Here's one will charm your true love true
        Forever and a day;
      Good sir, I pray you buy!

      Oh, no, he will not buy.

      My songs to sell, sweet maid!
        I pray you buy.
      This one will teach you Lilith's lore,
        And this what Helen knew.
      And this will keep your gold hair gold,
        And this your blue eyes blue;
      Sweet maid, I pray you buy!

      Oh, no, she will not buy.

      If I'd as much money as I could tell,
      I never would cry my songs to sell.
      I never would cry my songs to sell.
                  Vendor's Song — Adelaide Crapsey[6]

(e)   The moon's a devil jester
      Who makes himself too free.
      The rascal is not always
      Where he appears to be.
      Sometimes he is in my heart —
      Sometimes he is in the sea;
      Then tides are in my heart,
      And tides are in the sea.

      O traveler, abiding not
      Where he pretends to be!
                  The Traveler — Vachel Lindsay[7]

(f)   Whirl up, sea —
      Whirl your pointed pines.
      Splash your great pines
      On our rocks.

----

[6] Reprinted from *Verse* by Adelaide T. Crapsey, by permission of Alfred A. Knopf, Inc. Copyright 1934 by Adelaide T. Crapsey.
[7] From *Modern American Poetry,* edited by Louis Untermeyer. Published by Harcourt, Brace and Company, Inc.

> Hurl your green over us —
> Cover us with your pools of fir.
>
> *Oread — H. D.* [8]

2. Harmonize at least one of the following melodies for soprano, alto, and bass. Can any one of them be treated as a round?

Russian Folk Song

Allegretto

(a)

Allegretto

Folk Song

(b)

Bohemian Folk Tune

Moderato

(c)

M. PRAETORIUS

Moderato

(d)

Fine

D.C. al Fine

[8] From *The Collected Poems of H. D.*, published by Liveright, New York; copyright 1925, Boni and Liveright.

(e) **Allegretto** — Swedish Folk Song

Reprinted by permission from The Home and Community Song Book, Concord Series No. 2.
Published and copyrighted by the E. C. Schirmer Music Company.

(f) **Adagio** — MOZART

3. Harmonize several of the following melodies for piano, using any of the preceding accompaniment figures, or new ones which you consider effective. Identify the form of each melody used.

Presto — MENDELSSOHN, *Etude* (Adapted)

(a)

(or V$^4_3$)

(b) **Moderato** · Dutch Folk Song

Use acc. of *(a)* above

(c) **Allegretto** · German Folk Song

(d) **Moderato** · Italian Folk Song

GASTORIUS, Chorale (1670)

(e)

Fine

IV

D.C. al Fine

Greek Folk Song

(f) Moderato

1.

2.

Fine (C$_4^6$) (G$_7$) *D.C. al Fine*

II — *Assignment for Playing*

1. Harmonize any of the melodies in the *Assignment for Writing* (3).

2. Improvise melodies in period form, modulating to C minor at the semicadence, and returning to F minor for the final cadence. Repeat from memory and harmonize.

3. Improvise a mazurka in *A–B–A* form, using the following outlined period for part I. Make parts II and III each a phrase as indicated. Remember to lead back into F minor through its V_7 chord at the end of part II.

TCHAIKOVSKY, adapted from *Album for the Young,* Op. 39, No. 10

A Tempo di mazurka

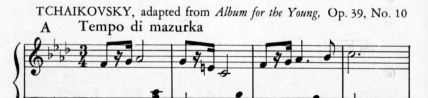

4. Play by ear the first period of *In Old Madrid* in the key of F minor. Repeat, supplying harmonic background. (See Gartlan, *High School Songs,* page 289.)

5. Learn to harmonize the ascending and descending harmonic minor scale, thus:

6. Learn the following modulations and devise some original ones. Repeat in other keys with embellishments.

*Note the quality of the VII and II chords in the minor mode. Both are used only thus in the first inversion.

7. Transpose simple melodies and passages in this chapter up a major third (F minor to A minor, and A flat major to C major).

In transposing a third, note that the music can be shifted up or down to the next line or space. Also experiment in reversing the clefs — that is, in reading the upper staff as if it were written in the bass clef, and vice versa. This device automatically transposes one staff when making a shift of a third in either direction. Naturally the new key signature must also be kept in mind.

III — Assignment for Listening

1. *Oral dictation:* harmonic recognition only. (Name chords by quality, letter, and Roman numeral.)

High School Songs (Gartlan), Out on the Deep (Lohr) (9-23), p. 84;

"Toreador Song" from Carmen (Bizet) (9-16), p. 113;

In Old Madrid (Trotere) (1-24), p. 289.

Chopin, *Waltz*, Op. 69, No. 2, B Major section;
  Polonaise, Op. 71, No. 3 (1-4; 27-30);
  Mazurka, Op. 59, No. 3 (1-8).
Beethoven, *Piano Sonata*, Op. 57, Finale, Presto section (1-18).
Schubert, *Impromptu*, Op. 142, No. 1, F Minor section (19-21;
 last 53 measures);
  Impromptu, Op. 142, No. 4 (1-8).
2. *Written dictation (quality, bass, melody, and name of chord).*
 High School Songs (Gartlan), *Integer Vitae*, p. 147.
 Home and Community Song Book: Night Song (1-8), page 85.
 Schumann, *Lieder* (Breitkopf & Härtel, Ed.), No. 33, page 62.

IV — Assignment for Analysis

Mozart, *Variations on a Theme by Grétry*, K352, Variation V;
  Variations on a Folk Song, K613, Variation VIII, Coda.
Beethoven, *Piano Sonata*, Op. 2, No. 1, Prestissimo (1-13).
Pergolesi, *Stabat Mater*, No. 2.
Tchaikovsky, *Romance*, Op. 5 (1-7).
Schubert, *Impromptu*, Op. 142, No. 1 (17-21).

The following passages for analysis have been selected from the above list. Identify cadences, chords, and nonharmonic tones, noting especially the pivotal and modulatory chords.

MOZART, Variations on a theme by Grétry, Var. V

*Neopolitan sixth, a chromatic chord, used cadentially.

MOZART, Variations on a Folk Song, Var. III

Allegretto

(b)

etc.

FINALE

BEETHOVEN, *Piano Sonata*, Op. 2, No. 1

Prestissimo

(c)

It. 6th

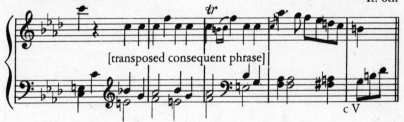

[transposed consequent phrase]

c V

Largo assai   G. B. PERGOLESI, *Stabat Mater,* No. 12

(d)

TCHAIKOVSKY, *Romance*, Op. 5

Andante cantabile

(e)

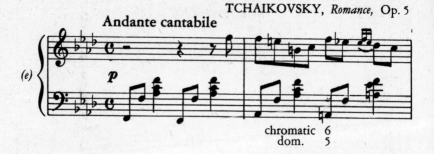

chromatic 6
dom.   5

Chapter XIX

THE MELODIC MINOR SCALE:
RELATIVE MODULATIONS

Ex. 143

BACH (1685—1750) Air, *French Suite*, No. 2

AMONG BACH'S best known clavier compositions are two sets of idealized dances known, for rather obscure reasons, as *French* and *English Suites*.[1] The above measures from one of them suggest the light, graceful style associated with the French music of the period. Notice how skilfully the music is woven from simple rhythmic and melodic patterns. Compare, for example, the rhythmic designs and the relation between the melody

[1] Authorities have never agreed on the origin of these terms. Possibly so named, in the case of the *English Suite*, because the prelude of the first suite is based on a *gigue* by Dieupart, a popular teacher and composer living in England. Both sets of suites probably date back to Bach's Cöthen period (1722).

of measure 1 and the bass of measure 3. Yet such organization does not seem to interrupt the free-flowing character of the music.

Determine aurally the key and the mode of Example 143. Do they remain unchanged? Name the keys used and decide exactly where and how the change is made.

This modulation, up a third from a minor to its relative major key, occurs frequently — perhaps more so than any other type except that to the dominant key from either mode (see Chapter XVIII).[2]

Example 143 is also a good example of *counterpoint,* noted before. Here there are two definite melodic lines of almost equal interest. Bach was a master of counterpoint, which was to him as natural a means of expression as was a purely harmonic idiom to Chopin or Debussy.

Compare the accidentals used in measures 1 and 2 (Example 144), especially in the bass clef, noting how they differ from each other and from the harmonic minor scale, thus:

Ex. 144

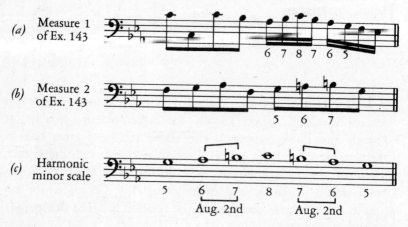

These changes affect the sixth and seventh degrees. Thus, in both measures the sixth and seventh degrees of the harmonic

---

[2] Learn this signature of three flats (B flat, E flat, and A flat) for C minor, noting that it is "borrowed" from its relative E flat major scale.

minor scale are now spaced a major second apart *to facilitate melodic progression.*[3] Consequently, this version is known as the *melodic minor* scale. Using the accidentals in measures 1 and 2, Example 144, construct the complete melodic minor scale and compare it with the harmonic minor scale by singing both, thus:

Ex. 145

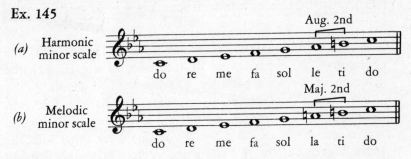

Example 145 shows that the only *essential* distinction between the major and minor modes is the lowered third step in the minor mode, since the sixth step is not always lowered. Note that the augmented second, which is not characteristic of Western music, may be avoided by raising or lowering *both* the sixth and seventh steps. What principle determines the choice of accidentals?

Consider the following passage from Bach's *Well-Tempered Clavier,* in which both the raised and lowered sixth and seventh steps of the minor scale are used, thus:

Ex. 146   BACH, *Well-Tempered Clavier,* Book 1, Fugue II

[3] The augmented second is a characteristic of certain Oriental scales from which our harmonic minor scale may have been derived historically. See Chopin, *Mazurka,* Op. 24, No. 1 (1-8); Chapter XX, *Assignment for Analysis,* (d); Chapter XVIII, Example 140, page 304.

The use of accidentals is determined by three factors: (1) The consecutive and separate use of the notes A and B; (2) the direction of the scale passages; (3) the implied chords.

For example, in measure 1, whenever the sixth and seventh steps appear consecutively, the interval of the augmented second is avoided. Note also that the accidentals used agree with the prevailing chord: the A flat for the A flat major and F minor chords in the first half of the measure, and the B for the implied G_7 chord at the end. In measure 2, the augmented second is again avoided. Here, however, since the chord for the second half of the measure is I, both the sixth and seventh steps are nonharmonic tones. In such cases, the choice of accidentals is optional, but, in general, is determined by the direction of the scale line, raised sixth and seventh for ascending and lowered for descending passages.

This analysis demonstrates that:

(1) The melodic minor scale is used only for the consecutive progressions 6-7 or 7-6 *when one or both are nonharmonic tones.*

(2) The choice of the raised or lowered sixth and seventh steps depends upon the implied chord.

(3) The harmonic minor is used for the consecutive progression 6-7 or 7-6, *when both are chord tones,* and occasionally when the second of the two is a nonchord tone.[4]

In the following passage, the augmented second occurs in measure 3 because the consecutive sixth and seventh steps are both harmonic tones.

---

[4] Mozart, *G Minor Symphony,* K550, First Movement; compare measures 4 and 8. See also Chopin, *Sonata,* Op. 58, Finale, measure 9.

Ex. 147   BEETHOVEN, *Sonata*, Op. 10, No. 1

However, these general principles will not cover all cases, and the *educated* ear must be the ultimate guide here as always. Often several choices are possible. Test both aurally. For example, here is a continuation of the Bach fugue, Example 146, but without accidentals. The passage is in C minor and uses the various forms of the minor scale. Experiment inserting suitable accidentals.

Ex. 148   BACH, *Well-Tempered Clavier*, Book 1, Fugue II

Review:

1. The key signature of C minor.
2. Two scales and keys that use the signature of three flats.
3. A common type of modulation from minor keys.
4. Where the modulation occurs in Example 143.
5. Why Example 143 is said to be contrapuntal.
6. The distinctive pitch between major and minor scales.
7. Why the melodic minor scale is so called.
8. What two scale steps are always altered similarly in the melodic minor scale.
9. How the melodic and harmonic minor scales differ in construction.
10. What determines the use of accidentals for the sixth and seventh steps.
11. When Bach wrote his *French* and *English Suites.*

For Further Study, Determine:

1. The form of Example 143.
2. The dances most frequently included in the suites of Bach's time.
3. What the word "clavier" means.
4. What the word "air" means when applied to a musical composition.
5. Some differences between the styles of Bach and Chopin (compare Examples 138-143).
6. The meaning of the signs ℀ and ⌢ .
7. Of what the *Well-Tempered Clavier* consists, and why it was so named.
8. What a *fugue* is.
9. What accidentals are usually used for a melodic scale passage whose chord background is the I, the IV, the V, the VI, or the VII₆ chord.
10. Why the lowered third step is the most characteristic pitch of the minor mode.

I — Assignment for Writing

1. Scan the following stanzas and set at least one of them to music for three voices — soprano, alto, baritone, or bass. Use the minor mode, preferably either F or C minor if appropriate. (Accompaniment optional.)

> (*a*)   I asked the heaven of stars
> What I should give my love —
> It answered me with silence,
> Silence above.

I asked the darkened sea
  Down where the fishermen go —
It answered me with silence,
  Silence below.

Oh, I could give him weeping,
  Or I could give him song —
But how can I give silence
  My whole life long?

Night Song — Sara Teasdale[5]

(*b*) Pretty Futility
     Always declares
     There's nothing so good
     As a basket of pears.

     Nothing so tranquil,
     Nothing so sweet,
     As eating ripe pears
     In the quiet of heat.

     She straightens her ruffles,
     And smiles as she swings,
     And when she has eaten
     Futility sings.

Pretty Futility — Elizabeth J. Coatsworth[6]

(*c*) With rue my heart is laden
      For golden friends I had.
    For many a rose-lipt maiden
      And many a lightfoot lad.

    By brooks too broad for leaping
      The lightfoot boys are laid;
    The rose-lipt girls are sleeping
      In fields where roses fade.

With Rue My Heart is Laden — A. E. Housman[7]

---

[5] From Sara Teasdale, *Rivers to the Sea*. Copyright, 1915 by the Macmillan Company and used with their permission.

[6] Reprinted from *Compass Rose* by Elizabeth Coatsworth; copyright 1929 by Coward-McCann, Inc.

[7] From *A Shropshire Lad* by A. E. Houseman. Reproduced by permission of Henry Holt & Company, Inc.

(*d*) When descends on the Atlantic
    The gigantic
Storm-wind of the equinox,
Landward in his wrath he scourges
    The toiling surges,
Laden with seaweed from the rocks:

Ever drifting, drifting, drifting
    On the shifting
Currents of the restless main;
Till in sheltered coves, and reaches
    Of sandy beaches,
All have found repose again.
> *Sea Weed — H. W. Longfellow*

(*e*) The brooklet came from the mountain,
    As sang the bard of old,
Running with feet of silver
    Over the sands of gold!

Far away in the briny ocean
    There rolled a turbulent wave,
Now singing along the sea-beach,
    Now howling along the cave.

And the brooklet has found the billow,
    Though they flower so far apart,
And has filled with its freshness and sweetness
    That turbulent, bitter heart!
> *The Brook and the Wave — H. W. Longfellow*

(*f*) They are not long, the weeping and the laughter,
    Love and desire and hate;
I think they have no portion in us after
    We pass the gate.

They are not long, the days of wine and roses:
    Out of a misty dream
Our path emerges for a while, then closes
    Within a dream.
> *Envoy — Ernest Dowson*[8]

---

[8] Reprinted by permission of Dodd, Mead & Company, Inc., from *The Poems of Ernest Dowson.*

2. Write a short trio, for instruments played by members of the class, in *A–B* or *A–B–A* form, using either an old or a contemporary dance rhythm, and have it performed.

3. Harmonize at least one of the following melodies for soprano, alto, and bass. Can any of them be treated as a round?

ZELTER

(Melody in bass)

Russian Folk Song

(Melody in bass)

(Melody in Sop.)

GRÉTRY, *Lucile*

Moderato — Hungarian Folk Tune

Moderato — Finnish Folk Song

Moderato — REISSIGER

Andante — Unknown

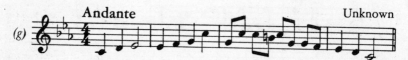

Reprinted by permission from A Book of Songs, Concord Series No. 14. *Published and copyrighted by the* E. C. Schirmer Music Company.

4. Harmonize several of the following melodies for piano, using appropriate accompaniment figures. Identify the form of each melody used.

MOZART, *C Minor Piano Sonata*, K457

Allegro assai

Finnish Folk Song

Allegretto

(b)

Polish Folk Song

Moderato

(c)

Chorale

(d)

Russian Folk Song

Moderato

(e)

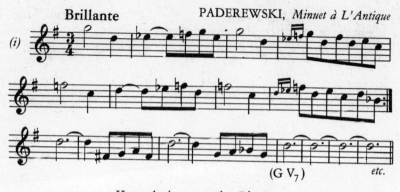

Brillante   PADEREWSKI, *Minuet à L'Antique*

(i)

(G V₇)   etc.

II — *Assignment for Playing*

1. Harmonize any of the melodies in the *Assignment for Writing* (4).

2. Improvise melodies in *A–B–A* form, each part a phrase in length. Use the melodic form of the C minor scale. Repeat from memory. Experiment harmonizing some of the best ones.

3. Improvise a tango in *A–B–A* form, using the following motive for Part I (a period modulating to the dominant key). Part II will be a phrase ending on the V₇ chord of C minor. Part III will also be a phrase beginning like Part I, but ending in the tonic key.

Moderato   Cuban Tune

4. Play by ear, in the key of C minor, the melody of the Russian folk song, *Dark Eyes*. Repeat with accompaniment.

5. Learn these harmonizations of the melodic minor scale:

(a)

(IV⁶₄)

6. Learn the following modulations and devise original ones. Use these patterns to modulate between familiar major and minor keys. Repeat each phrase in piano style with embellishments.

7. Transpose simple melodies and passages in this chapter down a minor third (C minor to A minor, and E flat major to C major). Review notes on transposition in *Assignment for Playing,* Chapter XI, page 183, and Chapter XVIII, page 314.

III — Assignment for Listening

1. *Oral dictation:* harmonic recognition only. (Name chords by quality, letter, and Roman numeral.)

> *Songs We Sing: Pretty Minka,* No. 95
> Haydn, *Surprise Symphony,* Andante, Minore (1-8);
> > *C Minor Symphony IX* (Peters Edition), Menuetto (1-18);
> > *E flat Major Symphony I* (Peters Edition), Andante (1-8).
> Beethoven, *Egmont Overture,* principle theme, Allegro.
> Schubert, *Piano Sonata, E flat Major,* Op. 122, Menuetto (1-12);
> > *Impromptu,* Op. 90, No. 1 (5-8; 13-16) ;
> > *The Hunter* (5-8).
> Schumann, *Album for the Young,* Op. 68, No. 38 (1-4),
> > > > No. 39 (1-24).

2. *Written dictation* (*quality, bass, melody, and name of chord*).
   Purcell, *Dido and Aeneas*, No. 1 (18-30),
                 No. 4,
                 No. 28, *Sailor Song.*
   Mendelssohn, *Ruy Blas Overture,* Lento (1-4), Allegro molto
     (1-32).
   New Episcopal Hymnal, No. 556, *St. Andrew of Crete,*
                 No. 147, *Old One Hundred Twelfth.*
   Home and Community Song Book. (Concord Series No. 2).
     Avenging and Bright (5-8), page 64.
   Bach, *371 Chorales,* Nos. 122, 149, 173, 196 (1-2).
   Sing!: Mother Volga (1-8), page 29.
   Golden Book: Go Down Moses, page 97.

IV — Assignment for Analysis

Purcell, *Dido and Aeneas,* No. 1 (1-18),
                No. 2 (1-8).
Pergolesi, *Stabat Mater,* No. 1 (1-11).
Bach, *Partita No. 2,* Allemande (1-6),
             Sarabande (1-8),
             Rondeau (1-16) ;
   Well-Tempered Clavier, I, Fugue 2 ;
   Two-Part Inventions, No. 2;
   Three-Part Inventions, No. 2;
   French Suite No. II, Courante (1-8),
             Sarabande (1-8),
             Minuet (1-8),
             Gigue (1-23);
   First Lessons (Carroll), March, No. 16, Book I.
Mozart, *Twelve Variations on a French Air,* K265, Variation 8
     (1-8) ;
   Piano Concerto, K491 (Peters Edition) ; First Movement
     (58-63), Finale (128-136).
Beethoven, *Symphony V,* Op. 67, First Movement (1-21; 396 to
     end);
   Bagatelles, Op. 119, No. 5 ;
   Sonata, Op. 2, No. 1, Menuetto (1-14).
Mendelssohn, *Songs Without Words,* No. 14 (1-8).
Schubert, *Allegretto in C Minor* (1-8) ;
   Impromptu, Op. 90, No. 1 (5-8; 13-16);
   Moment Musical, Op. 94, No. 3.

Chopin, *Mazurka*, Op. 30, No. 1 (1-8),
     Op. 56, No. 3 (1-9);
  Polonaise, Op. 40, No. 2 (1-11);
  Nocturne, Op. 48, No. 1 (1-8);
  Etude, Op. 10, No. 12 (10-18);
  Rondo, Op. 1 (5-20);
  Prelude, Op. 28, No. 20 (1-4);
  Fantasie, Op. 49 (1-11).
Herbert, *Badinage* (8-16).
Weber, *Invitation to the Dance,* Op. 65, Vivace (1-8).

The following passages for analysis have been selected from the above list. Identify form, chords, and nonharmonic tones. Note especially pivotal and modulatory chords.

BACH, *French Suite* No. 2, Menuet

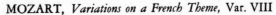

MOZART, *Variations on a French Theme,* Var. VIII

SCHUBERT, *Impromptu*, Op. 90, No. 1

Allegro molto moderato

SCHUBERT, *Moment Musical*, Op. 94, No. 3 (Adapted)

Allegro moderato

CHOPIN, *Fantasie*, Op. 49

Tempo di marcia (Grave)

(e)

HERBERT, *Badinage* (Adapted)

Allegro

(f)

Chapter XX

THE NATURAL MINOR SCALE:
MEDIANT MODULATIONS

Ex. 149

Old American Song

When John-ny comes march-ing home a-gain, Hur-rah!___ Hur-rah!___ We'll give him a heart-y wel-come then, Hur-rah, Hur-rah! The men will cheer, the boys will shout, The la-dies they will all turn out, And we'll

all feel gay when John-ny comes march-ing home.

SING THIS folk melody, noting its form and mode. It consists essentially of two phrases: the first rather short with a modified repetition, and the second somewhat longer due to sequential extensions. The mode is clearly minor, but it differs somewhat from both the harmonic or melodic minor scales previously studied. Note that the last four measures include all the tones used in the melody. When arranged consecutively, they form this incomplete scale:

Ex. 150

The last measure of Example 149 gives G as its tonic. It is similar in appearance to the descending melodic minor scale (except that the E flat is omitted), but it differs in sound. This difference is due to the use of F natural (instead of F sharp) *in the final cadence.* Let us consider briefly the origin of its use.

The cadential use of the lowered leading tone (F natural) is derived from the Church modes,[1] the immediate predecessors of our present major and minor scales. Many folk songs, particularly those of eastern Europe and of early American settlers, use these old modal forms because the melodies have been handed down, in some cases, for hundreds of years. The Church modes in turn were derived from Oriental and Mediterranean melodies of great antiquity, and served as the basis for the ecclesiastical Gregorian Chant, or Plainsong. During the Middle Ages, scholarly monks

---

[1] See A. Madeley Richardson, *The Mediaeval Modes* (New York: The H. W. Gray Co., 1933).

compared the Church modes to the modes of the ancient Greeks and gave them Greek names, which, though little used in the Church, are widely current in contrapuntal texts today. Unfortunately, the names were misapplied, so that today Greek and Church modes of the same name differ in construction.

The Church modes may be represented by the white key scales on the piano without accidentals. There were four *authentic* modes beginning on D (Dorian), E (Phrygian), F (Mixolydian), and G (Lydian), paralleled by their *plagal* modes (distinguished by their prefix, *hypo-*) which began on pitches a fourth lower respectively (except where F or B natural were concerned), and which ended on the same *final* as the authentic mode of the same name, thus:

Ex. 151

(a) Dorian   *(b)* Hypo-dorian

Final   Final

These eight modes sufficed until 1547 when Glareanus, the Swiss theoretician, added four additional modes: the Aeolian on A and the Ionian on C, each with its *hypo*-parallel.

Ex. 152

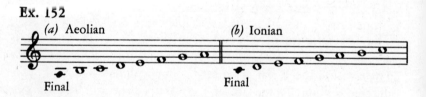

(a) Aeolian   *(b)* Ionian

Final   Final

The Church never recognized officially these additions to its Plainsong. Although sometimes used, they were analyzed as one of the four official modes. Glareanus' addition of the Aeolian and Ionian modes was only a recognition of established practice.

The point of interest for us is that two of these added modes (the Ionian and Aeolian) are of the same interval construction as the major and minor modes in use today and, when written without accidentals, are identical in pitch with our C major and "natural" A minor scales. The stress upon the relative, rather than the parallel, relationship of major and minor scales, as well as the use of the term "natural" minor, is probably due to this historical background.

Thus, today, *three* forms of the minor scale are used: the Natural (or Aeolian Minor), and the Harmonic and Melodic Minors with their chromatic alterations according to the context. Let us compare the notation of the Natural (Aeolian) Minor scale, as given in Example 152 (*a*), with its notation in the key of G minor used in this chapter, thus:

Ex. 153

Consider again the folk song (Example 149, page 338), and listen to its harmonization. Since this melody is definitely modal, the harmony should utilize the distinctive tone of the mode: F natural instead of F sharp. This F natural accounts for the unusual effect at the cadences. Experiment using an F sharp. Both are possible, especially in measures 8 and 12. Identify the chords in measures 7 and 10. Compare their sound and quality in the harmonic minor scale.

Aside from the consistent use of the natural minor scale for modal effects, as in Example 149, page 338, composers often use it harmonically to avoid the augmented second in any voice, thus:

Ex. 154   MOZART, *Requiem Mass*, Offertorium

Note especially measures 3 and 6. The major III chord (measure 3) is used more frequently than is the minor V_6 (measure 6), probably because the descending scale is more common in the soprano than in the bass. Observe that when the scale steps 8-7-6 occur melodically, the seventh step may either be treated as a passing tone or be harmonized with the major form of the III chord as in Example 154, measure 3.

To summarize the facts in Chapters XVII-XX regarding the various forms of the minor mode: they were presented from an *aural* rather than historical standpoint as the harmonic, melodic, and natural minor scales. For purposes of review, however, the order will be reversed beginning with the oldest historical form.

(1) The minor mode developed late historically from the Aeolian mode (1547), and corresponds to the white key scale of the piano beginning on A. It is known as the *natural* or *Aeolian minor scale.*

(2) For cadential reasons, the seventh step of the Aeolian minor scale may be raised one half tone, thus forming the *harmonic minor scale.*

(3) For melodic reasons, both the sixth and seventh steps of the natural minor scale may be raised one half tone, thus forming the *melodic minor scale.* The descending form of this scale corresponds to that of the natural minor.[2]

(4) The signature used for all three forms of the minor

---

[2] Some theorists regard the descending melodic scale as equivalent to the natural minor scale (since its pitches are identical), and, therefore, recognize only the ascending form. However, the essentially different functions of the two scales seem to warrant a distinction between them.

scale is that of the major scale beginning on its third step, that is, of the minor scale. This signature is adequate for the natural minor scale, but necessitates the raising, by one half tone, the seventh degree of the harmonic minor scale and both the sixth and seventh degrees of the melodic minor scale. The descending melodic minor (natural minor) scale requires no alteration, unless preceded by other forms of the scale.

(5) Major and minor scales using the same signature are termed *relative scales*.

(6) Major and minor scales having the same key tone are termed *parallel scales*. Aurally, this is the most important relationship.

In order to clarify these differences, note carefully the three forms of the minor scale, thus:

Ex. 155

(1) Aeolian or Natural minor

(2) Harmonic minor

(3) Melodic minor

As an example of modulation in connection with minor scales, consider the old Russian national hymn, beginning:

Ex. 156

etc.

Sing the melody from memory. Study the opening key and mode, and determine aurally whether either is changed before the end. Clearly there is a shift to the minor mode twice during the course of the melody. Sing the following passage in four parts to clarify these changes of tonality:

Ex. 157* **Maestoso**   LWOFF

God ev-er glo-ri-ous, Sov-'reign of all Vouch-safe Thy bless-ing on our own dear land Thine is the vic-to-ry, and Thine the king-ly pow'r Sent forth to de-liv-er by Thy might-y hand.

*See Tchaikovsky's *Marche Slave*, Op. 31, Più Mosso section, measure 19, in which this melody is used as a bass for the Più Mosso theme — a wonderful example of counterpoint.

Here we have a definite swing to G minor, the mediant key (measures 7 and 8), and to C minor (measures 11 and 12). Note how the complete cadence in C minor is avoided. Observe especially the modulation from E flat major to G minor (the mediant), which is a new type.

This passage (Example 157) sums up the most usual modulations from major to minor keys, namely to those keys whose tonics are a third above or below the original key tone; in other words, up to the mediant and down to the submediant (or relative) key.

The principle of modulation by thirds from the tonic is also used in the minor mode, but only *up* a third to the relative major as we have seen (Chapter XIX, page 319). The modulation down a third is rarely used and has not been illustrated, although a familiar example is to be found in Schubert's *Unfinished Symphony*, first movement, in which the second theme is in the submediant key.

To summarize: it was found (Chapters IX-XX) that the most general types of modulation were:

Ex. 158

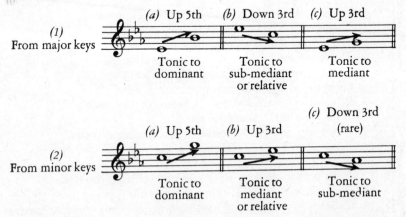

It can be said, then, that in either mode, modulations to the dominant relative keys are common, while those up a third from major and down a third from minor are progressively more rare.

One will undoubtedly hear other types, but these are the most frequent modulations to *diatonic* keys and the only ones to be considered at present. Modulations to *chromatic* keys rightly belong to a discussion of chromatic harmony.

Review:

1. The signature of G minor.
2. Why Example 149 sounds modal.
3. Why F sharp is more usual at the cadence than is F natural.
4. Why many folk tunes are modal.
5. Which two medieval modes have survived and are in general use today.
6. The construction of the Aeolian, or natural minor, scale.
7. Its relation to the harmonic and melodic minor scales.
8. Why Example 149 should be harmonized modally.
9. Two ways of treating the scale steps 8-7-6 in the minor scale.
10. The differences between the natural, harmonic, and melodic minor scales.
11. With what scale the descending melodic minor agrees in pitch.
12. A new type of modulation from a major to a minor key.
13. The two most used modulations from both major and minor keys.
14. Another name for the Aeolian minor scale.

For Further Study, Determine:

1. What the word "mode" meant in medieval Europe.
2. What is meant by the Gregorian modes.
3. The difference between modal and minor harmony.
4. The names and final notes of the medieval modes.
5. How accidentals were introduced into modal music.
6. Other modal melodies than those cited above.
7. Whether composers today are influenced by the modes.
8. What the word "tetrachord" means.
9. How many tetrachords are in the major and minor scales.
10. Whether modes had cadences.
11. Another name for the mediant key from a minor tonic.
12. What the diatonic keys are in relation to C major and C minor.
13. How their signatures differ in relation to C major.
14. The two scale steps upon which our major-minor system of tonality depends, and why.
15. The difference in function between the natural and the *descending* melodic minor scales.

I — Assignment for Writing

1. Scan the following stanzas and set at least one of them to music for three voices — soprano, alto, and baritone or bass. Experiment using the minor mode, modulating up a third to the relative key, or the major mode, modulating up a third to the mediant key. Some of the poems of medieval character may suggest setting in the Aeolian mode.

(a) Oh, the sun was brightly shining,
      Blue the sky and soft the air,
      As with mandoline I wandered,
      Through Savoira's land so fair.

      And when ev'ning shades were falling,
      Like an angel, rob'd in light,
      From her balcony she bade me,
      Softly bade me sweet good-night.
                The Page's Song — Eichendorff[3]

(b) My love for him shall be
        Fair love and true:
        For he loves me, I know,
      And I love him, pardie!

      And for I know that he
        Doth love me so,
        I should be all untrue
      To love but him, pardie!
           My Love for Him — Medieval Norman Songs
           (Translated by John Addington Symonds)

(c) Fair in a western brookland
        That bred me long ago,
      The poplars stand and tremble
        By pools I used to know.

      There, in the windless night-time,
        The wanderer, marveling why,
      Halts on the bridge to hearken
        How soft the poplars sigh.
          Far in a Western Brookland — A. E. Housman[4]

---

[3] Reprinted from *Mendelssohn's Songs,* Universal Edition, No. 713, by permission of Associated Music Publishers, Inc.

---

[4] From *A Shropshire Lad* by A. E. Houseman. Reproduced by permission of Henry Holt & Company, Inc.

(*d*) White in the moon the long road lies,
The moon stands blank above;
White in the moon the long road lies
That leads me from my love.

The world is round, so travelers tell,
And straight though reach the track,
Trudge on, trudge on, 'twill all be well,
The way will guide one back.

But ere the circle homeward hies
Far, far it must remove:
White in the moon the long road lies
That leads me from my love.

White in the Moon — A. E. Housman[5]

(*e*) Take, O take those lips away,
That so sweetly were forsworn;
And those eyes, the break of day,
Lights that do mislead the moon:
But my kisses bring again,
Bring again;
Seals of love, but sealed in vain,
Sealed in vain.

Measure for Measure — Shakespeare

2. Continue writing small pieces for instrumental combinations found in class. For example, a violinist and a pianist might collaborate in writing a composition for both instruments. Make the form simple and clear by strong cadences. Use the *A–B* or *A–B–A* pattern. Experiment writing canons for two or more instruments. Perform these compositions in class.

3. Harmonize at least one of the following melodies for soprano, alto, and bass. If any of them can be treated as rounds, do so.

Slowly   Slavonic Folk Song

(*a*)

---
[5] From *A Shropshire Lad* by A. E. Houseman. Reproduced by permission of Henry Holt & Company, Inc.

The four preceding selections are reprinted by permission from 140 Folk-Songs, Concord Series No. 3. Published and copyrighted by the E. C. Schirmer Music Company.

Allegretto

TELEMANN

Moderato

Old Ballad

Chorale

(g)

BACH, *Chorale* (Adapted)

(b)

Allegretto   Old French Air

(i)

4. Harmonize one or more of the following melodies for piano, using appropriate accompaniment figures. Identify the form of each melody used.

Allegro   English Folk Song

(a)

Allegretto

English Folk Song

(b)

supply bass

(c) Allegretto — Bohemian Folk Song

(d) Andante — Russian Folk Song

(e) Allegretto — Swiss Folk Song

Reprinted by permission from The Home and Community Song Book, Concord Series No. 2. *Published and copyrighted by the* E. C. Schirmer Music Company.

II — Assignment for Playing

1. Harmonize any of the melodies in the *Assignment for Writing* (4).

2. Improvise melodies in G minor in the *A–B–A* form. Make each part a phrase, and use any of the three forms of the minor scale. Repeat from memory with simple harmonic background. (Optional.)

3. Improvise a chorale in G minor (see Schumann's *Album for the Young*, Op. 68, No. 4), the first phrase modulating to B flat major and the second returning to G minor. Experiment using the natural minor scale.

4. Learn this harmonization of the natural minor scale and apply it to other minor keys:

Compare the above harmonization with that in Chapter XIX, *Assignment for Playing*, (5b), page 333.

5. Learn the following mediant modulations and devise original ones. Use the same patterns to modulate between other major and minor keys previously studied. Repeat each phrase in piano style with embellishments.

E♭ to G

6. Play by ear, in the key of G minor, the melody of *We Three Kings of Orient Are*. Repeat with suitable harmonic background.

7. Transpose simple melodies and harmonic passages in this chapter up and down a major second. Review notes on transposition in *Assignment for Playing*, Chapters XI, page 183, and XVIII, page 314.

III — Assignment for Listening

1. *Oral dictation:* harmonic recognition only. (Name chords by quality, letter, and Roman numeral.)

Mendelssohn, *Songs Without Words*, No. 6 (3-17);
Piano Concerto No. 2, Op. 40, Finale (1-6).
Schubert, *The Erlking* (1-24).
Schumann, *Album for the Young*, Op. 68, No. 39, Trio.
Chopin, *Mazurka*, Op. 24, No. 1 (1-8);
Nocturnes, Op. 37, No. 1 (1-8),
Op. 55, No. 1 (1-8),
Op. 15, No. 3 (1-12; 89-104).
Tchaikovsky, *Barcarolle in G Minor* (1-12);
Chanson Triste in G Minor (1-8).
Rachmaninoff, *Prelude in G Minor*, Op. 23, No. 5 (1-34).
Bach, *First Lessons* (Carroll) Book I, Minuets 1, 2, 6, 8, Polonaise
No. 4, Gavotte, No. 14,
Book II, Polonaises, Nos. 1, 6.
Home and Community Song Book. Concord Series No. 2.
Glory to God (Palestrina);
Hymn to St. Raphael (Brahms); Nos. 23, 31, 64, 71, 87.
High School Songs (Gartlan), *Then You'll Remember Me* (Balfe) p. 100.

2. *Written dictation* (*quality, bass, melody, and name of chord*).
Purcell, *Dido and Aeneas*, No. 31 (1-8), p. 55,
No. 37 (1-10), p. 63,
No. 38, pages 65-66.
Home and Community Song Book. Concord Series No. 2.
The Coasts of High Barbary, page 26;
Spanish Ladies, page 35;
The Parable of the Sinful Rich Man, page 70.
New Green Book, Twice 55: Matona (Orlando Lassus), No. 156.
Green Book, Twice 55: No. 158, *Oh Come, Immanuel.*
New Episcopal Hymnal, No. 2, *Veni, Emmanuel,*
No. 68, *Bangor,*
No. 71, *Herzliebster,*
No. 417, *St. Bride,*
No. 410, *Burford,*
No. 501, *Walsall,*
No. 268, *St. Patrick and Deidre*
No. 99, *O Filii et Filliae.*
Bach, *371 Chorales*, Nos. 72, 174 (1-8).

IV — Assignment for Analysis

Schumann, *Sonata*, Op. 22, First Movement (4-9), Scherzo (1-4) ;
Bird as Prophet, Op. 82, No. 17;
Album for the Young, Op. 68, Nos. 36, 37, 39.
Mozart, *G Minor Symphony*, K550, principal theme and closing
section of First Movement.
Brahms, *Hungarian Dance No. 1* (1-11; 49-60), No. 15, Animato;
Ballade in G minor, Op. 118, No. 3 (1-5);
Symphony III, Op. 90, Finale, principal theme.
Schubert, *Violin Sonata*, Op. 137, No. 3, First Movement (1-12),
p. 33.
Liadow, *Birioulki*, Op. 2, No. 4 (1-4).
Chopin, *Mazurka*, Op. 24, No. 1 (1-8),
Op. 67, No. 2 (1-16).
Kuhlau, *Sonatina*, Op. 55, No. 2, Allegro (27-34).
Mendelssohn, *Piano Concerto No. 2*, Op. 40, Finale (1-4), p. 55.
Beethoven, *Sonatina*, Op. 49, No. 1 (1-15) ;
String Quartet, Op. 132, Molto adagio (Lydian mode).
Tchaikovksy, *Symphony V*, Op. 64, Introduction to slow movement.
Bach, *First Lessons* (Carroll), Book I, Nos. 2, 4, 6, 8,
Book II, Nos. 1, 4, 6;
371 Chorales, No. 174 (1-5) ;

Violin Sonata II, Bourrée;
Two-Part Invention, No. 11;
Three-Part Invention, No. 11.
Rachmaninoff, *G Minor Prelude*, Op. 23, No. 5.

The following passages for analysis have been selected from the above list. Identify forms, chords, and nonharmonic tones. Note especially the various types of minor scales used and the pivotal and modulatory chords.

BRAHMS, *Hungarian Dance*, No. 15 (Adapted)
Animato

Allegro energico   BRAHMS, *Ballade*, Op. 118, No. 3

CHOPIN, *Mazurka*, Op. 67, No. 2

Allegro

BEETHOVEN, *Sonatina*, Op. 49, No. 1

Andante

Allegretto

BACH, *Minuet* (Carroll I)

(e)

Moderato

BACH, *Minuet,* Trio (Carroll I)

(f)

Moderato

LIADOW, Op. 2, No. 6 (Transposed)

(g)

Chapter XXI

FOUR-PART VOCAL WRITING

Ex. 159   J. S. BACH, (1685 – 1750)

From Chorale Collection, *by Elvera Wonderlich, published by Appleton-Century-Crofts, Inc.,* 1946.

SING, in four parts, Bach's harmonization of this melody in the Dorian mode, first published about 1546. Since the melody, with the exception of the G sharp, is predominantly modal, and not transposed, it has no *key* signature. However, Bach has harmonized it chiefly in the tonality of D minor,[1] rather than modally,

---

[1] The key signature of D minor is one flat (B flat). Write the three forms of the D minor scale, first using accidentals, then with its signature of one flat. Sing each form from memory.

modulating to A minor at the end of the first phrase, and returning to D minor for the second phrase. Note the final D major chord. This typical medieval device was used because, traditionally, compositions could only end upon a consonance, and the minor third of the tonic chord (D–F in this case) was not so regarded until made reputable by the theoretician, Zarlino, in 1558[2]. Such a major ending for a composition in minor is called a *Tierce de Picardie*, or *Picardian Third*, for some unknown reason. Its use has persisted, as in the ending of Bach's *Passacaglia*, Schubert's *Serenade*, or the theme of Elgar's *Enigma Variations*.

This chorale illustrates many important principles of four-part vocal writing and is well worth detailed study. Though its general texture is homophonic, the movement of the individual voices is also contrapuntal. Medieval Plainsong was *monophonic* (a single melody). When composers first combined two different sounds, they wrote in parallel fourths and fifths, known as *organum*. Gradually, however, the texture became *polyphonic* (a combination of melodies), and, after the Renaissance, the stress was chiefly on *homophonic* texture (a melody supported by chords). Since the classic period, both the last two textures have been used, either alone or in combination.

The chorales of Bach represent a nearly perfect balance between the homophonic and polyphonic styles. Analyze the chords in Example 159, page 361, first generally in terms of their color and progression, and then specifically with regard to details. Note how the tonality of A minor is introduced in the first phrase, and also how the two forms of the minor scale (melodic and natural) are used in the bass of the second phrase. Locate and identify all nonharmonic tones.

This passage is harmonized for four voices: soprano, alto, tenor, and bass, whose range in this portion of the chorale is rather

---

[2] In Zarlino's *Le Institutioni Harmoniche* (1558). However, the validity of ending on a minor chord was not accepted generally even in the time of Bach.

narrow. In general, the total average ranges of the four voices are:

Ex. 160

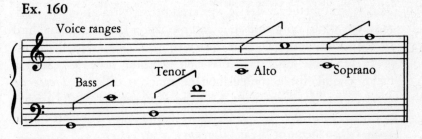

Thus the men's voices are approximately an octave lower than the corresponding women's voices: the range of the tenor being about an octave lower than the soprano, and the bass an octave lower than the alto. Note that the women's voices (soprano and alto) are written on the upper staff, and the men's voices (tenor and bass) on the lower staff. When these four voices are used, the harmonization is said to be for *mixed voices.* (Review note to Example 31, page 48, regarding the distinction between open and close harmony.)

In four-part harmony, the *position* of the chord is determined by the chord tone in the soprano. Thus, we speak of root position, position of the third, position of the fifth, and so on. Of course, the *inversion* of the chord is determined by the bass tone.

Three- and four-part writing are quite similar, although the latter naturally is somewhat more difficult. Four-part writing has special problems in regard to the spacing and progression of the voices and the doubling of certain chord tones. Consider the chorale (Example 159, page 361) with these three points in mind:

(1) *Spacing:* None of the adjacent voices is more than an octave apart except the tenor and bass in measure 7. Since there are no other instances of such wide spacing, we may assume that the *bass* is the only voice that may be separated by more than an octave from its neighbors. Conversely, adjacent voices rarely cross or overlap either in the same or consecutive chords.

(2) *Progression:* Are there any wide skips in the alto or tenor between different chords? How is such smooth voice leading obtained? Note that the chords whose roots are separated by a third or more have one or two

tones in common (I-IV or I-VI), while chords on adjacent roots have none (IV-V). In general, the three upper voices move to the *nearest position* of the next chord, usually either by holding the *common* tone in the same voice or by moving in contrary motion to the bass if the roots are adjacent. If the common tone is not held in the same voice, the nearest position is defined as the one which does not involve a skip of more than a third in any voice. Whenever the melody makes it impossible to do either, special voice leading is necessary.

(3) *Doubling* depends both upon the type of chord used and the effort to obtain smooth progression of the individual voices. Measures 1 to 4 illustrate these points. As regards the type of chord used, it will be recalled that the *root* is usually doubled in triads (the fundamental form and first inversion of the II, VI, and III often appear with a doubled third however), the *root* or fifth in chords of the sixth, and the fifth in $^6_4$ chords. This means, broadly speaking, that the *bass tone* may be doubled, except in first inversions. The root of the fundamental V_7 is often doubled also, but no tone is doubled in its inversions.

In applying these three principles, questionable parallel fifths or octaves sometimes occur (see Chapter XVI, page 265). They are usually due to faulty doubling or voice leading and can be eliminated by special attention to these points. In this connection, however, it should be noted that the only valid basis for such criticism is *stylistic*: all technical points are to be judged in relation to the style of the period represented by the music. No procedure is right or wrong *per se*, but only in terms of its idiom and historical perspective.

Let us begin the study of four-voice harmonization by singing the opening measures of the following chorale:

Ex. 161   Attributed to HASSLER (1601)

O sa-cred head now wound-ed With grief and care bowed down.

Sing the remaining phrases from memory. The final phrase ends on A and the entire melody is in the Phrygian mode. Composers have harmonized the melody either in F major or D minor. Test the following basses first by singing each alone, and then with the melody, thus:

Ex. 162

* Omit eighth note D with bass 4.

Note that since the unit of rhythm is a quarter note, only one of the eighth notes, measure 3, is harmonized. Observe also the new use of accidentals below the bass notes and the figure 𝄽 in Ex. 162. These belong to a system of musical shorthand known as *figured bass* or *thorough bass*, which was used by composers of the 17th and 18th centuries to indicate the desired chords. The system was also known as *basso continuo* in instrumental music.

The principles of figured bass are simple since numbers are used to indicate each chord interval above the bass note. They may be summarized thus:

1. A bass note without a number indicates a fundamental triad.

2. All numbers are counted upward from the bass note.

3. An accidental indicates that the third above the bass is altered accordingly, unless there is a specific number to the right to which it applies.

4. A line through a number indicates that the corresponding pitch is raised one half step ($\cancel{6}$)

5. Several horizontal numbers under a single bass note indicate the progression of the upper voices as $^6_4$ $^5_3$, meaning that 6 moves to 5, and 4 to 3.

6. A dash (—) after a number indicates that the corresponding note is to be held in the same voice.

7. Bass figurations are always given in order beginning with the highest number, but the vertical order of the voices does not necessarily correspond to that of the numbers. Thus, $^6_4$ means simply that the upper voices will be those intervals *from the bass* in any convenient order as determined by the context.

Now to return to Example 162, page 365, determine which bass is preferable. Note that, though the first cadence may be harmonized either in D minor or F major, the second cadence, as well as the whole second phrase, is definitely in D minor.

Having completed the bass line (bass I) first, *write the entire alto part next.* In doing so, it will be necessary to consider the chords used. Remember to keep the common tone stationary, or move to the nearest position of the next chord. This is a new technique that requires practice; but, once mastered, it will result in better voice leading than will completing each chord as a separate unit.

Ex. 163

with alto added

Bass 1

IV₆   6   7

Note that in measures 1 and 2 the alto is written as high as possible to prepare for the upward leap in the soprano to the E after the fermata.[3]

Try using F in the alto at the beginning of measure 1. Is this equally satisfactory, and why?

The following example completes the harmonization by adding the tenor voice. Why is the chord third (F) doubled in the second chord of measure 3?

Ex. 164

Sing the result and study carefully the spacing, voice leading, and doubling. Experiment adding the alto and tenor to the other basses in the same manner; that is, write first the entire alto and then add the tenor voice. Effective choral writing depends to a large extent on the smooth melodic flow of the individual voices. In your own writing, keep this point in mind. Make each voice as melodic as possible, and test by singing it alone before combining it with other voices. Having added the tenor to Example 164, check the results by singing as before.

This chorale melody has been used by many composers. Bach himself made 18 harmonizations of it, some of which are to be found in *The Passion According to St. Matthew,* and *The Christmas Oratorio.* One of his contemporaries, C. H. Graun (1701-1755), began his Passion-Cantata, *The Death of Jesus,* with this harmoni-

---

[3] A musical sign ⌢ showing that the note or chord is to be held, hence called a *fermata* (hold). The sign is used in chorales to denote the end of the musical phrase. Whether it also meant a pause in Bach's day is a moot point.

zation of the melody (bass 4, Example 162):

Ex. 165

Compare this harmonization with the other suggested in Example 162, page 365. The use of eighth notes in the lower voices (measure 1) is to improve the bass and alto lines. The suspension in measure 2 (alto) is for rhythmic continuity. Note the changes of chord for the repeated melody tones in measure 3, the exceptional doublings and bass figurations.

Some of the differences between two-, three-, and four-voice writing are shown in the following passage from Handel's oratorio, *Judas Maccabaeus,* the two-part version of which we examined in Chapter XI, Example 95, page 173.

Ex. 166   **Allegro**   HANDEL

* In the two-part version, the missing chord-third is supplied by the accompaniment.

(c) 4 voices

Sing these three versions, observing their differences. Compare the above four-voice version with the styles of Example 159 and 165, in regard to the treatment of repeated and nonharmonic tones in the melody, for example.

In conclusion, remember that the definite statements made above, regarding four-voice writing, are all *general principles* subject to many exceptions. But follow them rather closely at present, testing *all doubtful cases aurally*. For vocal music, singing is a better test than playing. It is well to search for *the best* rather than merely for an adequate or *theoretically correct* solution. Do not be confused by details; work for the broad general effect.

Review:

1. The pitches and signature of the D minor scale.
2. The ranges of the soprano, alto, tenor, and bass voices.
3. How four-part vocal music is distributed between two staves.
4. What determines the *position* of a chord in contrast to its *inversion*.
5. The three factors in four-part writing aside from choice of chord.
6. The distance between adjacent voices in four-part writing.
7. Two ways of securing smooth voice progression.
8. What is meant by the *common tone*, and how it is treated.
9. What the nearest position of the next chord is when the common tone is not held.

10. How the three upper voices progress between chords having adjacent roots.

11. Two factors that determine doubling.

12. The doubling used for fundamental and inverted triads and seventh-chords.

13. Which voice is doubled most frequently.

14. How questionable parallels may be avoided.

15. After the chords are determined, in which order the alto, tenor, and bass are written, and why.

16. The name for the sign ⌒• and what it means.

17. The principle of figured bass.

18. Some differences in style between Examples 159, 165, and 166.

19. Why each voice should be interesting melodically.

20. What is meant by harmonizing for mixed voices.

21. What the terms "monophonic," "polyphonic," and "homophonic" mean.

22. What the *Tierce de Picardie* (Picardian Third) is.

For Further Study, Determine:

1. Why music for mixed voices is usually written in four parts, and whether more than four parts are ever used.

2. Why only the bass may be more than an octave from the adjacent voice.

3. Whether adjacent voices often overlap or cross.

4. Whether wide skips are possible between different positions of the same chords.

5. How many *common tones* are possible between different triads.

6. How inversion affects the progression of chords having adjacent roots.

7. In what inversion the bass tone is seldom doubled.

8. In what class of chord is the bass tone rarely doubled.

9. In what periods of musical history parallel fifths were considered good taste.

10. Why the chorale melody, *Oh Sacred Head* (sometimes called the *Passion Chorale*), is said to be in the Phrygian mode.

11. Whether the best results are obtained by completing each chord vertically or by writing each voice horizontally.

12. The difference between a chorale and a hymn.

13. The difference between *choral* and *chorale*.

14. Why the melody of Example 159 is said to be in the Dorian mode, and that of Example 161 in the Phrygian mode.

I — *Assignment for Writing*

1. Using the given harmonization of familiar songs, hymns, or chorales, arrange them for soprano, alto, tenor, and bass, or rearrange for these four voices melodies that were previously harmonized for three voices. Sing these arrangements in class.

2. Experiment with arrangements or original compositions for instrumental quartets made up of two trebles, a tenor, and a bass instrument. The form of these original compositions should be *A–B* or *A–B–A*, clearly defined by strong cadences. These arrangements, or compositions, are to be performed in class.

3. Add the alto and tenor voices (in that order) to at least one of the following passages:

Unfigured basses:

Meisterchorale No. 17

(a)

Meisterchorale No. 19

(b)

Meisterchorale No. 30

(c)

Moderato PURCELL, *Dido and Aeneas,* No. 20 (Adapted)

(d)

Meisterchorale No. 32

Figured bass:

(e)

4. Harmonize at least one of the following melodies for soprano, alto, tenor, and bass:

Allegretto Piedmontese Folk Song

(a)

Moderato *   English Folk Song

(b)

or V_3^4 I_6 V_3^4

*Here the three upper voices (second and fourth beats) are nonchord tones.

Adagio   Russian Folk Song

(c)

Allegretto   GLINKA

(d)

CRÜGER (1649)

Chorale (1524)

BACH, Chorale

Andante   HAYDN, *The Creation*, No. 3

5. Harmonize at least one of the following melodies for piano, using any of the preceding accompaniment figures or others that are appropriate:

Reprinted by permission from The Home and Community Song Book, Concord Series No. 2. Published and copyrighted by the E. C. Schirmer Music Company.

II — *Assignment for Playing*

1. Harmonize any of the melodies in the *Assignment for Writing* (5).

2. Improvise a sarabande[4] in *A–B–A* form, using the following motive for part I. Part II is to be a phrase (8 measures as in part I), ending either in F major or A minor. Repeat the consequent phrase of part I for part III.

3. Improvise melodies in two- or three-part form, details optional. Repeat from memory and harmonize.

4. Experiment playing familiar vocal or instrumental minor melodies by ear. (For example, Schubert's *Serenade*.)

---

[4] The *sarabande,* one of the dances in the classic Suite, first appeared in the 16th century. It was probably of Moorish or Spanish origin.

5. Transpose the following modulatory chord patterns into all the major and minor keys previously studied. Devise original modulatory patterns from major to the dominant, mediant, or relative keys, and from minor to the dominant or the relative keys. Repeat in piano style with embellishments.

6. Transpose simple melodies and harmonic passages in this chapter down a major or minor second. Review note on transposition, Chapters XI and XVIII, pages 183 and 314, respectively, *Assignment for Playing*

III — Assignment for Listening

1. *Oral dictation:* harmonic recognition only. (Name chords by quality, letter, and Roman numeral.)

Mozart, *Violin Sonata*, K377, Andante, Variation VI.

Beethoven, *Symphony IV*, Op. 60, First Movement, Theme II, (107-121);

Symphony IX, Op. 125, Scherzo (57-77),

Adagio, theme II,

Finale, principal theme (164-179).

Mendelssohn, *In Autumn*, Op. 9, No. 5 (1-8).

2. *Written dictation (quality, bass, melody, and name of chord).*

New Episcopal Hymnal, No. 455, *St. Peter*.

Bach, *Minuet*, No. 10, *First Lessons* (Carroll), Book I, page 8; No. 5, *First Lessons* (Carroll), Book II, page 7.

Mendelssohn, *Elijah*, No. 11 (1-4).

Home and Community Song Book. Concord Series No. 2.

The Monks' March, page 44.

IV — Assignment for Analysis

Mozart, *String Quartet in D Minor*, K421, First Movement (1-4);

Violin Sonata, K377, Variation VI.

Beethoven, *Symphony IX,* Op. 125, First Movement, principal
theme (16-22);

Violin Concerto, Op. 61, Allegro (43-58), Rondo,
subordinate theme I.

Schubert, *Violin Sonatina,* Op. 137, No. 2, Minuetto (1-12).

Schumann, *The Strange Man,* Op. 68, No. 29 (1-12).

Brahms, *Violin Sonata,* No. II, Op. 100, Second Movement, Vivace
(1-19);

Liebeslieder, No. 11 (1-8).

Meyerbeer, *Coronation March* (cf. 1-9 with 35-42).

Gounod, *Funeral March of the Marionettes* (1-16).

Meisterchorale, No. 79.

The following passages for analysis have been selected from the above
list. Identify form, chords, and nonharmonic tones. Note especially the
various types of minor scales used and the pivotal and modulatory chords.

BEETHOVEN, *Violin Concerto,* Op. 61 (Principal Theme)

Con energia e forza   SCHUMANN, Op. 68, No. 29

(b)

BRAHMS, *Violin Sonata*, Op. 100 (Adapted from Second Movement)

MEYERBEER, *Coronation March (The Prophet)*

Molto maestoso

GOUNOD, *Funeral March of the Marionettes*

Misterioso

*Chromatic chord.

Meisterchorale, No. 79

(Study carefully as an example of part writing and modulation.)

Chapter XXII

THE V₆ CHORD

Ex. 167

BEETHOVEN, (1770—1827), *Seventh Symphony,* Op. 92

Allegretto   (Second Movement)*

*This theme was originally intended for the second movement of the *String Quartet,* Op. 59, No. 3, and is to be found among the sketches for that quartet in 1806. Beethoven later considered changing the tempo to Andante quasi Allegretto. (See Grove, *Beethoven and his Nine Symphonies,* pages 251, 255.)

Beethoven completed both his *Seventh* and *Eighth Symphonies* in 1812, when he was forty-two years old, only twelve

years after the performance of his *First Symphony*. Another twelve
years were to pass before the appearance of his monumental *Ninth
Symphony,* so that the year 1812, though midway in point of
time, really marks the close of his most productive symphonic
period. Both the *Seventh* and *Eighth Symphonies* are unique in
having an *Allegretto* in place of the usual slow movement; but
while the *Allegretto* of the *Eighth Symphony* is whimsical, the
corresponding movement of the *Seventh Symphony* seems more
melancholy than many second movements in the conventional slow
tempo. Hear the entire movement, especially measures 1 to 102, in
which Beethoven repeats the theme with fascinating insistence.
Immediately after the passage quoted in Example 167, this counter
melody appears in the violas and cellos, thus:

Ex. 168

It is taken up by other instruments until it dominates the music.

Which is the most prominent element in Example 167, the
melody, harmony, or rhythm? Before the counter melody enters,
the melodic element is reduced to a minimum. In the second half
(measures 11 to 18), the harmonic changes are subtle and beautiful, featuring the contrast between major and minor quality. And
yet, on the whole, the insistent rhythmic pattern (♩ ♫) is
perhaps the most prominent element in the passage.

After the rhythm, probably the next most prominent element is
the harmony, at least at the beginning of the movement (Example
167). How does Beethoven achieve his effects so simply? Determine the key and the mode,[1] and identify the chords by their

---

[1] Note that the key of A minor has no signature, being the relative of C major.
Write the three forms of the A minor scale in treble and bass and sing them from
memory.

letter and quality names: for example, measures 1 and 2 consist of an A minor $^6_4$ chord, a most unusual beginning. The E₆ chord (measure 4) is V₆ in the prevailing tonality. The V₆ chord is often used as it is here in place of the fundamental V. Spell it upward from its bass tone, and then arrange it in thirds. Sing the chord and its resolution in *arpeggio* form, thus:

Ex. 169

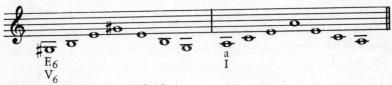

E₆
V₆

(Repeat in parallel major key)

Since Example 167 is three-part writing, it is unnecessary to double any part of the chord; but in four-part writing, the root or fifth is usually doubled in preference to the third, which is the leading tone of the scale.

As an example of the use of the V₆, sing the following chorale melody and the various basses alone, then together, thus:

Ex. 170   NEUMARK (1657)

Which is preferable? The composer used bass 3, completed thus:

Ex. 171

Sing the completed version, and justify the doubling in each chord. The repetition of a chord or bass tone over a bar, in chorales, is often used for a preliminary beat of a phrase, as in Examples 170 and 171, but it rarely, if ever, occurs during the course of a phrase. Contrast this with the use in instrumental music, Example 167, page 383, and Example 173, page 387. Note the use of the VI (measure 3) in place of the I. Is the doubling in the progression V-VI over the bar unusual, and, if so, why is it necessary here?

It is evident, then, that the most satisfactory results are obtained by doubling either the root or the fifth in the V₆ since its third is the leading tone of the scale which should not be stressed by doubling.

Now listen to the following melody, singing one bass note to each measure:

Ex. 172

Allegro   MOZART, *Viennese Sonatina*, No. 2, Rondo

The mode is obviously minor, centering around A at the beginning and around E at the end. Hence, the first phrase is in the tonality of A minor, and the second in E minor, the dominant key — a very common type of modulation. How is this modulation made? Note that the second phrase begins sequentially. Is it in the new key? Since this is a short passage from the middle of the movement, the key signature of the entire movement (A major) is used. Study Mozart's harmonization, as follows:

Ex. 173

Identify the chords, cadences, and resulting form. What is the prevailing motive? Explain how the entire passage is developed from it. Experiment with this principle in your own work. In measure 3, substitute the fundamental for the inverted V chord, and determine which is preferable.

To summarize: (1) the V₆ is useful as a substitute for the fundamental V, except at the perfect authentic cadence; (2) a modulation may be made from any minor to its dominant key simply by using the two tonic chords consecutively, especially after a cadence, as in Example 173.

For some time, we have been writing A–B–A (three-part) forms. The length of the individual parts may vary, provided there is a definite return to the beginning after the contrasting section.

Here are several examples showing these differences:

Ex. 174*

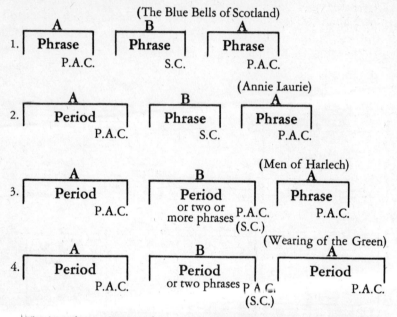

*The imperfect authentic cadence is sometimes substituted for the semi- or perfect cadence in the period form. In this example, if Part II of either 3 or 4 is to be a genuine period, it must be ended by a perfect cadence in the dominant key.

Of these *A–B–A* forms, the second is probably the most frequently used, at least for small compositions. Find other music written in these forms, for example, see Schumann's *Album for the Young,* Op. 68, Mendelssohn's *Songs Without Words,* or familiar folk melodies.

From short *A–B–A* forms, longer ones can be made by repetitions of one or more of the parts. Usually part I is repeated alone, and parts II and III are repeated together, forming the design *A–A–B–A–B–A.* The repetitions may be either exact or modified. If exact, they need not be written out a second time, but may be merely indicated by repeat marks, thus: *A* ⫽ *BA* ⫽. Experiment with both types of repetitions in your own compositions.

There are so many kinds of *A–B–A* form that it is best to concentrate on the essential points of *statement, contrast,* and *restatement,* and then note how the various types fit into this fundamental pattern.

Review:

1. The construction and use of the V_6 chord.
2. What choice of doubling is possible in the V_6 chord.
3. How Example 173 is developed from a short motive.
4. The construction and signature of the A minor scale.
5. The most usual modulations from A minor.
6. Four types of the *A–B–A* form.
7. How to extend the *A–B–A* form.
8. Where the modulation occurs in Example 173.
9. Why the third of the V_6 chord is seldom, if ever, doubled.

For Further Study, Determine:

1. Whether the V_6 chord is used in cadences.
2. What the effect is of omitting the chord third in Example 167, page 383, measure 5; and of the $\frac{6}{4}$ chord in measures 1 and 2.
3. Why it differs from the II_6 chord in respect to doubling (see Example 171).
4. What form of the minor scale is used in Example 167.
5. How many modulations are made in Example 167.
6. Some examples of the *A–B–A* form outlined in Example 173, both with and without repeated parts.
7. What the rhythmic pattern ♩ ♫ is called in poetry.
8. When a bar tone may be repeated in chorales.

I — Assignment for Writing

1. Continue arranging familiar vocal music for mixed voices, using the composers' chords or rearranging three-voice harmonization for four voices.

2. Continue making arrangements or writing original compositions for instrumental quartets made up of two treble, a tenor, and a bass instrument. In original work, experiment extending the *A–B–A* form by repeating one or more of the parts. Choose one of the forms in Example 173. Perform these arrangements or compositions in class.

3. Add the alto and tenor parts (in that order) to at least one of the following passages:

Figured basses:

BACH, *371 Chorales*

(a)

BACH, *371 Chorales*

(b)

Unfigured basses:

BACH, *371 Chorales*

(c)

BACH, *371 Chorales*

(d)

4. Harmonize at least one of the following melodies for mixed voices:

Moderato — Russian Folk Song

(a)

Reprinted by permission from A Book of Songs, Concord Series No. 14. Published and copyrighted by the E. C. Schirmer Music Company.

Andante — Swedish Folk Song

(b)

Moderato　　　　　　　　　　Bohemian Folk Song

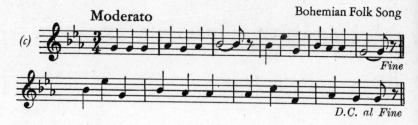

Fine

D.C. al Fine

Lively　　　　　　　　　　French Folk Tune

KUFFERATH

Chorale (1540)

(V₆)

(E♭)(C)　(G)

Chorale (1680)

(g)

(C)   (D)

Chorale (1648)

(h)

5. Harmonize at least one of the following melodies for piano, using any of the preceding accompaniment figures, or others that are appropriate. Note new accompaniment figure used in (a):

Andante

Irish Folk Song

(a)

_p_

Moderato — Norwegian Folk Song

(b)

(C)

The two preceding selections are reprinted by permission from The Home and Community Song Book, *Concord Series No. 2. Published and copyrighted by the E. C. Schirmer Music Company.*

Alla Turca
Allegretto — MOZART, *Piano Sonata*, K331

(c)

BEETHOVEN, *Ruins of Athens,* Turkish March

(d)

II — Assignment for Playing

1. Harmonize any of the melodies in the *Assignment for Writing* (5) above.

2. Improvise a *Cradle Song* (*Berceuse*), using the following motives. Part I is to be a period; part II, a phrase in A minor. Repeat the con-

sequent phrase of part I for part III (see Example 174, No. 2).

Andante   HAUSER, *Cradle Song*
Part I   Part II

3. Improvise melodies in A minor according to Example 174, No. 1. Experiment with modulation to C major or E minor. Repeat from memory and harmonize.

4. Continue playing by ear familiar minor melodies, for example, *La Cinquantaine*. (Gabriel-Marie.)

5. Transpose the following modulatory chord pattern into all the minor keys previously studied. Devise original modulations according to Chapter XX, Example 158, page 345. Repeat both phrases in piano style with embellishments.

(a)   *(b)*

6. Transpose simple melodies and harmonic passages in this chapter up and down a major and minor third, that is, from A to F or C. Review notes on transposition in the *Assignment for Playing*, Chapter XI, page 183, and Chapter XVIII, page 314.

III — *Assignment for Listening*

1. *Oral dictation:* harmonic recognition only. (Name chords by quality, letter, and Roman numeral.)

Gabriel-Marie, *La Cinquantaine*, Trio.

Gautier, *Le Secret,* A Minor section.
Chaminade, *Gavotte,* Op. 9, No. 2 (1-9).
Strauss, *Vienna Life Waltzes,* No. 2 (Universal Edition), p. 20.
Schumann, *Vienna Carnival-Scene,* Op. 26, Scherzino (17-24);
    Album for the Young, Op. 68, Nos. 6, 12, 27.
Beethoven, *Piano Sonata,* Op. 7, Allegro molto (1-13),
                         Largo (1-8),
                  Op. 31, No. 2, First Movement (1-6);
    Violin Sonata, Op. 96, Poco Allegretto (1-8).
Clementi, *Sonatina,* Op. 36, No. 2, Allegretto (1-8); Second
    Movement (entire) ; Allegro (1-32).

2. *Written dictation (quality, bass, melody, and name of chord).*
    Green Book, Twice 55: No. 139, *Lo, What a Branch of Beauty;*
                    No. 89, *Good King Wenceslas* (1-12);
                    No. 73, *Holy, Holy, Holy* (1-8).
    Golden Book: Go Down Moses.
    Anniversary Chorales, No. 13 (cf. V₆ with V).
    New Episcopal Hymnal, No. 577, "Awake My Soul."

IV — Assignment for Analysis

Arensky, *Basso Ostinato* (1-5).
Beethoven, *G Major Piano Concerto,* Op. 58, First Movement
    (1-14);
                Für Elise (1-22);
                Piano Sonata, Op. 7, Largo (1-8),
                          Op. 31, No. 2, First Movement (1-6).
Chopin, *Mazurka,* Op. 56, No. 2 (29-36),
               Op. 59, No. 1 (1-12).
Bach, *French Suite No. 3,* Minuet and Trio;
    English Suite No. 2, Sarabande (1-5).
Schumann, *With Myrtle and Roses* (1-4);
    Album for the Young, Op. 68, No. 27.
Schubert, *Fantasia,* Op. 78, Andante (1-8);
    A Minor Sonata, Op. 42, Scherzo (1-10).
Brahms, *Intermezzo,* Op. 76, No. 7 (1-8).
Grainger, *Country Gardens* (1-4).
Clementi, *Sonatina,* Op. 36, No. 2 (1-32).
Gabriel-Marie, *La Cinquantaine,* Trio.
Mozart, *Symphony in G Major* (See footnote, Ex. 114, page 229).
The following passages for analysis have been selected from the above

list. Identify form, chords, and nonharmonic tones. Note especially the various types of minor scales used and the pivotal and modulatory chords.

CHOPIN, *Mazurka*, Op. 56, No. 2

SCHUBERT, *Piano Sonata*, Op. 78

SCHUBERT, *Sonata*, Op. 42, Scherzo

Allegro vivace

(e)

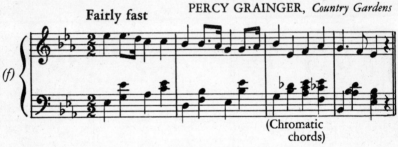

PERCY GRAINGER, *Country Gardens*

Fairly fast

(f)

(Chromatic
chords)

Copyright, 1919, by Percy Grainger. Reprinted by permission of G. Schirmer, Inc.

GABRIEL-MARIE, *La Cinquantaine*

Andante
[Trio]

(g)

MOZART, *G Major Symphony**

Menuetto

(h)

*See note to Ex. 114.

Chapter XXIII

THE IV₆ CHORD AND OTHER
CHORDS OF THE SIXTH

Ex. 175   **Allegro**   Old English Carol

Reprinted by permission from The Home and Community Song Book, *Concord Series No. 2.*
Published and copyrighted by the E. C. Schirmer Music Company.

*Chromatic chord.

402

ti - dings of   com - fort and   joy, com-fort and

joy,   O   ti - dings of   com - fort and   joy.

SING THIS old English carol in four parts, listening to the cadences and general harmonic color. Although the signature (one sharp) suggests G major, the prevailing impression is of E minor[1] since it begins and ends on this chord. As there are no accidentals in the melody, it is in the natural form of the minor scale corresponding to the Aeolian mode. (See Chapter XX.) This accounts for the general modal effect, although the harmony itself is not modal.

Name all the chords by letter and Roman numeral, noting especially the A minor chord in the first inversion (or IV_6) at the end of measure 3. Spell it upward from its root in thirds, then sing the inverted chord and its resolution in *arpeggio* form, as in Example 176.

This IV_6 chord in measure 3, Example 175, is obviously used as a substitute for the fundamental IV, just as the V_6 was substituted for the fundamental V in Chapter XXII, page 385. The doubling is also similar, since either the root or the fifth may be

---

[1] Note the signature of one sharp (F sharp) for E minor. Write the three forms of the E minor scale in treble and bass, first with accidentals, then with this signature. Sing each from memory.

duplicated, but rarely the third. Like all first inversions, the IV₆ is useful in writing a smooth, melodic bass line.

Ex. 176

(1) as in Ex. 175   (2) arranged   (3) sing and repeat in parallel major
                     in 3rds   key.

E: IV

E: IV₆

E: IV₆   V

(Note the difference in quality.)

Note the improvement in the bass line of Example 175 by the use of other chords of the sixth previously discussed:

I₆, Chapter VI, page 76
II₆, Chapter IV, page 46
V₆, Chapter XXII, page 383
VII₆, Chapter XIII, page 207

These, with the IV₆, are the most frequently used first inversions of triads. The others, III₆ and VI₆, are rarely used except either sequentially or consecutively along a scale line bass, Example 177 (*b*), thus:

Ex. 177   Allegro   BOTTOMLEY, *Madrigal*

Allegro vivace   BACH, *G Major Toccata*

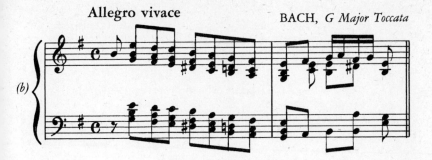

(b)

In measures 5 and 6 of this jolly madrigal, we hear chords of the sixth used as part of a short sequence. Note the voice leading. The passage from the Bach *Toccata* shows the consecutive use of these chords of the sixth to harmonize a scale passage. Identify the mode of each passage. Their consecutive use is further illustrated by the following passages:

Ex. 178

Andante   PINSUTI, *Goodnight, Goodnight, Beloved*

(a)

II_5^6

Adagio   MOZART, *Requiem,* "Sanctus"

(b)

BACH, *371 Chorales,* No. 106

(c)

After naming the chords, note the part-writing. How many voices move in similar motion? Which are the parallel voices when four voices are used? A general statement regarding the voice leading in consecutive chords of the sixth may be formulated thus: since the two outside voices and a third voice move in *similar* motion, the fourth voice moves stepwise in *contrary* motion to them, following either a two- or a three-note pattern.

Study Example 178 (*b*) and (*c*) with these points in mind; then harmonize the E major scale for mixed voices, using only consecutive sixths. Begin with any one of several patterns, depending on the meter, thus:

Ex. 179

(*a*)   (*b*)   (*c*)

Usually, as here, the *outside* voices move in parallel sixths. The important point is to arrange the inner voices so that one moves in similar and the other in contrary motion to the outside voices.

Consecutive sixths are rather rare and are seldom found in a passage of more than half a dozen chords. They sound like harmonized passing tones, but are effective if used occasionally. Consecutive chords of the sixth are generally used to harmonize scale passages.

To determine principles for using these first inversions of triads, either alone or consecutively, sing the following melody to determine its general harmonic background, and then add the bass suggested in Example 180:

Ex. 180

TCHAIKOVSKY, *Songs for Young People* "A Legend" Op. 54, No. 5

Moderato

From High School Songs for Every Occasion, *by Gartlan and Donnelly. Published by Hinds, Hayden & Eldredge, Inc.*

Are other bass lines possible? Determine the key, mode, and form. Notice how effective the fundamental triads are in the second half. The inner voices for the first phrase might be added thus:

Ex. 181

This solution is rather elaborate but shows some of the possibilities. Work out the alto and tenor parts in the same style for the remainder of the passage, and sing the completed version in four parts.

Although the composer did not use them, the melody might also be almost entirely harmonized by consecutive sixths, as in measures 5 and 6, Example 182. This is frequently done in three-voice writing but seldom when four voices are used, thus:

Ex. 182

In this chapter, therefore, we have noted how the first inversions of all triads are used, either separately or together. Like the other first inversions, the IV_6 is useful in writing melodic bass lines. Either the root or the fifth may be doubled — rarely the third. Consecutive sixths are usually used stepwise, or in a sequential manner. Three voices move in similar and one in contrary motion. The doubling results from this contrary motion in one of the inner voices. Single chords of the sixth are good anywhere except at final cadences, but consecutive sixths are more generally limited to scale passages. The VI_6 and III_6 are seldom used except in a sequence or in a line of consecutive sixths.

In your own work, determine the general harmonic background $(I–IV–V)$ as usual; then use the IV_6, and possibly consecutive sixths, to improve the bass line. Let the use of all new chords be determined aurally rather than theoretically.

Review:

1. Which form of the minor scale is used in Example 175.
2. To what old mode Example 175 corresponds.
3. The construction and signature of E minor scale.
4. How the IV_6 chord is used.
5. The doubling used in the IV_6 chord.
6. How many chords of the sixth are found in Example 175.
7. The most frequently used chords of the sixth.
8. How the III_6 and VI_6 chords are used.
9. How to use chords of the sixth consecutively.
10. The doubling and voice progression used for consecutive chords of the sixth.
11. The general effect of consecutive sixths.
12. For what melodic progression consecutive sixths are used.
13. Which voice determines the doubling in consecutive sixths.

For Further Study, Determine:

1. The difference between a *carol* and a *chorale*.
2. Whether Example 175 modulates.
3. Why the harmony of Example 175 is not modal.
4. Why all voices do not move in similar motion in consecutive sixths.
5. Why the III_6 and VI_6 chords are not much used except in sequence.
6. Why consecutive sixths may not be used as a part of the perfect authentic cadence.

7. How many chords of the sixths are to be found in familiar music.
8. What *toccata* and *madrigal* mean and how they are applied to music.
9. The quality of the IV₆ in the major mode.

I — Assignment for Writing

1. Continue arranging familiar vocal music for mixed voices, using the composers' chords; or rearrange three-voice harmonizations for four voices, for example, *Elijah,* "Lift Thine Eyes" (Mendelssohn).

2. Continue rearranging or writing original compositions for instrumental quartets. In original work, experiment with one of the *A–B–A* forms given in Example 174, page 388. Perform original work in class.

3. Add the alto and tenor parts (in that order) to at least one of the following passages:

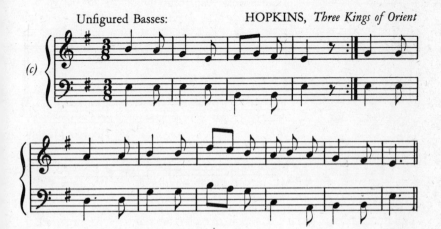

Unfigured Basses: HOPKINS, *Three Kings of Orient*

(c)

MENDELSSOHN, March from *Athalie,* Trio

Allegro

(d)

4. Harmonize at least one of the following melodies for mixed voices:

Chorale

(d)

RODNEY

Allegretto con moto

(e)

Note melody in bass

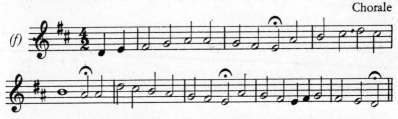

From High School Songs for Every Occasion, by Gartlan and Donnelly. Published by Hinds. Hayden & Eldredge, Inc.

Chorale

(f)

5. Harmonize at least one of the following melodies for piano, using any of the previous accompaniment figures or others that are appropriate. Note new accompaniment figure used in (a).

Presto

Flemish Folk Song

(a)

(b) Allegretto — Finnish Folk Tune

(c) Moderato — Folk Song

(d) Tempo di valse — SCHUBERT, Op. 18a, No. 4

(e) Tempo di valse — SCHUBERT, Op. 127, No. 10

G: V₆   B♭: IV₆

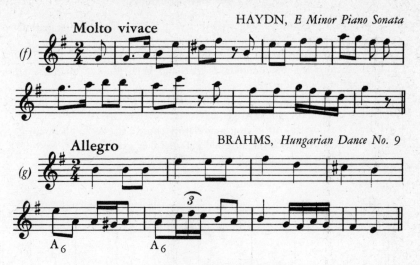

II — Assignment for Playing

1. Harmonize any of the melodies in the *Assignment for Writing* (5). above.

2. Improvise a *tarantelle*[2] *in A–B–A form*, using the following motives.

Part I

Part II

---

[2] *Tarantelle* is an Italian dance in $\frac{6}{8}$, named from the town, Taranto. It was once regarded as a means of curing the disease called *tarantism*.

Use any of the forms suggested in Example 173. Try making part III a modified version of part I.

3. Improvise melodies in E minor according to Example 174, No. 2. Experiment with modulations to diatonic keys. Repeat melodies from memory and harmonize.

4. Continue playing by ear familiar minor melodies. Recall music in the key of E minor; for example, Massenet's *Elegie*, Op. 10.

5. Transpose the following modulatory chord patterns to all minor keys previously studied. Devise original modulations according to Chapter XX, Example 158. Repeat both phrases in piano style with embellishments.

6. Transpose simple E minor melodic and harmonic phrases up a minor second to F minor, and down a major second to D minor. Review notes on transposition in *Assignment for Playing*, Chapters XI and XVIII.

III — Assignment for Listening

1. *Oral dictation:* harmonic recognition only. (Name chords by quality, letter, and Roman numeral.)

Bach, *English Suite No. 5*, Sarabande (1-4).
Beethoven, *Symphony II*, Op. 36, Trio (1-8).
Handel, *Messiah*, No. 30, "Behold and See," complete;
No. 36, "Thou Art Gone up on High" (10-24);
No. 36, "Thou Art Gone up on High" (10-24);
No. 3, "Every Valley" (15-20).
Mozart, *Violin Sonata*, K304, Allegro (12-20),
Tempo di Minuetto (1-8);
String Quartet in D Minor, K421, Minuetto (1-10).
Gluck, *Iphigenie en Tauride*, Chorus (*Play a Tune*), page 45.
Schubert, *Violin Sonatina*, Op. 137, No. 3, Finale, Letter D;
Violin Sonatina, Op. 137, No. 1, Finale (1-8);
Valses Nobles, Op. 77, No. 10.
Rossini, *The Barber of Seville*, Overture, Allegro, principal theme (1-24).

Schumann, *Vienna Carnival-Scene*, No. 1, p. 8 (1-16) ;
  Scenes from Childhood, Op. 15, No. 9 (1-8),
       No. 11 (1-8),
       No. 24 (9-12).
Chopin, *Polonaise*, Op. 71, No. 3 (5-8).
Mozart, *Piano Sonata*, K545, Allegro (18-26) ;
  Piano Sonata, K310, Presto (1-20) and (37-44).
Grieg, *Sailors' Song*, Op. 68, No. 1 (1-8).
Dvořák, *New World Symphony*, Finale (1-4).
Tchaikovsky, *Symphony V*, Op. 68, Introduction (1-4).
Brahms, *Symphony IV*, Op. 98, Andante moderato, subordinate
 theme (1-4).
Folk Songs of Many Peoples, Vol. I, *The Sun is Low*, page 113.

2. *Written dictation (quality, bass, melody, and name of chord)*.
 Choralbuch, Nos. 23, 36, 38, 47, 49, 60, 61, 186.
 High School Songs (Gartlan), *The Redemption, Lovely Appear*
 (Gounod), p. 212 (11-18); *Send Out Thy Light* (Gounod),
 p. 38 (1-20).
 Green Book, Twice 55: No. 133, *Fine Knacks for Ladies* (1-8) ;
      No. 132, *Oh Thou Whose Feet;*
      No. 8, *Christ the Lord Has Risen Today*
      (1-4) ; .
 See *Assignment for Writing*, 3 (*c*).
 Home and Community Song Book. Concord Series No. 2. Nos. 86,
 87 (1-12), 100, 101, 116 (1-8).
 Bach, *371 Chorales*, Nos. 102, 206 (phrases 1-2).
 New Episcopal Hymnal, No. 564, *Lyons* (1-8),
      No. 51, *We Three Kings of Orient Are,*
      No. 284, *Windsor,*
      No. 55, *Heinlein,*
      No. 77, *Isleworth.*
 Graun, *The Death of Jesus* (Peters Edition), No. 7, Chorus, p. 29.
 Beethoven, *Piano Concerto IV*, Op. 58, Andante con moto (6-13;
 19-26).
 Chopin, *Nocturne*, Op. 15, No. 3, Religioso (1-8).
 Mendelssohn, *Songs Without Words*, No. 44 (1-8).
 Schumann, *Album for the Young*, Op. 68, No. 4.

IV — *Assignment for Analysis*

Bach, *French Suite No. 3*, Sarabande (1-8);
 First Lessons (Carroll), Gavotte, No. 14 (1-8).

Purcell, *Dido and Aeneas,* Act II, No. 22, p. 38; No. 23, p. 39.

Mozart, *D Minor Piano Concerto,* K466, First Movement (77-87).

Handel, *Messiah,* No. 2, "Comfort Ye My People" (1-4).

Haydn, *The London Symphony,* No. 104, First Movement, principal
       theme (1-8);
       The Clock Symphony, Finale (1-8);

Beethoven, *Bagatelle,* Op. 126, No. 5 (1-16);
       Piano Sonata, Op. 10, No. 1, Adagio molto (1-8),
                 Op. 10, No. 3, Rondo (1-8),
                 Op. 79, Vivace (1-8),
                 Op. 109, Vivace (1-8),
                 Op. 81*a,* Allegro (1-5).

Schubert, *Unfinished Symphony* (VI), Andante con moto (1-7);
       Symphony in C major (VII), Andante con moto, second
       theme.

Schumann, *Little Lullaby,* Op. 124, No. 6 (1-16).

Mendelssohn, *The Page's Song* (1-22).

Brahms, *Ballade,* Op. 118, No. 3 (10-14);
       Waltz, Op. 39, No. 12 (1-12), No. 11 (1-16);
       Symphony No. 1, Op. 68, Andante sostenuto (1-8).

Tchaikovsky, *Album for the Young,* Op. 39, No. 9, *The New Doll*
       (1-8).

    The following passages have been selected for analysis from the above
list. Identify the form, chords, and nonharmonic tones. Note especially
the use of the minor scale and the pivotal and modulatory chords.

BACH, *Third French Suite,* Sarabande

Andante con moto

BACH, *Gavotte* (Carroll I)

HANDEL, *Messiah*, No. 2, "Comfort Ye"

Allegro   HAYDN, *London Symphonies*, No. 7

(d)

BEETHOVEN, *Sonata*, Op. 79, Finale

Vivace

(e)

Compare with Beethoven *Sonata*, Op. 109, Vivace (meas. 1—9)

BEETHOVEN, *Sonata*, Op. 10, No. 3, Rondo

Allegro

SCHUBERT, *B Minor (Unfinished) Symphony*

Andante con moto

BRAHMS, *First Symphony*, Op. 68

Andante

chromatic

TCHAIKOVSKY, Op. 39, No. 9

*Chromatic chord.

SCHUBERT, *C Major Symphony,* No. 7

For additional examples of consecutive chords of the sixth, see:
Beethoven, *Piano Sonata,* Op. 2, No. 3, Rondo (diatonic); Chopin, *C sharp
Minor Prelude,* Op. 45, and *Piano Sonata,* Op. 35, Scherzo (chromatic).

Chapter XXIV

THE II⁶₅ CHORD

Ex. 183

HUGO WOLF(1860 – 1903), *Goethe Songs*, No. 35 (Adapted)

Bacchantish

Drunk - en must____we be more____ or less!

Youth ____ is a wine ____ less drunk - en

From Fifty Songs by Hugo Wolf, published by Oliver Ditson Company. Used by permission of Theodore Presser Co., Distributors.

THIS EXCERPT, from a set of 50 Goethe songs composed
between October, 1888 and February, 1889, was written by one
of the outstanding vocal composers of the century. In many
respects, Wolf's life parallels that of Schubert: his facility, his
sordid life in Vienna, his lack of family, and his tragically early
death. Wolf was an ardent disciple of Wagner. Perhaps for this
reason his accompaniments are rich and independent, to such a
degree that his songs are duos for voice *and piano,* since the latter
performs the same musical function as the Wagnerian orchestra.
Wolf's harmonic daring, rhythmic freedom, and melodic gift
stamp him as the last great master of the German *lied.*

The passage quoted (Example 183) has many points of interest.
This form is an extended parallel period. The tonality of the song
is minor[1] but both phrases modulate to the major mode. What is
the relationship of the two cadential major keys to the tonic key
of B minor? In the extended second phrase (5-12), the new
tonality of D major is reached through a series of chromatic
chords reflecting the mood of the text. Note, however, that the
B flat is retained to the end as a reminder of the prevailing minor

---

[1] Note the key signature of two sharps (F sharp and C sharp) used for B minor.
Write the three forms of the B minor scale in treble and bass, first with accidentals,
then with this signature. Sing each form from memory.

mode of the song. Here we see the composer molding his materials in order to obtain variety through contrast. Compare
measures 1, 2, and 3 and 5, 6, and 7 by playing and singing them.
At exactly what points are the changes made?

Let us examine the harmonic structure of Example 183, page
423, more closely. It contains a number of new harmonic effects,
two of which are of special importance to us: the second chord in
measure 1, and the stationary tones, F sharp in measures 5 and 6,
and D in measures 9 to 12.

First, in regard to measure 1: rhythmically the C sharp is the
essential tone. When the tones harmonizing C sharp are arranged
in thirds (including the B in the voice part), we have:

Ex. 184

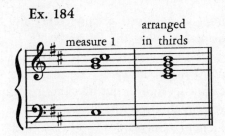

Name this chord in the key of B minor, then sing and resolve it
in *arpeggio* form to the chord of measure 2, thus:

Ex. 185

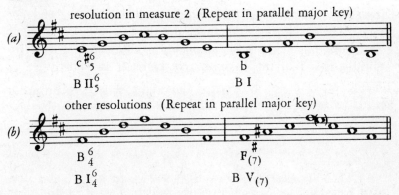

This new II⁶₅ chord[2] resembles the familiar V⁶₅ chord in appearance, but it differs in quality in each mode owing to the size of its intervals. (See Chapter XXVII, page 505, the II₇ chord.) Note also its likeness to the II₆ and IV chords; in fact, it may be regarded as a combination of them, thus:

Ex. 186

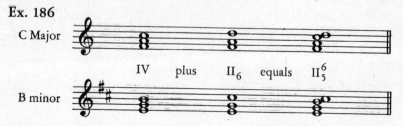

These similarities give a clue to its use, especially at cadences. Experiment using it for either the IV or the II₆ by adding only one tone to each of these chords[3]. What tone must be added to each chord? Note that in both cases, the addition produces a II⁶₅ chord. The dissonant seventh in the II⁶₅ either remains stationary, as a common tone in the next chord (Example 183, page 423, measures 1 and 2), or resolves downward one degree, as is customary in seventh-chord dissonances.

Second, in regard to the stationary tones in Example 183, F sharp in measures 5-6 (melody), and D in measures 9-12 (bass): these stationary tones are foreign to the prevailing chords and, consequently, produce new dissonances. Any such tone that is held, irrespective of the momentary chord, is called an *organ,*[4] or *pedal, point.* The F sharp is a dominant and the D a tonic organ point. The pedal point may occur in any voice, although it is most frequently found in the bass. In rare cases, it is embellished by

---

[2] See the first measures of Beethoven's *Piano Sonata in E flat Major,* Op. 31, No. 3 and Mendelssohn's *Wedding March* for a diatonic and chromatic example respectively of compositions beginning on this II⁶₅ chord.

[3] This is why certain ⁶₅ chords are sometimes explained as triads with an *added sixth.* The effect is much used by the impressionistic composers, Debussy, Ravel, Cyril Scott, and Palmgren, as well as by many writers of contemporary popular music.

[4] So called because of the ease with which it is possible to hold a tone on the pedal keyboard of the organ while moving to different chords on the manuals.

neighboring tones. Sometimes both the tonic and dominant tones
are held together, forming a *double* or *pastorale pedal point.*
(Example 183, measures 5 and 6.) Whether single or double, the
stationary tone or tones may be either repeated or tied. In analysis,
the pedal point is recognized, but the chords are named from the
other voices without inversion, of course, unless the pedal point
is in an upper voice. Since the stationary tone usually begins and
ends as the root of a chord, a pedal point often gives the effect of
chord expansion, and so is useful at the cadence to lengthen either
the V₇ or the I chords.[5] The pedal point is more used in instrumental than in vocal music.

BACH, *371 Chorales,* No. 336

Ex. 187

(To be completed by the student)

(To be completed by the student)

---

[5] Sometimes entire compositions are written over a stationary bass, as Bach's
organ *Pastorale in F Major,* whose bass is a series of pedal points. The stationary
E flat in Wagner's *Rheingold Prelude* is harmonic, since the entire composition is
based on the E flat major chord. The effect, however, is that of a pedal point.

To continue with Example 183, page 423, at present, discussion of the chromatic chords in measures 7 and 8 will be omitted since they represent a use of the "twelve-tone scale" beyond the province of this discussion. However, it is interesting to note aesthetically the expressive use of this type of harmony, as well as that of the vocal line.

Sing the chorale melody in Ex. 187, first alone, then with the suggested basses. Complete basses 4 and 5. Notice how the II⁶₅ is used at cadences and the treatment of foreign tones in both parts.

Add the alto and tenor parts to one of the above basses, making the inner voices as simple as possible. Foreign tones may occasionally be used to fill in skips, but they are rarely used together except in parallel thirds and sixths. Example 188 shows how the composer added the inner voices to bass 3.

Ex. 188

BACH

*Note the chromatic embellishing chords.

Sing Example 188 in four parts. The two marked chromatic chords might have been diatonic. Do they sound equally well without the accidental G sharp? Note that the melody in both phrases ends 2-1, the repeated second step being harmonized by the II⁶₅, followed by the V or V₇. This cadential use of the II⁶₅ is very frequent, especially in chorale style. The II⁶₅ is also often followed by the I⁶₄, as in Examples 183 and 185.

What of the doubling and the resolution of the chord-seventh in the II⁶₅? Formulate a statement about these points based on the music that we have examined. Does the II⁶₅ differ from the V⁶₅ in these respects?

In conclusion, remember the cadential use of the II⁶₅ based on its likeness to the IV and II₆ discussed above. Use all four tones of the chord — none is omitted or doubled. Find examples of the organ — or pedal — point in instrumental music. It is easily recognized as a stationary tone that begins and ends as a consonance, but that becomes a dissonance as the chords change. It usually occurs in the bass on the tonic or dominant of the scale, beginning and ending as a chord root. Sometimes both tones are sustained together. Harmonically, a pedal point gives the effect of chord expansion. Experiment with it in original work to extend the V_7 or the I chords of the final cadence.

Review:

1. The signature and construction of the B minor scale.
2. The construction and resolution of the II⁶₅ chord.
3. The relationship between the II⁶₅ and the IV and II₆ chords.
4. What is meant by *added sixth* chords.
5. How the II⁶₅ is used in melody harmonization.
6. What an organ, or pedal, point is.
7. In what voice and on what scale steps it usually occurs.
8. What a *pastorale* organ point is.
9. Why an organ point gives the effect of harmonic extension.

For Further Study, Determine:

1. How *you* would express the poem of Example 183 in music.
2. How the II⁶₅ differs in quality in the two modes.
3. Why the first inversion of the seventh-chord is called a ⁶₅ chord.
4. Why no tone is doubled in the II⁶₅ chord.
5. Why the organ, or pedal, point is so called.
6. What instrument is so constructed that it plays a *pastorale* organ point as a bass for melody harmonization.
7. The difference between an organ point and a common tone.
8. The difference between organ pedals and piano pedals.

I — Assignment for Writing

1. Scan the following poem and set it to music for four mixed voices, preferably in the key of B minor. If an accompaniment is added, use the rhythmic figure in Example 183. Experiment by putting the melody in the bass. The entire poem contains two more stanzas that should be included if a complete setting is desired.

> Gaily bedight,
> A gallant knight,
> In sunshine and in shadow,
> Had journeyed long,
> Singing a song,

In search of Eldorado.
   But he grew old —
   This knight so bold —
And o'er his heart a shadow
   Fell as he found
   No spot of ground
That looked like Eldorado.

Eldorado — *Edgar Allen Poe*

2. Write a Spanish dance for four stringed instruments (guitar, mandolin, or string quartet) in the style of Example 183. If there are not sufficient stringed instruments in the class, write for violin and piano. (Form optional, but probably some *A–B–A* type.) The work should be performed in class.

3. Add the alto and tenor voices (in that order) to at least one of the following passages:

Figured basses: FREYLINGHAUSEN (1704)

FREYLINGHAUSEN (1705)

French Melody (13th Century) "Draw Nigh, Immanuel"
Unfigured bass:

4. Harmonize at least one of the following melodies for mixed voices:

B major

SULLIVAN, *The Mikado*

Allegretto con spirito   SULLIVAN, *The Mikado*

(c)   Soprano only _ _ _ _ _ _ _ _ _ Harmonize

(d)   Chorale

(e)   Chorale

5. Harmonize at least one of the following melodies for piano, using any of the preceding accompaniment figures or others that are appropriate. Note new accompaniment figure used in (*a*).

Tempo di bolero

TROTERE

From *High School Songs for Every Occasion, by Gartlan and Donnelly. Published by Hinds, Hayden & Eldredge, Inc.*

BIZET, *Carmen*, "Toreador Song"

Allegro moderato

Andante   VERDI, *Il Trovatore*, No. 12

(c)

BALFE, *The Bohemian Girl*, "Then You'll Remember Me"

Andante cantabile

(d)

Moderato   VON FLOTOW, *Martha*, "Ah! So Pure"

(e)

Moderato   German Folk Song

(f)

SCHUBERT, *Menuette No.* 7, Op. Posth.

Tempo di minuetto

(g)

Alegretto   MOZART, *Don Giovanni*, No. 16, "Deh vieni"

(b)

II — *Assignment for Playing*

1. Harmonize any of the melodies in the *Assignment for Writing* (5).
2. Improvise a bolero[6] in *A–B–A* form, using the following motive. Experiment with modulation by ending part I in B minor. Part II should end on the V₇ of D major in order to lead back to part III, which will begin like part I. Part III may be a modified version of part I.

Part I   MOSKOWSKI, *Spanish Dances*, Op. 12, Bolero

Con spirito

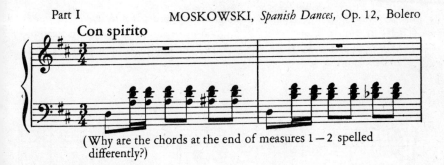

(Why are the chords at the end of measures 1 — 2 spelled differently?)

───────

[6] A brisk Spanish dance in $\frac{3}{4}$ whose accompaniment is based on the castinet rhythm ♩♩ ♩♩♩♩ or ♩♩♩♩ ♩♩♩♩ See Chopin, *Bolero*, Op. 19, for piano and Ravel's *Bolero* for orchestra.

Part II

3. Improvise melodies in B minor, as Example 174, No. 3. Experiment with modulation to diatonic keys suggested in Example 150 (Chapter XX, page 345. Repeat melodies from memory and harmonize.

4. Continue playing familiar melodies by ear. Recall music in the key of B minor; for example, Schubert's *Unfinished Symphony*. Play its opening (bass) phrase beginning on B.

5. Transpose the following modulatory chord patterns to all the minor keys previously studied. Devise original modulations suggested in Example 158 (Chapter XX, page 345). Repeat each phrase in piano style with embellishments.

6. Transpose simple B minor melodic and harmonic phrases down a major or a minor second to G and A minors. Review notes on transposition in *Assignment for Playing*, Chapter XI, page 183, and Chapter XVIII, page 314. Experiment transposing passages in other minor keys to B minor.

III — Assignment for Listening

1. *Oral dictation:* harmonic recognition only. (Name chords by quality, letter, and Roman numeral.)

Beethoven, *Piano Sonata,* Op. 31, No. 3, Allegro (1-8),
      Op. 28, Andante, Poco animato,
      Op. 26, Trio (1-8) ;
   Bagatelles, Op. 33, No. 2, Adagio contabile (1-8);
   Symphony II, Op. 36, Scherzo (1-16) ;
   Symphony III, Op. 55, Marcia funebré, C major section;
   Symphony VI, Op. 68, First Movement, principal theme.
Haydn, *Symphony in E flat (Drum Roll),* Minuetto (1-10);
  London Symphony, Minuetto (1-16) ;
  Clock Symphony, First Movement, principal theme (1-10).
Mozart, *Violin Sonata,* K377, Tempo di Minuetto (1-8).
Schubert, *G Major Fantasia,* Op. 78, Andante (1-29),
         Menuetto (1-18) ;
  Moment Musical, Op. 94, No. 6 (1-16).
Bach, *French Suite No. 6,* Gavotte (1-8).
Mendelssohn, *Ruy Blas Overture,* Op. 95, Section 5 ;
    Athalia Overture, Op. 74 (1-8);
    Elijah, No. 21, "Hear Ye Israel" (1-13) ;
    Songs Without Words, No. 10 (1-34);
Schumann, *Album for the Young,* Op. 68, No. 21 (1-4).
Chopin, *Waltz,* Op. 34, No. 1 (60-64),
    Op. 64, No. 3 (1-16) ;
  Mazurka, Op. 30, No. 2 (1-8).
Brahms, *Violin Sonata No. 2,* Op. 100, Allegretto grazioso (1-12).
Wagner, *Die Meistersinger,* Act I, "By Silent Hearth" (1-17).
Dvořák, *Slavic Dance,* Op. 72 (1-8).

2. *Written dictation (quality, bass, melody, and name of chord).*
Green Book, Twice 55: No. 149, *Crossing the Bar* (1-4).
Home and Community Song Book. Concord Series No. 2.
 Where E'er You Walk, page 94;
 The Jolly Miller, page 25;

The Foggy Dew, page 57.
Golden Book: Oh Come All Ye Faithful (1-8), page 72;
              At Pierrot's Door, page 86;
              Singing in the Rain (1-8).
Sing!: Thou'rt Like a Lovely Flower, page 25.
Schumann, *Lieder Album,* No. 8 (Breitkopf & Härtel Edition).
Mozart, *Violin Sonata,* K304, Minuet, E Major section (1-16).
Grieg, *Watchman's Song,* Op. 12, No. 3 (1-8).
Choralbuch, Nos. 96, 101.
Bach, *371 Chorales,* No. 334;
    The Passion According to St. Matthew, No. 31, Chorale
    (1-4).
New Episcopal Hymnal, No. 500, *Supplication,*
                No. 32, *Ebeling,*
                No. 519, *Ton-y-Botel.*

IV — Assignment for Analysis

Bach, *The Christmas Oratorio,* No. 51 (1-4);
    Organ Prelude in G Major (Peters Edition), Vol. VIII.
Mozart, *Violin Sonata,* K304, Tempo dimenuetto, E Major section;
    Violin Sonata, K302, Rondo (1-8);
    E flat Major String Quartet, K428, Menuetto (1-6).
Handel, *Messiah,* "Every Valley," No. 3 (1-8).
Beethoven, *Piano Sonata,* Op. 31, No. 3, First Movement (1-8);
    Rondo a Capriccio, Op. 129 (1-8).
Schubert, *Death and the Maiden* (1-8);
    Impromptu, Op. 142, No. 3 (1-4);
    Violin Sonatina, Op. 137, No. 3, Allegro moderato (1-8).
Mendelssohn, *G Minor Piano Concerto,* Op. 25, Andante;
    Songs Without Words, No. 35;
    Organ Sonata, Op. 65, No. 5, Andante con moto
    (1-4).
Schumann, *Symphony No. 3,* Op. 97, Lebhaft (1-8);
    Scenes from Childhood, Op. 15, No. 3.
Chopin, *Waltz,* Op. 69, No. 2 (9-16);
    B Minor Sonata, Op. 58, Allegro maestoso (1-4);
    Prelude, Op. 28, No. 6, fourth phrase.
Brahms, *To a Nightingale* (1-7);
    Symphony III, Op. 90, Poco allegretto (1-12);
    Cradle Song (*Golden Book*), p. 81.
Strauss, *Tales from Vienna Woods,* Waltz, No. 2.

Bizet, *L'Arlesienne Suite,* Fourth Movement (1-12).
Mozart, *Jupiter Symphony,* K551, Finale (1-8).
Dvořák, *Silhouette,* Op. 8, No. 4, Meno mosso.
Schubert, *Waltzes,* Op. 18a, No. 9;
     German Dances, Op. 33, No. 5.
Brahms, *Treachery,* Op. 105, No. 5 (4-7).
Chopin, *B Minor Sonata,* Op. 58, First Movement (1-4).
Schumann, *Novelletten,* Op. 21, No. 8, Trio II.
Beethoven, *Missa Solemnis,* Op. 123, *Agnus Dei* (2-8).

The following passages have been selected for analysis from the above list. Identify the form, chords, and nonharmonic tones. Note especially the various types of minor scales used, and the pivotal and modulatory chords.

BACH, *Praeludium* (Peters Ed., Vol. VIII)

HANDEL, *Messiah*, No. 3 "Every Valley"

Andante

Moderato   SCHUBERT, *Death and the Maiden*

MENDELSSOHN, *Piano Concerto*, Op. 25

Andante

CHOPIN, *Piano Sonata*, Op. 58 (Adapted)

Allegro (1st move. Pr. Th.)

Poco allegretto   BRAHMS, *Third Symphony*, Op. 90

MOZART, *Jupiter Symphony*, K551, Finale

Allegro molto

Chapter XXV

EMBELLISHING $^6_4$ CHORDS
(THE IV$^6_4$)

Ex. 189

BRAHMS (1833 – 1897), *Hungarian Dance No. 5* (Adapted)

Allegro

FOLK SONGS and dances have attracted many composers, from Haydn to Bartók, but no one has used them more skilfully than has Brahms in his arrangements of 21 *Hungarian Dances,* from which the above passage is adapted. Listen to it again, noting its vigor and passionate intensity. The beginning seems to suggest the low, dark tones of the violin or viola played by a gypsy fiddler. Note the effect of the change of register in measure 9, and the acceleration made by the rushing sixteenth notes from measure 13 onward. Has the mood of the melody been heightened by the chords and cadences as well as by this change of register and pace? Observe that the mode is minor, and since F sharp is the key tone, the borrowed key signature of A major is used.[1]

The chord background is naturally simple, in keeping with the folk tune. Sing the essential bass notes while the melody is being played, noting the relatively few harmonic changes in the first phrase (measures 1 to 8), and the consecutive inversions in the second phrase (measures 13 and 14). What chord is defined by the pattern of notes in the accompaniment figure of the first measure? In this case, the first tone indicates the harmony, the others being largely rhythmic in effect. The clash in measure 3 is due to the pedal point in the bass, the real chord being a seventh chord built on E sharp. (See Chapter XXX.) In measure 5, this stationary bass tone forms a new chord. Listen to its quality and arrange its tones, F sharp–B–D, in thirds, as in Example 190.

---

[1] Learn the F sharp minor scale with its signature of three sharps (F sharp, C sharp, and G sharp). Write the three forms of the scale in treble and bass, first with accidentals, then with this signature. Sing each form from memory.

Ex. 190

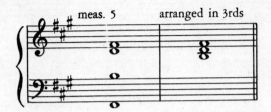

Obviously it is a B–D–F sharp chord whose chord-fifth (F sharp) is in the bass, forming a B minor chord in the second inversion, notated B$^6_4$. Name it in the key of F sharp minor, and then sing and resolve it in *arpeggio* form to the chord of measure 5, thus:

Ex. 191

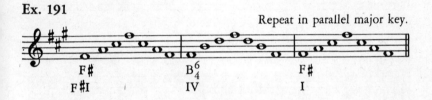

Repeat in parallel major key.

Observe that this new IV$^6_4$ chord (Example 191, measure 2) has the same bass tone as the I chord, and so it is often used, as here, between two fundamental tonic chords for harmonic variety. Sing the following passages with this point in mind:

Ex. 192   OLIVER

Sicilian Folk Song

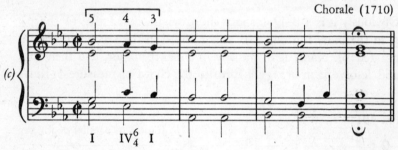

Chorale (1710)

Scotch Folk Song

BACH, Chorale

PRAETORIUS (1609)

I   IV$\frac{6}{4}$ I

Plagal Cadence

Chorale (1800)

IV   IV$\frac{6}{4}$ I

Consider the points of likeness and the differences in regard to voice leading and rhythmic location of the IV$\frac{6}{4}$ in Example 192. Note that in each passage, unessential tones are harmonized — either neighboring tones as at (*a*) and (*b*), passing tones as at (*c*) and (*d*), or repeated tones as at (*e*), (*f*), and (*g*). From this example, it is clear that the chord-fifth (the bass tone) is as in the I$\frac{6}{4}$. In the group I–IV$\frac{6}{4}$–I, observe that the bass and the voice that doubles in both remain *stationary* while the other two voices move stepwise. Rhythmically, the IV$\frac{6}{4}$ occurs either on strong or weak pulses, usually the latter.

Play or sing Example 192 again, substituting a fundamental IV for each IV$\frac{6}{4}$. The second inversion of the IV chord, which resolves on a stationary bass tone, does not give the effect of chord *progression,* but merely a sense of chord *expansion.* This test shows very clearly the nonessential harmonic quality of the IV$^6_4$ Consequently, it is often called an *embellishing $^6_4$ chord,* since its effect is to decorate and expand the effect of the I-chord.

Locate the IV$^6_4$ chord in one or more of these songs or in other familiar music:

> *America*
> *The Vacant Chair*
> *The Battle Cry of Freedom*
> *Keep the Home Fires Burning*
> *Home Sweet Home*
> *Old Folks at Home*
> *Massa's in the Cold Ground*
> *Darling Nelly Gray*
> *Carry Me Back to Old Virginny* (chorus)
> *There's Music in the Air*
> *Long, Long Ago*
> *Oh Wert Thou in the Cauld Blast*
> *Sweet and Low*
> *Killarney*
> *Wearing O' the Green*
> *The Harp That Once Through Tara's Halls*
> *Kathleen Mavoureen*
> *Silent Night*

Obviously it is most frequently found in simple music in which the bass is rather inactive. It is very rarely used in chorale style where the bass is treated melodically.

Consider the melodic and rhythmic use of the IV$^6_4$ used. Although a number of ways are suggested in Example 192, perhaps the most typical are those in (*a*) and (*b*). Note the scale numbers of these progressions, then sing this phrase from an old chorale:

Ex. 193   CRÜGER (1598–1662)

Sing the chord roots while the melody is being played, then, using them as guides, construct a good bass for the tune. After deciding on a bass line, compare it with the following by singing each bass alone first, then both parts together, thus:

Ex. 194*

*The entire chorale, "Now Thank We All Our God," may be found in *The Home and Community Song Book* (E. C. Schirmer Co.), page 177; *The Golden Book* (Hall and McCreary), page 65; and *The Sixth Book of Songs*, Foresman (American Book Co.), page 290. If possible, compare these three versions.

A comparison of these basses leads to the following conclusions:

Bass 1 is monotonous and shows the weakness of too frequent use of the IV$^6_4$ in chorale harmonization.

Bass 2 is better, especially in the last two measures, although the repeated bass tone D, anticipating the cadence, is weak.

Bass 3 is more interesting.

Bass 4 is somewhat similar to bass 3, and is considerably improved when the inner voices are added, thus:

Ex. 195

Bass 4

Bass 5, however, is by far the best, judged from the general effect and smoothness of the individual voice leadings, thus:

Ex. 196

Bass 5

Compare these different versions carefully by singing and listening to them. All accidentals outside the key are optional. Test their effect by omitting them. The figurations are given to illustrate the use of this system of musical shorthand. (See Chapter XXI, page 366.) Identify all chords and nonharmonic tones.

To summarize the use of the IV$^6_4$ chord: note that the bass and the voice doubling it remain stationary, while the other two voices move stepwise. Frequently, this stepwise movement results in the melodic patterns 3-4-3 or 5-6-5. Sometimes, however, the upper tones of these groups are treated as nonharmonic rather than as harmonic neighbors of the I chord. The effect is entirely different.[2] The IV$^6_4$ is also used to harmonize the fourth scale step when it connects the third and fifth steps in a tonic chord, or for the repeated key tone at a cadence. It gives the effect of expanding, or embellishing, the tonic chord and in so doing loses its subdominant value. Because of this nonharmonic effect, the IV$^6_4$ is more generally used on the unaccented part of the beat or measure as a substitute for the fundamental I chord. In melodies it is useful for harmonizing an upper neighboring tone or a passing tone over a stationary tonic bass. In writing test all its effects aurally by singing or playing the passage.

Review:

1. The signature and construction of the F sharp minor scale.
2. The construction and resolution of the IV$^6_4$ chord.
3. The doubling and rhythmic locations of the IV$^6_4$ chord.
4. What is meant by an embellishing $^6_4$ chord.
5. Whether the IV$^6_4$ gives a feeling of harmonic progression, and why.
6. The types of melodic progression for which it is most frequently used.
7. The voice leading in the IV$^6_4$ chord.
8. In what type of vocal music it is most used, and why.

For Further Study, Determine:

1. Between what pitches the augmented second occurs in the F sharp harmonic minor scale.
2. The difference in quality between the IV$^6_4$ in the major and minor modes.
3. Why the IV$^6_4$ usually occurs on a weak or subdivided beat.
4. Why the IV$^6_4$ gives the effect of harmonic embellishment rather than progression.
5. Why two of the upper voices of the IV$^6_4$ usually resolve stepwise.

---

[2] See Beethoven, *Hammerklavier Sonata*, Op. 106, First Movement (1-4).

6. Whether the bass of the chord succession I–IV$^6_4$–I forms a pedal point, and why.

7. One strong and one weak point in each bass of Example 194.

I — Assignment for Writing

1. Scan the following poem and set it to music for mixed voices with violin *obbligato,* preferably in the key of F sharp minor. Try to suggest the mood of the dance, noting suggestions for meter and combination of melodies in the poem. (Accompaniment optional.)

> Now let the sleep-tune blend with the play-tune,
> Weaving the mystical spell of the dance;
> Lighten the deep tune, soften the gay tune,
> Mingle a tempo that turns in a trance.
> Half of it sighing, half of it smiling,
> Smoothly it swings, with a triplicate beat;
> Calling, replying, yearning, beguiling,
> Wooing the heart and bewitching the feet.
>
> *Dance Music — Henry van Dyke*[3]

2. Arrange the theme of one of Brahms' *Hungarian Dances* (possibly Example 189 transposed to G minor), or similar folk dances for four instruments played by members of your class, and have it performed. (Optional.)

3. Add the alto and tenor voices (in that order) to at least one of the following passages:

Figured Basses: BACH, Chorale

---

[3] Reprinted from *Music and Other Poems* by Henry van Dyke; copyright 1904 by Charles Scribner's Sons, 1934 by Henry van Dyke; used by permission of the publishers.

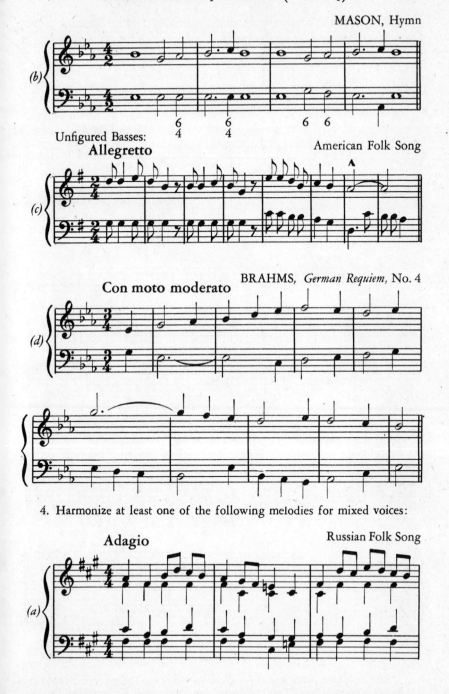

4. Harmonize at least one of the following melodies for mixed voices:

Fine   D.S. al Fine

Chorale

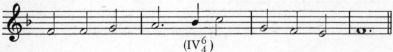

Chorale (1666)

(IV$^6_4$)

Chorale (1797)

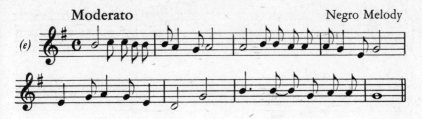

(e) Moderato   Negro Melody

(f) Allegro   Traditional

(g) Allegro   SULLIVAN, *Gondoliers,* Finale

(h) Moderato   SILCHER

(i) Adagio — SCHUBERT, *In the Red of Evening*

(j) Molto lento — SCHUBERT, *By the Sea*

Harmonize with the melody in the tenor voice

(k) Maestoso — HAYDN, *Chorale of St. Anthony*

Reprinted by permission from A Book of Songs, Concord Series No. 14. Published and copyrighted by the E. C. Schirmer Music Company.

5. Harmonize at least one of the following melodies for piano:

BRAHMS, *Hungarian Dance No. 5* (Adapted)

(a) Allegro

F$\sharp$V$^6_5$ VI

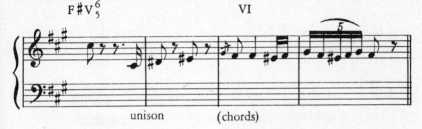

unison   (chords)

BRAHMS, *Hungarian Dance No. 4*

Poco sostenuto

II$^6_5$

V

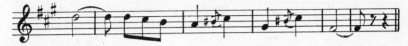

BRAHMS, *Hungarian Dance No. 7*

Allegretto vivace

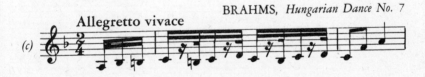

(Theme II)

Allegretto   MOZART, *A Major Piano Sonata*, K331

(d)

Moderato   SCHUBERT, *Ecossaisen*, Op. 18a, No. 3

(e)

IV$\frac{6}{4}$ V$_7$

Fine   *D.S. al Fine*

American Folk Song

Moderato

(f)

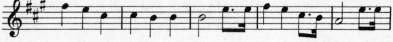

Allegretto   P. SCHARWENKA, *Moment Musical*

(g)

Acc. fig.

II — *Assignment for Playing*

1. Harmonize any of the melodies in the *Assignment for Writing* (5).
2. Improvise a Hungarian Dance in *A–B–A* form, using the following motives. Make part I a phrase, repeated in F sharp minor. Part II will be a phrase ending on the V$_7$ of B minor, and part III will be a single phrase without repetition. Repeat parts II and III together and extend at the end (see Chapter XXII, page 388).

Vivace   BRAHMS, *Hungarian Dance No, 13* (Adapted)

Part I

continue by transposing phrase to F♯ minor.

Part II

Figure   Sequence

3. Improvise melodies in F sharp minor as in Example 174, No. 4 (Chapter XXII, page 388). Experiment with modulations to diatonic keys suggested in Example 158 (Chapter XX, page 344). Repeat melodies from memory and harmonize.

4. Continue playing by ear familiar minor melodies. Recall music in the key of F sharp minor, for example, the minor section of Dvořák's *Humoresque*.

5. Transpose the following modulatory chord patterns to all minor keys previously studied:

6. Devise original modulatory patterns as suggested in Example 158 (Chapter XX, page 344). For example, experiment using a motive in sequence, thus:

(Sing in four parts, noting use of motive.)

7. Transpose simple F sharp minor melodic and harmonic phrases in this chapter up a minor third to A minor. Review notes on transposition in *Assignment for Playing,* Chapter XI, page 182, and Chapter XVIII, page 312. Experiment transposing passages in other minor keys to F sharp minor.

III — Assignment for Listening

1. *Oral dictation:* harmonic recognition only. (Name chords by quality, letter, and Roman numeral.)

> *Home and Community Song Book.* Concord Series No. 2. Nos. 44, 45, 60, 69.
>
> *Golden Book:* pp. 23, 44, 52, 59, 60, 61, 62, 64, 66, 67, 71, 76, 102, 104, 114.

Schumann, *Lieder,* Nos. 19, 24;
      Album for the Young, Op. 68, Nos. 8, 19 (1-4), 20.
Mozart, *Violin Sonata VIII,* K296, Andante sustenuto (1-8);
      Violin Sonata XVII, K526, Presto, subordinate theme;
      Piano Sonatas, K545, Andante (1-8),
               K309, Rondo (1-8),
               K498a, in B flat, Rondo (1-16);
      Viennese Sonatina, No. 1, Trio (1-4),
               No. 4, Andante grazioso (1-8).
Schubert, *C Major Symphony VII,* Trio (1-16);
      German Dances, Nos. 3, 6;
      Valses Nobles, No. 6 (1-8);
      Ecossaises, Nos. 1, 2;
      Moment Musical, Op. 94, No. 5 (1-8).
Haydn, *C Minor Symphony* (Peters Edition), No. 9, Trio;
      Military Symphony, Allegro (9-16); Allegretto (1-8).
Sullivan, *The Mikado,* "Brightly Dawns our Wedding Day"
      (ending);
      The Pirates of Penzance, "With Catlike Tread."
Schubert, *B flat Piano Sonata,* Molto moderato (1-8),
               Scherzo (1-8).
Beethoven, *Piano Sonata,* Op. 27, No. 1, Adagio (1-4);
      Symphony IV, Op. 60, Adagio (1-8);
      Symphony V, Op. 67, Finale, subordinate theme (1-4);
      Polonaise, Op. 89, principal theme (1-8).
Foresman Manual, "Amarylis," page 51;
      IV, Light Cavalry Overture (von Suppe), page 26;
      III, Lullaby (Mozart), page 50.
Mendelssohn, *Songs Without Words,* Nos. 5 (1-5), 12, 32 (1-15).
Tchaikovsky, *Symphony V,* Op. 64, Valse, Trio (1-4);
      Album for the Young, Op. 39, Nos. 3 (*The Hobby*
      Horse), 5 (*March of the Tin Soldiers*).
Dvořák, *Humoresque,* Op. 101, No. 7, Più lento (1-4).
Brahms, *Variations on Hungarian Song,* Op. 21, No. 2 (1-4).
Gluck, "Dance of the Happy Spirits" (*Orpheus*) (*Play a Tune,*
      p. 45).

2. *Written dictation (quality, bass, melody, and name of chord).*
    Foresman VI, Chorale (1-12), page 286.
    Home and Community Song Book. Concord Series No. 2. Nos. 17,
      19, 26, 120.
    Green Book, Twice 55: Nos. 81, 82
    Brown Book, Twice 55: No. 76 (1-4), 77, 131 (1-8), 143
      (chorus), 147.
    Golden Book: Dip Boys, Dip the Oar, page 102.
    Play a Tune, Slavonic Dance, Op. 46, No. 1 (Dvořák), page 78.

Mozart, *F Major Piano Sonata*, K332, Allegro (71-76).

IV — Assignment for Analysis

Brahms, *Symphony I*, Op. 68, Finale (1-8) ;
    Hungarian Dances, No. 17 (1-16), No. 13 (1-6) ;
    Intermezzo, Op. 118, No. 2 (1-4) ;
    Waltz, Op. 39, No. 15 (1-4).
Mozart, *Piano Sonata*, K545, Allegro (1-4) ;
    The Violet, K476 (1-7) ;
    String Quartet, K575, Andante (1-8).
Schubert, *Valses Sentimentales*, Op. 50, No. 5 (1-8) ;
    German Dances, Op. 33, Nos. 3, 6, 12;
    Grand Sonata No. 2 in A Major, Andantino (1-18),
      Trio ;
    Symphony VII in C Major, Trio (1-16).
Raff, *Cavatina* (1-4).
Schumann, *Carnival*, Op. 9, March (1-8).
Chopin, *Polonaise*, Op. 44 (9-16) ;
    Waltz, Op. 34, No. 3 (17-24) ;
    Mazurka, Op. 59, No. 3 (1-8),
      Op. 33, No. 4 (1-12).
Haydn, *E flat Symphony* (*Kettle Drum*), I, Allegro con spirito
    (1-4) ;
    G Major Symphony (*Surprise*), Introduction (1-4).
Mendelssohn, *Elijah*, No. 26, "It is Enough" (2-9).
Liszt, *Les Préludes*, A Major section.
Beethoven, *Andante in F*, B flat section.
Wolf, *Drunken Must We Be* (1-4).
Grieg, *Norweigian Dance*, Op. 46, No. 3.
Dvořák, *Valse Gracieuse*, Op. 54, No. 1, C sharp Minor section.
Sullivan, *The Mikado*, "Tit Willow" (4-11).

The following passages have been selected for analysis from the above list. Identify form, chords, and nonharmonic tones. Note the types of minor scales used, and the pivotal and modulatory chords.

BRAHMS, *First Symphony*, Op. 68, Finale

Allegro non troppo, ma con brio

(a)

BRAHMS, *Hungarian Dance No. 17*

Andantino

(b)

etc.   cadence thus, meas. 15 — 16

BRAHMS, *Intermezzo*, Op. 118, No. 2

Andante teneramente

(c)

etc.

MOZART, *Piano Sonata*,. K545

Allegro

(d)

MOZART, *String Quartet*, K575 (Adapted)

Andante

SCHUBERT, *Symphony No. 7 in C Major*, Trio

Allegro vivace

SCHUMANN, *Carnival*, Op. 9, March (Adapted)

Non allegro

MENDELSSOHN, *Elijah*, No. 26, "It is Enough"

Adagio

Chapter XXVI

PASSING $\frac{6}{4}$ CHORDS

(THE V_4^6)

Ex. 197

BEETHOVEN (1770—1827) *Piano Sonata,*
"Quasi una Fantasia," Op. 27, No. 2 (1802)

Adagio sostenuto*

*Preceded by four measures of introduction.

OF ALL Beethoven's piano works, none is better known than the *Moonlight Sonata,* from which this excerpt is quoted. There are many reasons for its popularity, the chief being, of course, its wide musical appeal. The principal theme quoted above is far too short to convey this appeal adequately. To fully appreciate it, hear the entire work. The second movement, beginning thus:

Ex. 198 Allegretto

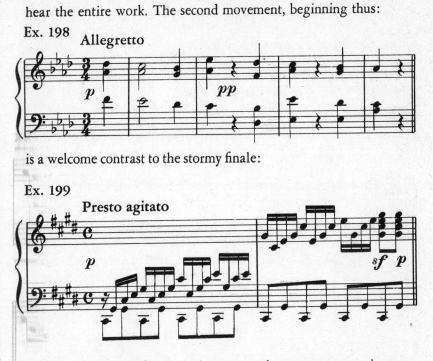

is a welcome contrast to the stormy finale:

Ex. 199

Presto agitato

and has been called a lyric intermezzo between two tragic nocturnes, or, as Liszt said, "A flower between two abysses."

But in addition to the work's musical appeal, there are other reasons for its fame. The title has probably increased the enjoyment for many, although Beethoven himself did not name the work.[1]

To return to Example 197, the first chord establishes the mode and key, obviously C sharp minor.[2] Name all the chords and decide through which one the cadential modulation to E major is made.

<hr />

[1] See Grove, *Beethoven and His Nine Symphonies*, p. 51. (London: Novello & Co., Ltd., 1896.) The *Moonlight Sonata* was probably named by the contemporary critic and poet, Rellstab.

[2] Write the three forms of the C sharp minor scale in treble and bass, first with accidentals only, then with its signature of four sharps (F sharp–C sharp–G sharp–D sharp). Sing each form from memory.

Consider this later variant of the theme:

Ex. 200

*Chromatic chord.

It begins in F sharp minor and ends in C sharp minor. Analyze the modulation. Name the chords, especially the last chord in measure 2. Compare this passage with Example 197, page 470.

Here we have a $\frac{6}{4}$ chord used as a *passing chord* between two essential harmonies. How do the bass and soprano differ from those of the embellishing $\frac{6}{4}$ chords discussed in Chapter XXV, page 455? In passing $\frac{6}{4}$ chords the outside voices often are the same tones in reverse order: in this case, the soprano moves *up* B sharp–C sharp–D sharp, while the bass moves *down* D sharp–C sharp–B sharp. The $\frac{6}{4}$ chord harmonizes the middle tone (C sharp) which appears in both bass and soprano.

Sometimes, however, the outside voices either move in similar motion as consecutive sixths (see Example 198), or the soprano remains stationary, as in the coda of the last movement of this sonata, thus:

Ex. 201

Presto agitato

Chord scheme

$$F^{\#}_6 \quad C^{\#} {}^6_4 \quad F^{\times}_{07}$$

It will be observed that these passing $^6_4$ chords occur on the weak pulse of the measure in Example 200, page 472, and on the strong pulse in Example 201. Though they are found on both, probably they occur most often on weak or subdivided pulses. This is because the passing $^6_4$, like the embellishing $^6_4$ chords, are not essential chords either harmonically or rhythmically.

The doubling in passing $^6_4$ chords is no problem, as the chord-fifth is automatically doubled when the voices progress stepwise.

Thus far, we have examined the passing use of $^6_4$ chords in instrumental music. Now observe how they are used vocally, by singing the following passage from Haydn's oratorio, *The Creation*:

Ex. 202

Allegro

Find the passing $\frac{6}{4}$ chord and name it in the key. Here the outside voices move in typical contrary motion between a triad and its first inversion. It is easy to hear the unessential quality of the V_4^6 chord, since the tone D in the outside voices gives the effect of a passing tone, and the tone B in the tenor, the effect of a lower neighbor. Note that the progression of the voices automatically doubles the fifth of the V_4^6 chord. Find other passages in choral music that use this chord pattern. Sing and resolve the V_4^6 in *arpeggio* form as used in Example 202, thus:

Ex. 203

$$C_6 \qquad\qquad G_4^6 \qquad\qquad C$$
$$C: I_6 \qquad\qquad V_4^6 \qquad\qquad I$$

(Repeat in parallel minor key)

Examples 198-202 inclusive show the use of the I, IV, and V chords as passing $^6_4$ chords. Of these, the V^6_4 chord is the one most generally used in musical literature. The other triads (II, III, VI, and VII) are rarely used in the second inversion as either passing or embellishing chords. This emphasis on the use of the principal triads as passing or embellishing $^6_4$ chords is probably due to their harmonic importance in the key, as discussed in Chapter III, page 31. The unessential harmonic character of· $^6_4$ chords has been noted above, and, consequently, being inherently weak, they appear as variations of the strongest chords in the key — the I, IV, and V.

We have noted the stepwise melodic progression typical of passing $^6_4$ chords.[3] Use them in harmonizing this melody. Sing the tune alone first, trying to sense the general harmonic background, thus:

Ex. 204   ORLANDO GIBBONS (1583 – 1625)

Repeat, singing the indicated chord roots, while the melody is being played. From this background, construct a good bass line, perhaps using the passing $^6_4$ for ascending and descending three-tone scale passages as in Example 205.

---

[3] Both passing and embellishing $^6_4$ chords rarely are used in chorales, as both involve three repeated tones in one of the upper voices, which hinders the melodic flow of that part. Hence, the VII$_6$ is usually found in chorales rather than the V^6_4.

Ex. 205

*What passing $\frac{6}{4}$ is suggested by the melodic line in measure 5, and why is it not used?

    We have changed somewhat our original chord background, as is sometimes necessary in working out a bass, because of the opportunity to use the passing $\frac{6}{4}$ chords in measures 1 and 3, the passing $\frac{4}{3}$ in measure 5, and the II$\frac{6}{5}$ to avoid chord repetition in the last measure. Have both voices sing together and suggest improvements. Fill in first the tenor, then the alto. Why is the doubled F sharp necessary on the first beat of measure 2?

    This version is adequate as far as it goes, but it falls short musically of the composer's harmonization as given in Example 206.

Ex. 206

Sing it in four parts, listening to the movement of other voices. Note that, although the melody in measures 1, 3, and 5 is sequential, the harmonization is not, for reasons best known to the composer. Explain the exceptional doubling in the IV chord on the last beat of measure 5. Compare measures 6 in Examples 205 and 206. Which is preferable? Contrast the use of the passing $^6_4$ chords in these two examples.

To summarize, then, the second inversions of the I, IV, and V chords are useful as *passing chords* between a triad and its first inversion in either order or between two chords whose bass notes are a third apart. Often the outside voices use the same tones in reverse order. Although the bass always moves stepwise three tones, the soprano *either* remains stationary *or* progresses to its lower neighbor and back again. Two of the upper voices move stepwise, which doubles the chord-fifth. The passing $^6_4$, like other $^6_4$ chords, is unessential harmonically, and most often occurs on unaccented or subdivided beats. Of the passing $^6_4$ chords, the V$^6_4$ is perhaps the most frequently used and is employed thus: I–V$^6_4$–I$_6$, or I$_6$–V$^6_4$–I, the soprano being usually 1-2-3 or 3-2-1.

Remember that fluency in using these chords will come not

from memorizing rules, but from the development of taste through feeling, and, as Haydn said, "an educated ear."

Review:

1. The signature and construction of the three forms of the C sharp minor scale.
2. The construction and resolution of the V_4^6 chord.
3. The doubling and rhythmic location of the V_4^6 chord.
4. Why the V_4^6 is unessential harmonically.
5. What is meant by a passing $\frac{6}{4}$ chord, and which chords are so used.
6. How each voice progresses in a passing $\frac{6}{4}$ chord.
7. The most typical melodic progression resulting from the use of the passing $\frac{6}{4}$ chord.
8. Why both the embellishing and passing $\frac{6}{4}$ chords are rarely used in chorales.
9. What chord is usually substituted for the V_4^6 in chorales.

For Further Study, Determine:

1. Why the leading tone of the C sharp harmonic minor scale is B sharp rather than C natural.
2. The quality of the V_4^6 in both modes.
3. Whether the chord-fifth is always doubled in passing $\frac{6}{4}$ chords. (See Example 206.)
4. Why the inner voices are shifted in Example 202, measure 1.
5. Whether $\frac{6}{4}$ chords are ever used consecutively.
6. What type of $\frac{6}{4}$ chord is sometimes entered by a skip in the bass.

I — Assignment for Writing

1. Scan the following poem and set it to music for mixed voices, preferably in the key of C sharp minor. Why would the *A–B* form be appropriate for this poem? (Accompaniment optional.)

I am the God Thor,　　　　Here amid icebergs
I am the War God,　　　　Rule I the nations;
I am the Thunderer!　　　This is my hammer,
Here in my Northland,　　Miolner the mighty;
My fastness and fortress,　Giants and sorcerers
Reign I forever!　　　　　Cannot withstand it!

The Saga of King Olaf — *H. W. Longfellow*

2. Arrange the *Allegretto* (measures 1-36) from Beethoven's *Moonlight Sonata,* Op. 27, No. 2, for four instruments played by members of your class, and have it performed. (Optional.)

3. Add the alto and tenor voices (in that order) to at least one of the following passages:

Figured basses:

Chorale (1795)

(a)

Chorale (1833)

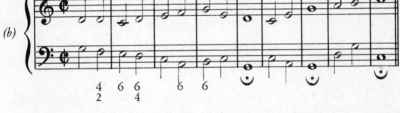

(b)

Unfigured basses:

BACH, *371 Chorales*

(c)

Hebrew Melody (arr. by Costa)

From High School Songs for Every Occasion, *by Gartlan and Donnelly. Published by Hinds, Hayden & Eldredge, Inc.*

4. Harmonize at least one of the following melodies for mixed voices:

5. Harmonize at least one of the following melodies for piano. Note new accompaniment figure in (a) and (b). Identify form of each melody used.

Allegretto   SCHUBERT, *Impromptu,* Op. 90, No. 4

(a)

Non allegro   SCHUMANN, *Little Lullabye,* Op. 124, No. 6

(b)

Allegro   SCHUBERT, *C Minor Piano Sonata*, Finale

Tempo giusto   CHOPIN, *Waltz*, Op. 64, No. 2

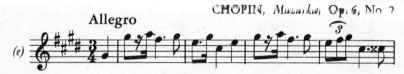

Allegro   CHOPIN, *Mazurka*, Op. 6, No. 2

Moderato   English Folk Song

II — *Assignment for Playing*

1. Harmonize any of the melodies in the *Assignment for Writing* (5).

2. Improvise an *A–B–A* form in the style of the *Assignment for Writing* (5a), or Example 197, using either of the following motives. (Details of form and modulation optional.)

3. Improvise melodies in C sharp minor, *A–B–A* form. (Details optional.)

4. Play by ear in the key of C minor, first the melody alone, then with accompaniment, the folk tune, *Charlie Is My Darlin'* (Example 141). Repeat in C sharp minor. Recall music written in C sharp minor, for example, Rachmaninoff's *C sharp Minor Prelude.*

5. Play and transpose the following modulatory chord patterns to all minor keys previously studied:

6. Devise original modulatory patterns as suggested in Example 158, Chapter XX. For example, experiment using a motive in sequence, thus:

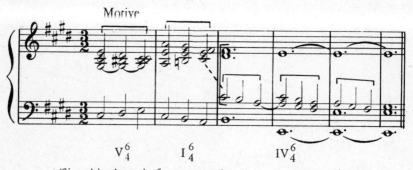

(Sing this phrase in four parts to hear how the motive is used.)

7. Transpose simple C sharp minor melodic and harmonic phrases in this chapter down a major third to A minor. Review notes on transposition in *Assignment for Playing,* Chapter XI, page 183, and Chapter XVIII, page 314. Experiment transposing passages in other keys to C sharp minor.

III — Assignment for Listening

1. *Oral dictation:* harmonic recognition only. (Name by quality, letter, and Roman numeral.)

Beethoven, *Piano Sonata,* Op. 2, No. 3, Trio.
Schumann, *Lieder,* No. 46 (18-14 from end);
   Hunting Song, Op. 82, No. 8 (1-8).
Schubert, *Gratzer Walzer,* Op. 91a, No. 3;
   Wanderer Fantasie, Op. 15, Adagio (1-18);
   Impromptu, Op. 90, No. 4, Trio;
   Moment Musical, Op. 94, No. 4 (1-8);
   Unfinished Symphony Andante (66-81) subordinate
    theme.
Chopin, *B flat Minor Scherzo,* Op. 31, C sharp Minor section;
   Rondo, Op. 16, Introduction (1-8);
   Prelude, Op. 28, No. 10; No. 15 (C sharp Minor section),
    Op. 45 (1-4).
Brahms, *Love Lasts For Aye,* Op. 43, No. 1 (1-12).

2. *Written dictation (quality, bass, melody, and name of chord).*

Golden Book: My Faith Looks up to Thee, p. 59;
   Abide With Me, p. 59;
   While Shepherds Watch, p. 74;
   Lead Kindly Light, p. 64;
   Men of Harlech, p. 102.
High School Songs (Gartlan), *The God of Abraham Praise,* p. 35.
New Episcopal Hymnal, No. 264, *Webb,*
    No. 440, *Aberystwyth* (also in *Green
     Book,* No. 83),
    No. 584, *Materna,*
    No. 589, *O Quanta Qualia.*
Choralbuch, Nos. 21, 53, 61, 62, 100, 107, 116, 127, 156, 162,
 169, 178, 204.

IV — Assignment for Analysis

Mozart, *C Major Piano Sonata,* K330, Andante (1-4);
   A Minor Piano Sonata, K310, Andante (1-4).
Beethoven, *Piano Sonata,* Op. 14, No. 1, Allegretto (1-8),
     Op. 32, No. 2, Largo (1-6);
   Phantasie, Op. 77, Allegro mo non troppo (1-8).
Schubert, *The Wanderer* (23-31);
   Waltzes, Op. 18a, No. 3.

Chopin, *Mazurka,* Op. 68, No. 2, Poco più mosso (1-8),
         Op. 41, No. 1 (1-8),
         Op. 67, No. 4, A Major section;
     Polonaise, Op. 40, No. 1 (9-12);
     Waltz, Op. 64, No. 2, Più moso (1-8).
Schumann, *Symphonic Etudes,* Op. 13, theme (1-4);
     Romance, Op. 28, No. 3, Intermezzo I (1-9).
Brahms, *Waltzes,* Op. 29, No. 7,
         Op. 16, No. 16;
     Ever Gentler Grows My Slumber, Op. 105, No. 2 (1-3).
Dvořák, *Silhouette,* Op. 8, No. 4 (1-8).

The following passages have been selected for analysis from the above list. Identify the form, chords, and nonharmonic tones. Note the types of minor scales used, and the pivotal and modulatory chords.

MOZART, *C Major Piano Sonata,* K330

Andante cantabile

(a)

BEETHOVEN, *Sonata,* Op. 14, No. 1

Allegretto

(b)

*Chromatic chord.

BEETHOVEN, *Piano Sonata*, Op. 31, No. 2

*Chromatic embellishment.

SCHUBERT, *The Wanderer*

*Chromatic chord.

SCHUMANN, *Symphonic Etudes,* Op. 13, Theme (Adapted)

(e)

DVOŘÁK, *Silhouette,* Op. 8, No. 4

(f)

For additional examples of the passing $^6_4$ chord, see Beethoven, *Sonata Pathétique,* Op. 13, Introduction (1, 5, 6), and *Piano Sonata,* Op. 31, No. 2, Allegro (33-42).

Summary III

Examination of musical literature in Part III (Chapters XVII-XXVI), showed many ways in which composers solved their melodic, harmonic, and formal problems, and from this study certain techniques and standards of taste emerged. The facts learned may be summarized thus:

First, in regard to scales, two medieval patterns (modes) have survived as the principal basis of our music, the Ionian or C major scale, and the Aeolian or A minor scale. For harmonic and melodic reasons, three different forms of this minor scale are used today:

(1) The original Aeolian, or natural minor, corresponding to the white keys on the piano beginning on A.

(2) The harmonic minor, which added a raised leading tone (G sharp) to the natural minor scale.

(3) The melodic minor, which added both the raised sixth and seventh steps (F sharp–G sharp) ascending, but which retained the natural form of the scale descending.

From their modal origin, it is clear why both C major and A minor today use the same key signature, since they both consist of the same pitches (the white keys on the piano). Such major and minor scales, using the same key signature, are called *relative scales.*

But there was another and closer connection between the two modes — that of a common tonal center, or key tone. This relationship was confirmed by the comparative use of the two modes as found in musical literature. Thus, aurally, the minor scale became an alteration of the major scale beginning on the same pitch. The one essential alteration for minor was the lowered third step — the lowered sixth and seventh steps being optional. These major and minor scales, which had the same tonic, were named *parallel scales.*

Aurally, it was apparent that the parallel major and minor scales (same name) were more closely related than the relative scales (same signature). This is true because music is heard, not seen.

Thinking of the parallel relationship aided in playing, singing, and writing new minor scales, for it was found that any major scale could be made minor by lowering its third and sixth degrees one half tone, and then borrowing the key signature of the lowered third step. In using this borrowed signature, the accidentals necessary for the sixth and seventh steps depended on whether the harmonic or melodic forms of the scale were used.

Thus, though the historical sequence of the scales was found to be interesting, it was the aural (tonic) relationship that eventually proved to be the most practical.

The use of the various forms of the minor scale depended upon the melodic and harmonic context of the sixth and seventh scale steps as follows:

(1) The melodic minor scale was used only for 6-7, or 7-6, when one or both were foreign tones. The choice between the raised and lowered sixth and seventh steps depended on which step was harmonic. When both were foreign tones, over the I chord, they were altered according to the scale direction. Otherwise, they are altered similarly according to the chord used.

(2) The harmonic minor scale was used when both the sixth and seventh steps were chord tones.

Thus, in Chapters XIX-XXVI, the historical and aural relationships of the major and the minor modes were discussed, and may be summarized as follows:

Ex. 207

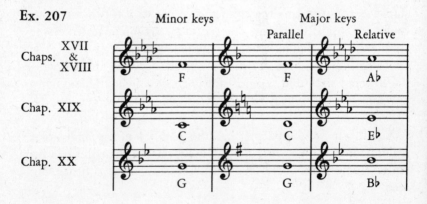

Minor keys   Major keys

Chaps. XVII & XVIII — F — F (Parallel) — Ab (Relative)

Chap. XIX — C — C — Eb

Chap. XX — G — G — Bb

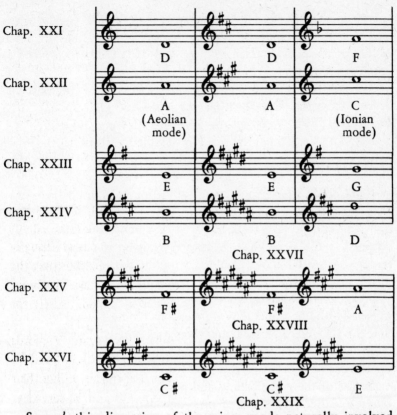

Chap. XXI

D   D   F

Chap. XXII

A   A   C
(Aeolian   (Ionian
mode)   mode)

Chap. XXIII

E   E   G

Chap. XXIV

B   B   D

Chap. XXVII

Chap. XXV

F♯   F♯   A

Chap. XXVIII

Chap. XXVI

C♯   C♯   E

Chap. XXIX

Second, this discussion of the minor mode naturally involved the question of *modulation* and the relative frequency of certain types. Modulations to the dominant were most frequent, and those to relative keys from both modes next in order. Modulations up a third to the mediant from major, and down a third to the submediant from minor were comparatively rare. The consecutive use of parallel keys (C major and C minor) were considered as an interchange of mode within the same tonality — not as a modulation. These statements conclude the discussion of diatonic modulations. Modulations to chromatic keys properly belong to the study of chromatic harmony.

Third, music was arranged in four parts for soprano, alto, .tenor, and bass (mixed voices). The distinction was made between the *position* of a chord (soprano) and its *inversion* (bass). This was a new technique of four-part vocal writing that involved problems of spacing, voice leading, and doubling, which may be summarized thus:

(1) All voices should be an octave or less from the adjacent voice, except the bass which may be more, and none should cross the adjacent voice in either the same or following chords.

(2) The bass tone was usually doubled, except in the first inversion of triads. No tone was doubled in inverted seventh-chords.

(3) Chords whose roots were a third or sixth apart have two tones in common; a fourth or fifth apart, one tone in common; and a second or seventh apart, none. Common tones are usually retained in the same voice. Where there is no common tone, the upper voices often move in contrary motion to the bass. However, all these general principles were frequently modified, usually for improvement in voice leading.

Finally, the first and second inversions of the IV and V chords and the II_6^5 were discussed, and their uses noted. The IV_6 and V_6 were used as substitutes for their fundamental chords. Either their chord root or chord-fifth was doubled. The IV_4^6 and V_4^6 served as examples of the embellishing and passing use of $_4^6$ chords respectively. Neither type sounded or progressed as *real* chords, since both gave the effect of a combination of neighboring or passing tones.

The use of these $_4^6$ chords was aided by recognizing certain typical melodic progressions which, for convenience, might be summarized thus:

Ex. 208

(a) Embellishing $_4^6$ chords

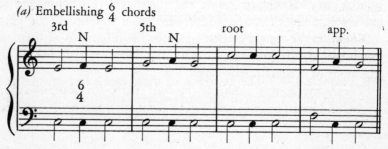

(b) Passing $\frac{6}{4}$ chords

N = neighboring tone; P = passing tone.

In these $\frac{6}{4}$ chords, all voices either moved stepwise or were stationary, and the chord-fifth was doubled in all cases.

The II$\frac{6}{5}$ was used as a substitute for both the II, II$_6$, and IV chords as the chord-seventh formed a link between the II and IV chords. The II$\frac{6}{5}$ harmonized any of its scale steps, 2, 6, or 8, and was resolved by progressing to the V$_7$, V$\frac{4}{2}$, or I$\frac{6}{4}$ chords.

The *organ* or *pedal point* was the only new foreign tone discussed (Chapter XXIV, page 426). Its stationary bass tone gives it a superficial resemblance to embellishing $\frac{6}{4}$ chords (Example 208) which disappears, however, when it is recalled that the pedal point is a foreign tone. The pedal point begins and ends, however, as a chord tone. Pedal points occurred most frequently in the bass on the 1 or 5 of the scale; but occasionally both tones were used together as a *double* or *pastorale pedal point,* or the pedal point appeared in other voices than the bass, and on other scale steps than the tonic or the dominant.

Original writing and improvisation of the various types of small *A–B–A* forms were continued. (See Chapter XXII, page 388, Example 174.) The extension of these forms through the repetition of one or more of the parts was noted; chiefly the repetition *A–A–B–A* or *A–A–B–A–B–A* in either exact or modified form.

Suggestions for Study

Find examples in musical literature of the following technical points discussed in Part III:

(1) Scales.

The harmonic, melodic, and natural minor scales.

(2) Chords.

The first inversion of all triads, the second inversions of the IV and V, and the II_5^6.

(3) Nonharmonic tones.

The single and double pedal point.

(4) Form.

Types of ternary (A–B–A) forms illustrated in Chapter XXII, Example 174, page 388.

Part IV

SECONDARY DISCORDS. ENHARMONIC SCALES

Chapter XXVII

THE II₇ AND OTHER
SECONDARY SEVENTH CHORDS

Ex. 209

Moderato — KREISLER, *Caprice Viennois* (Adapted)

(l.h.)

499

V₉

(See Chapter XXIX)

Permission to reprint this extract, based on an arrangement for piano by Guy Maier, has been granted by the copyright proprietor and publisher, Charles Foley, New York.

T HE MELODY quoted above with its indolent, graceful rhythm is typical of the 19th-century Viennese waltz, popularized by Schubert, and Brahms. Compare these composers' use of the dotted quarter note in their waltzes. (See *Assignment for Analysis,* page 519.)

The prevailing key center is B and the mode is major, indicated by the new key signature of five sharps used for B major.[1]

In passing, an important principle of musical spelling should be noted in connection with the key of B major. What other letter (with an accidental) would represent the same pitch as B when played on the piano? Although there is more than one possibility, C flat is the most practical. This use of two letters for the same pitch is called *enharmonic notation.*[2] It can be applied to scales and chords, and is also useful for modulation. This new scale of B major may be written *enharmonically* as C flat major, thus:

Ex. 210

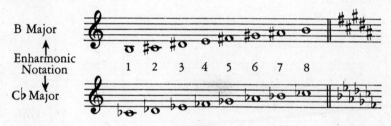

Theoretically, all scales may be written enharmonically, but practically, few are. Thus, in this case, it is obviously easier to use the signature of five sharps (B) than seven flats (C flat). Hence, the key of C flat major is rarely used, and is given here only for reference.

---

[1] Write the B major scale in treble and bass, first with accidentals only, then with its signature of five sharps (F sharp–C sharp–G sharp–D sharp–A sharp). Learn this signature, noting (as usual in major keys) that the name of the key corresponds to that of the tone above the last sharp.

[2] Scientifically B and C flat are different pitches. Their identity on the piano and in writing today is due to a compromise in tuning known as *equal temperament.* Bach's *Well-Tempered* [well-tuned] *Clavier* illustrates the utility of this system of tuning, which is universally accepted today.

In this connection, one must remember that, in order to make notation meaningful, it is necessary to spell consistently in the prevailing key, except in cases of enharmonic modulation. In other words, music is always written according to its meaning in context rather than simply by sound. This is similar to the principle used in the spelling of words, for example, *to, two,* and *too.*

Return now to Example 209, page 499. Play it again, listening especially to the tonality and the cadences. Note that the two-measure accompaniment figure tends to combine the ⁹/₈ measure into a larger metrical unit. Frequently, as here, the time signature does not truly represent the meter heard. The ear, not the eye, is the best judge. The true meter is often indicated by the length of the cadence chord, as in Example 209, since cadences are *harmonic* as well as *melodic* points of repose. With this in mind, identify the form. Would not the meter be clearer if the melody of Example 209 were rewritten either in ⁶/₈ or ¹²/₈, thus:

Ex. 211   KREISLER, *Caprice Viennois*

Are the chords appropriate to the style of the melody? Undoubtedly their rich color is due in part to the use of both dissonance and chromaticism. Find an example of each.

For the present, we shall discuss little of these technical details, and only note that most of the bass dissonances are due to a double pedal point in measures 1 to 16 (see Chapter XXIV, page 427), which is broken up into a two-measure accompaniment figure. Listen to the last four measures. What is the chord in the fourth measure from the end? Spell this chord upward in thirds from the bass tone (C sharp), identify it by letter and number, then sing and resolve it in *arpeggio* form, as in Example 212.

Ex. 212

C$\sharp_7$ F$\sharp_{7\,(9)}$ B

B: II$_7$ V$_{7\,(9)}$ I

(Repeat in parallel minor key)

This new II$_7$ is one of the most used of the *secondary* seventh chords, a term including all diatonic sevenths except the V$_7$. It resolves here to a dominant discord, but it may be followed equally well by the I$^6_4$, especially at a cadence. The voice leading of the II$_7$ is similar to that of the V$_7$, that is, the root may be doubled and the fifth omitted, and the chord seventh may either resolve downward one degree (to V$_7$), or be held stationary (to I$^6_4$).

Listen to the following passage, which contains some other less used diatonic dissonances:

Ex. 213

KUHLAU, *Sonatina,* Op. 88, No. 3

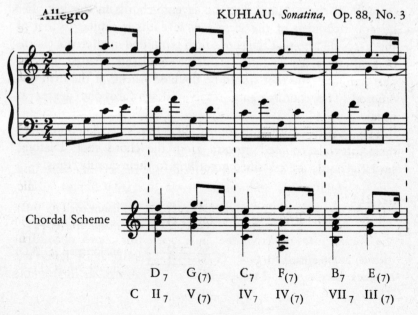

Chordal Scheme

         D$_7$ G$_{(7)}$ C$_7$ F$_{(7)}$ B$_7$ E$_{(7)}$
C   II$_7$ V$_{(7)}$ IV$_7$ IV$_{(7)}$ VII$_7$ III$_{(7)}$

A₇   D₍₇₎   G₇
VI₇   II₍₇₎   V₇

Would this look the same in C flat major? Would it sound the same?

Here we have a series of fundamental seventh-chords moving sequentially. Note that the sevenths of these chords sound like suspensions rather than like part of an essential chord. They include all the possible diatonic seventh-chords in the key. The general treatment of the secondary sevenths is similar to that of the V₇. Note also that the chord-fifth is omitted in alternate chords to facilitate voice leading. If this passage were written in four-part harmony, the root would be doubled whenever the fifth was omitted. The chord-seventh resolves downward one degree as usual.

The quality of seventh-chords, like triads, is determined by their intervals counted upward from the chord root. Diatonic seventh-chords are classified according to their quality, thus:

Ex. 214

(a) Major large 7th   major triad (G-B-D)
                                                       major 7th (G-F♯)

(b) Dominant 7th   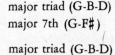   major triad (G-B-D)
                                                       minor 7th (G-F)

(c)   Small 7th 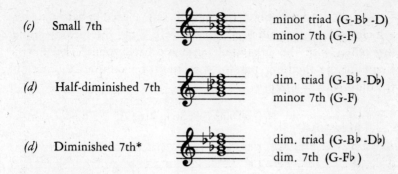 minor triad (G-B♭-D)
minor 7th (G-F)

(d)   Half-diminished 7th   dim. triad (G-B♭-D♭)
minor 7th (G-F)

(d)   Diminished 7th*   dim. triad (G-B♭-D♭)
dim. 7th (G-F♭)

*See Wedge, *Applied Harmony*, Book I, page 109, for a complete list of seventh chords with suggested symbols.

Applying these quality names to the diatonic seventh-chords in both modes, we have:

Ex. 215

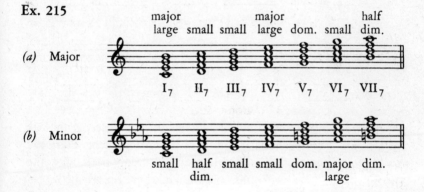

The natural (Aeolian), form of the I₇ and III₇ are given, as the harmonic form is rarely used. This is another indication of the possible cadential origin of the harmonic minor scale. (See Chapter XXX, page 572.)

The tables in Examples 214 and 215 are given for reference only. They enable one to name the differences in quality between the same seventh-chords in the two modes. For example, the II₇ can be identified as a small seventh-chord in major, and a half-diminished seventh-chord in minor.

Now let us consider how this new II$_7$ can be used in harmonizing a melody. Sing this old Netherlands folk song, the melody alone first, then with the suggested harmonic background (I–IV–V). Compare the rhythmic pattern with that of Example 209, noting the difference in effect.

Ex. 216   Netherlands Folk Song (1625), *We Gather Together*
Maestoso

This harmonic background is adequate, but it seems to lack variety and color, especially for a vocal arrangement. Here are two similar but slightly different versions. Sing both with the melody, thus:

Maestoso

Ex. 217

Perhaps there is little to choose between them, although, on the whole, bass 2 seems preferable. For example, the similar stepwise motion in measure 7 between bass 1 and the melody is probably not as desirable as is the fundamental progression in bass 2. Bass 1 could be improved by changing measure 6 to B (half note)– C sharp. But try also F sharp–E in this measure. In bass 2, the rhythm and augmented fourth in measures 13 and 14 are weak. Construct another bass combining the best features of both.

Note the interesting nonharmonic treatment of some of the melody tones and the use of the II₇ at each star (*). In general, the II₇ is used in place of a fundamental II or IV chord. Add the alto and tenor for bass 2 or for a combination of both, as suggested above.

Identify the cadences which determine this *A–B* or two-part form (See Chapter X, page 151). Here each part is a period in length, both ended by the strong perfect cadence (measures 8 and 16).

The parts of an *A–B* form are usually equal in length — either a phrase or a period, rarely a longer form. When extended by repetition, both parts are repeated thus: *A(A)–B(B)*. The two parts often end similarly, especially in older music, without, however, any suggestion of a return to the beginning.

Observe the departure from and return to the original tonality in Example 217, page 506, and the melodic or rhythmic similarities between the two parts. These often occur in corresponding measures of each part, thus contributing to the unity of the form as a whole.

To summarize: Examples 209 and 217 have shown the II$_7$ chord as an important fundamental dissonance, similar in treatment to the V$_7$ as regards the doubled root and stepwise downward resolution of the chord-seventh. The other secondary seventh-chords in the key were examined and classified according to their interval construction (Examples 213, 214, 215, pages 503, 504, and 505). In regard to quality, while the V$_7$ remains the same in both modes, the II$_7$ differs, being a small seventh in the major and a half-diminished seventh-chord in the minor mode.

In connection with the new key of B major (Example 209, page 499), the principle of enharmonic notation was discussed, and it was shown that, by applying this principle, B major (five sharps) could also be written enharmonically as C flat major (seven flats).

Finally, the construction of the *A–B* (two-part) form was recalled as consisting of two equal sections, each ending in a perfect authentic cadence with no return to the melody of the beginning. The parts were equal in length and could be extended by repetition.

Review:

1. The construction and signature of B major.
2. The parallel minor key of B major.
3. What is meant by *enharmonic notation.*
4. The enharmonic equivalent of the B major scale.
5. Why the enharmonic equivalent of the B major scale is seldom used.
6. Whether A sharp, as the leading tone of the B major scale, can be written enharmonically as B flat, and why.
7. What is meant by equal temperament.
8. The construction, doubling, and resolution of the II₇ chord.
9. For what two chords the II₇ is often substituted.
10. Some characteristics of the *A–B* form.

For Further Study, Determine:

1. The form of Example 209.
2. Some stylistic differences between the waltzes of Schubert and Chopin, or Brahms and Strauss.
3. The dominant and subdominant keys of B major.
4. The difference in meaning between enharmonic and inharmonic.
5. The reason for the key scheme of Bach's *Well-Tempered Clavier.*
6. A reason for and against the progression of bass 1, measure 7, Example 217.
7. Whether both parts of an *A–B* form must end in the same key.
8. The triads belonging enharmonically to both E major and C flat major. (For example, E major I-C flat major IV, etc.)

I — Assignment for Writing

1. Arrange Example 209, or another waltz, for a group of instruments in your class and have it performed.
2. Add the alto and tenor voices (in that order) to at least one of the following passages:

Figured basses: BACH, Chorale

Chorale (1668)

Unfigured basses: Chorale (1784)

MENDELSSOHN, *Elijah*, No. 5, "Yet doth the Lord"

Grave

3. Harmonize at least one of the following melodies for mixed voices:

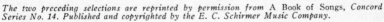

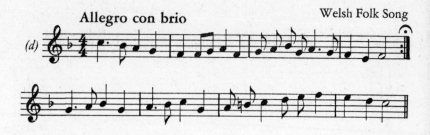

Allegro con brio   Welsh Folk Song

(d)

Moderato   French Folk Song

(e)

Fine

(II⁶₅)   (II₇)   *D.C. al Fine*

Reprinted by permission from A Book of Songs, *Concord Series No. 14. Published and copyrighted by the E. C. Schirmer Music Company.*

GOUNOD, *Gallia,* "O Turn Thee"

Andante maestoso

(f)

T.O.P. -

S

B II₇

Larghetto   MOZART, *Requiem Mass,* "Lacrymosa"

(g)

II₇

Bass

4. Harmonize at least one of the following melodies for piano. Identify the form of each melody used.

Tempo di marcia   Folk Song of Provençe

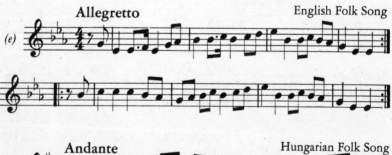

Reprinted by permission from The Home and Community Song Book, Concord Series No. 2.
Published and copyrighted by the E. C. Schirmer Music Company.

(This melody can be sung as a two-part round, the second voice
entering on the first pulse of the first complete measure.)

Allegretto   English Folk Song

Andante   Hungarian Folk Song

D II₇

A II₇

The two preceding selections are reprinted by permission from A Book of Songs, Concord *Series No. 14. Published and copyrighted by the E. C. Schirmer Music Company.*

GABRIEL-MARIE, *La Cinquantaine*

Andantine

(g)

SCHUBERT, *Fantasia,* Op. 15

Presto

(h)

BEETHOVEN, *Piano Sonata,* Op. 31, No. 1

Allegro vivace

(i)

II — *Assignment for Playing*

1. Harmonize any of the melodies in the *Assignment for Writing* (4).

2. Improvise an *A–B* form, using the following motives. Since the real meter is $\frac{6}{4}$, make each part a sixteen-measure period, extended by exact or modified repetition.

Part I

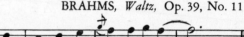

Part II

3. Improvise melodies in *A–B* form in the key of B major. Repeat from memory, and harmonize. (Optional.)

4. Transpose by ear familiar music into the key of B major. Experiment playing simple music written in B flat major (such as *The Star Spangled Banner*) in the key of B major, in order to become familiar with this new key (see Chapter XIV, page 241). Treat passages in C major similarly, transposing them to C flat major (see *Assignment for Analysis*, Chapters I-VIII).

5. Transpose the following modulatory chord pattern to all major keys previously studied:

6. Devise some original modulatory patterns from B major to its dominant key, using a motive in sequence (see Chapters XXV-XXVI, pages 447-490).

7. Transpose simple melodic and harmonic passages in B major down a major second to A major. Experiment transposing passages in other keys to B major.

III — Assignment for Listening

1. *Oral dictation:* harmonic recognition only. (Name chords by quality, letter, and Roman numeral.)

Haydn, *B flat Symphony, VIII,* Finale, development section (1-13).

Mozart, *Violin Sonata,* K481, Allegro molto (1-16).

Beethoven, *Bagatelles,* Op. 33, No. 6 (1-8).

Schubert, *German Dances,* Op. 33, No. 4;
   Unfinished Symphony, Andante, subordinate theme in
    bass.

Schumann, *Album for the Young,* Op. 68, No. 11, Trio; No. 43;
   Novelletten, Op. 31, No. 5, Vivo.

Chopin, *G Minor Ballade,* Op. 23, Moderato (1-4);
   Mazurka, Op. 67, No. 1, C Major section,
     Op. 30, No. 1 (1-8);
   B flat Minor Scherzo, A Major section (1-12),
     E Major section (1-8);
   Prelude, Op. 28, No. 11;
   Sonata, Op. 58, First Movement, theme II.

Löwe, *Nobody Saw,* Op. 9, No. 4 (1-4), *Song Classics,* p. 118.

Mendelssohn, *Yearning,* Op. 9, No. 7 (1-8);
   Elijah, No. 21, "Hear Ye Israel," Allegro maestoso
    (1-8);
   No. 32, "He That Shall Endure to the End."

Gounod, *Adore and Be Still* (5-14).

Moszkowski, *Spanish Dance in G Minor,* Op. 12, No. 2, part II.

Brahms, *Intermezzo,* Op. 118, No. 2, Poco lento (1-8);
   Hungarian Dances, No. 12, F Major section,
     No. 16 (1-4),
     No. 19, Più presto,
     No. 20 (1-8),
     No. 21 (1-8).

Wolf, *How Many Hours I've Wasted* (1-8).

Mascagni, *Cavalleria Rusticana,* Intermezzo (1-11).

Consecutive seventh-chords progressing by fifths:
Bach, *Passion According to St. Matthew,* No. 51, Introduction.
Schubert, *Wanderer Fantasie,* Op. 15, Allegro con fuoco (1-13).
Mozart, *F Major Piano Sonata,* K332, Allegro (60-67).
Chopin, *Mazurka,* Op. 67, No. 1, C Major section.
Brahms, *Requiem,* Op. 45, "Death Where Is Thy Sting?"
　　　　Symphony IV, Op. 98, Andante moderato (95-98).

2. *Written dictation (quality, bass, melody, and name of chords).*
　　Sing!: Keys of Heaven, page 75;
　　　　The Old Refrain (chorus), page 13;
　　　　Mother Volga, page 29;
　　　　Hail Poetry, page 109;
　　Brown Book, Twice 55: No. 66, *Vesper Hymn;*
　　　　　　　　　　No. 78, *Deck the Halls.*
　　Green Book, Twice 55: No. 85, *Abide With Me;*
　　　　　　　　　　No. 95, *Olaf Trygvason* (1-8);
　　　　　　　　　　No. 129, *My Bonnie Lass* (11-28);
　　　　　　　　　　No. 145, *Sweet Love Doth Now Invite*
　　　　　　　　　　(1-4).
　　Home and Community Song Book. Concord Series No. 2.
　　　Hark the Summons, page 43;
　　　Drink To Me Only, page 37;
　　　March of the Kings (8-16), page 71;
　　　Song of the Volga Boatman (1-4), page 76.
　　New Episcopal Hymnal, No. 275, *Capetown,*
　　　　　　　　　　No. 467, *Eventide,*
　　　　　　　　　　No. 367, *Laudes Domini,*
　　　　　　　　　　No. 74, *St. Cross,*
　　　　　　　　　　No. 285, *Leoni,*
　　　　　　　　　　No. 226, *Winkworth,*
　　　　　　　　　　No. 345 (2), *Dominus Regit Me.*
　　Chopin, *F Minor Fantasie,* Op. 49, Lento (1-4);
　　　　F Major Ballade, Op. 38, Andantino.
　　Gounod, *The Redemption,* "Lovely Appear" (23-34).
　　Schumann, *Fantasiestücke,* Op. 111, No. 2 (1-9);
　　　　　　Carnival, Op. 9, Reconnaissance, B Major section (1-8).
　　Mendelssohn, *Morning Song,* Op. 42, No. 7 (1-11);
　　　　Elijah, No. 22, "Be Not Afraid" (1-5).

IV — Assignment for Analysis

Handel, *Messiah*, No. 45, "I Know That My Redeemer Liveth";
   Rinaldo, Aria, "Leave Me In Sorrow" (1-8).
Schubert, *Piano Sonata*, Op. 122, Finale (after double bar);
   Waltz, Op. 18a, No. 2 (1-8).
Mozart, *F Major Piano Sonata*, K533, Rondo, Minore (1-4).
Mendelssohn, *Elijah*, No. 34, "Behold God the Lord" (end of E
   Major section);
   No. 21, "Hear Ye Israel," Allegro maestoso.
Schumann, *Pictures from Fairyland*, Op. 113, No. 3, B Major
   section.
Brahms, *Waltz*, Op. 39, No. 5 (1-8).
Wagner, *Tristan*, Act II, Introduction (1-3);
   Götterdämmerung, "Siegfried's Funeral March," E flat sec-
   tion.
Bizet, *Carmen*, "Toreador Song," F Major section.
Franck, *E Major Organ Chorale*, (1-4).
Massenet, *Elégie*, Op. 10 (1-5).
Grieg, *Sailor's Song*, Op. 68, No. 1 (17-24).
Rebikof, *Silhouette*, Op. 31, No. 1.
Mascagni, *Cavalleria Rusticana*, Intermezzo (1-4).
Elgar, *Salut d'Amour* (3-10).
Scharwenka, *Polish Dance*, Più mosso, C flat section.
Dvořák, *Humoresque*, Op. 101, No. 7, Più lento.
Strauss, *Blue Danube*, Waltz 5;
   Vienna Life, Waltz 1.
Grieg, *Ase's Death*, Op. 46, No. 2 (1-4).
Sibelius, *Valse Triste* (1-20).

The following passages have been selected for analysis from the above
list. Identify the form, chords, and nonharmonic tones. Note pivotal and
modulatory chords.

HANDEL, *Messiah*, No. 45, "I Know That My Redeemer Liveth"
   Larghetto

(a)

MASSENET, *Elégie,* Op. 10

Lento, ma non troppo

(b)

SCHUBERT, *Waltzes,* Op. 18a, No. 2

Tempo di valse

(c)

MENDELSSOHN, *Elijah,* No. 34, "Behold, God the Lord"

This passage should be sung by four voices.

Allegro molto

(d)

BRAHMS, *Waltz*, Op. 39, No. 5 (Adapted)

WAGNER, *Götterdämmerung* (Siegfried horn motive)

FRANCK, *Organ Chorale*, No. 1

HANDEL, *Rinaldo,* "Leave me in sorrow"

Andante

(b)

MASCAGNI, *Cavalleria Rusticana,* Intermezzo

Andante sostenuto

(i)

Andantino

ELGAR, *Salut d'Amour*

(j)

GRIEG, *Peer Gynt Suite,* Op. 46, No. 2, "Åse's Death"

Andante doloroso

(k)

Chapter XXVIII

THE II$_3^4$ AND II$_2^4$ CHORDS

Ex. 218

SCHUBERT (1797—1828), *Hedge-Roses*
(arr. for mixed voices), Original key—G major

Joy in his heart was glow-ing. Lit-tle wild-rose,

wild-rose red, In the hedge-row grow - ing.

SCHUBERT wrote this lovely song in 1815, when he was eighteen years old. Although he was teaching in his father's school that year he found leisure to write 146 songs (including the famous *Erlking*), two symphonies, three piano sonatas, a string quartet, and some church and operatic music. His amazing facility is shown by the composition of 30 songs in August, and over 20 in October, eight of which are dated October 15th, and seven more October 19th. During his short life, he wrote approximately 600 songs, in addition to a vast quantity of instrumental and choral music. Probably no one except Mozart ever gave the world so much great music in so short a time.

In Example 218, note new key signature of six flats for G flat major,[1] and the modulation to D flat major confirmed by the per-

---

[1] Write the G flat major scale in treble and bass, first with accidentals, then with its key signature. Note that the name of any flat major key corresponds to the next to the last flat in the signature.

fect authentic cadence in measure 10. Where does the modulation begin?

Analyze the song aurally for the number and types of cadences, including the *evaded cadence* (Chapter VII, page 93) in measure 8. These three phrases make a somewhat unusual form, a period extended by two different versions of the antecedent phrase (measures 1 to 4 and 5 to 10) followed by the concluding consequent phrase (measures 11 to 14). This type of period extension is known as an *antecedent* group. (See Haydn, *B flat Symphony* [Peters Edition], No. 12, Finale [1-12].) It is also possible to extend the end of a period in the same way by a *consequent group*. (See Beethoven, *Piano Sonata,* Op. 2, No. 1, Finale, Chapter XVIII, *Assignment for Analysis* [c].) Both types of extension are rare, however, and are mentioned only in connection with Example 218.

Here the entire song is in *strophic form,* that is, the same music is repeated for each verse. The other two structural designs for solo songs are the *through-composed* form, in which each verse has a new musical setting (see Schubert's *Erlking*), and the familiar *A–B* and *A–B–A* forms which are called *song-forms* because of their frequent use in song literature.

Sing the first two measures of Example 218 again, noting the chord in measure 2. Name the chord by letter and number, and then sing and resolve it in *arpeggio* form, thus:

Ex. 219

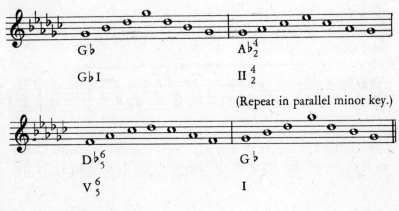

Now sing measures 5 and 6 (Example 218). How do they differ from measures 1 and 2? Name the chord in measure 6, and compare it with the II$^4_2$ chord in measure 2. Both these chords, being a third inversion of the A flat chord, are called $^4_2$ chords (see Chapter XIV, page 228, Example 113). Since they are inverted seventh-chords, no chord tone is omitted or doubled. The third inversion of a seventh-chord ($^4_2$) resolves downward to the first inversion of a triad or seventh-chord as here. Compare these chords with the last chord in measure 3 (V$^4_2$) whose third is omitted for better voice leading. Name the other chords (Example 218) and types of nonharmonic tones. Observe the similarity between the ending of the first antecedent phrase (measures 3 and 4) and the beginning of the consequent phrase (measures 11 and 12).

The II$^4_2$ (Example 218), like most inversions, is used as a substitute for its fundamental chord to facilitate voice leading and to vary the harmonic color.

Sing the following old chorale melody, listening for the cadences and general harmonic background:

Ex. 220

HENRICH ISAAC (d. 1519)

Since the key center, F sharp, is identical in pitch with G flat on the piano, the scale of F sharp major (six sharps) is the enharmonic equivalent of G flat major, thus:

Ex. 221

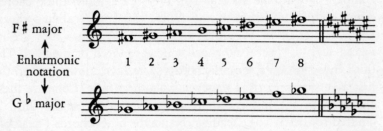

Note that both F sharp and G flat major require the same number of accidentals so that there is no advantage in using one or the other, as there was in the case of B and C flat major. (Chapter XXVII, page 499.)

Now to return to the chorale melody (Example 220). Work out a satisfactory bass for the last phrase, and compare it with these basses by Bach. Sing each bass first alone, then with the melody.

Ex. 222   J.S. BACH, Basses 2 to 7 inclusive*

*The complete harmonization may be found in Hall and McCreary, *Anniversary Chorales,* No. 11, *Kufferath,* Nos. 93, 94, 95, and Bach, *371 Chorales* (Peters Edition), Nos. 50, 63, 103, 117, 289, and 355. In all cases the repeated phrases are harmonized differently so that each phrase is actually harmonized twice.

These possibilities fall into two general types — basses 2-3 and
4-5-6. Bass 7 is somewhat different although it resembles the first
group. Bach adds the alto and tenor to it, thus:

Ex. 223   BACH

Note that the inner voices overlap to give the tenor greater
freedom. Sing the tenor line alone first, then add the other voices.
Using the same bass, rearrange the inner voices so that they do
not cross. Sing this version and compare it with Example 223.

Obviously, G is the root of the ⁶⁄₃ chord in measure 2. We have
already discussed the II⁶₅ (Chapter XXIV, page 423) and the II⅘
(Example 219, page 527). This second inversion (II⁴⁄₂) is the only
one that remains to be considered. Sing and resolve it in *arpeggio*
form, thus:

Ex. 224

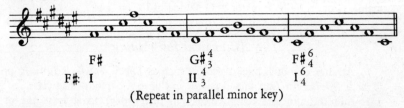

(Repeat in parallel minor key)

Note that, like the V⁴₃ (Chapter XII, Example 98, page 190),
no chord tone is omitted or doubled, and that the bass usually
resolves down stepwise to a fundamental triad or ⁶⁄₄ chord. (The
resolution of the II⅘ in Example 223, measure 2, is embellished.)
The II⅘, like the II⁶₅ and II⁴⁄₂, is used as a substitute for the fundamental II₇ or IV chord as seen above.

In general, the inversions of the other secondary seventh-chords
(I₇, III₇, VI₇, and VII₇) resolve similarly to those of the II₇
chord. They are quite rare, but are useful at times either for
harmonic color or for melodic line.

To summarize: the II⁶₅ is the most used form of the II₇ chord, but each inversion has unique possibilities for color and voice leading. All inverted seventh-chords resolve similarly, that is, by stepwise progression to the chord whose root is a perfect fifth lower. Use them naturally to make the outside voices as melodic as possible, always testing the result aurally.

Remember that the important point is not the use of a particular chord, but the effectiveness of the passage as a whole.

Review:

1. The construction and signature of the G flat and F sharp major scales.

2. Why the choice between F sharp and G flat is purely a matter of preference.

3. The parallel minor scale of F sharp major.

4. The form of Example 218.

5. The construction and resolution of the II⁴₃ and II⁴₂ chords.

6. How the II⁴₃ and II⁴₂ chords are used.

7. Which inversion of the II₇ is most frequently used.

8. What is meant by an evaded or deceptive cadence.

For Further Study, Determine:

1. How many compositions you know in F sharp or G flat major.

2. The dominant and subdominant keys in relation to G flat and F sharp majors.

3. Which triads belong enharmonically to both B major and G flat major. (For example, B major = G flat major IV, etc.)

4. All the chords and nonharmonic tones in Examples 218 and 223.

I — Assignment for Writing

1. Arrange one of Schubert's songs such as *The Serenade, To Music,* or *Who is Sylvia?* for four mixed voices and have it performed in class.

2. Add the alto and tenor voices (in that order) to at least one of the following passages:

Figured basses: KUFFERATH, Chorale

(a)

56   56   6   6   4 3   4   4   6   7
                                         2   2   5

KUFFERATH, Chorale

Unfigured basses:

BRAHMS, *German Requiem*, No. 3 "Lord, make me to know"

Andante moderato

MONK

3. Harmonize at least one of the following melodies for mixed voices:

BRAHMS, *German Requiem*, No. 2, "Behold all Flesh"

Moderato in modo di marcia

Andantino   MOZART, *Ave Verum* (K618)

SCHUBERT, *To the Lyre*

4. Harmonize at least one of the following melodies for piano. Identify the form of each melody used.

KUHLAU, *Sonatina,* Op. 88, No. 2

(Repeat in G♭ major)

BEETHOVEN, *Violin Sonata,* Op. 23

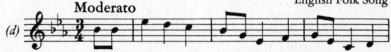

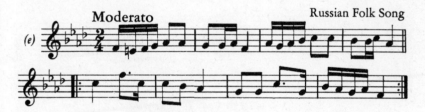

The four preceding selections are reprinted by permission from A Book of Songs, Concord Series No. 14. Published and copyrighted by the E. C. Schirmer Music Company.

II — *Assignment for Playing*

1. Harmonize any of the melodies in the *Assignment for Writing* (4).

2. Improvise an *A–B* form, using the following motives to be developed into two eight-measure periods. Make each part end similarly, and extend the form by repeating each.

Part II

3. Improvise melodies in G flat or F sharp major in *A–B* form. Repeat from memory and harmonize. (Optional.)

4. Transpose by ear familiar music to the keys of G flat or F sharp major. Continue playing music written in F or G major (for example, *America*), in the keys of F sharp and G flat major by thinking in terms of the changed key signature. (See Chapter IX, page 146, and Chapter XIII, page 223.)

5. Transpose the following modulatory chord patterns to all familiar major keys:

6. Devise some original modulatory patterns from G flat and F sharp major to their dominant keys. Experiment using a motive in sequence.

7. Transpose simple and harmonic passages in G flat and F sharp major up a major second to A flat major, and down a major second to E major (review notes on transposition). Experiment transposing passages from those keys to G flat and F sharp major.

III — Assignment for Listening

1. *Oral dictation:* harmonic recognition only. (Name chords by quality, letter, and Roman numeral.)

(*a*) Examples in F sharp major:

Schubert, *Death-Music,* E flat and F sharp sections.

Beethoven, *Piano Sonata,* Op. 78, First Movement (1-12).

Schumann, *Romance,* Op. 28, No. 2 (1-8).

Chopin, *Nocturne,* Op. 15, No. 2 (1-8).

Mendelssohn, *Songs Without Words,* No. 5, F sharp Major section (1-4).

Grieg, *To Spring,* Op. 43, No. 6 (1-10).

Grünfeld, *Romance,* Op. 45, No. 1 (1-4).

Rubinstein, *Kamennoi-Ostrow,* Op. 10, No. 22.

Dvořák, *Silhouette,* Op. 8, No. 4, Più mosso (1-4).

Brahms, *Hungarian Dances,* No. 4, Molto allegro,
                         No. 2 (1-16), Allegro non assai,
                         No. 5, Vivace,
                         No. 17, Meno presto (1-4),
                         No. 19, Più presto;
    Intermezzo, Op. 118, No. 2, Più lento.

(*b*) Examples in G flat major:

Beethoven, *Leonore Overture,* No. 3, Op. 72, Tempo I.

Schubert, *Marche Militaire,* Op. 51, No. 1, Trio;
    Impromptu, Op. 90, No. 3 (1-8).

Chopin, *Etude,* Op. 10, No. 5 (1-8),
             Op. 25, No. 9 (1-8);
    B flat Minor Sonata, Op. 35, Scherzo, Più lento (1-17);
    Polonaise, Op. 26, No. 2 (1-12).

Ilyinsky, *Cradle Song,* Op. 13 (II½ *sound,* not chord, in measure 2, caused by tonic organ point).

Paderewski, *Melodie,* Op. 16, No. 2 (3-18).

Dvořák, *Humoresque,* Op. 101, No. 7, G flat Major sections.

Chaminade, *The Flatterer* (1-16).

(*c*) Examples using the II⅔ or II½:

Bach, *Well-Tempered Clavier,* I, Prelude 2.

Tchaikovsky, *Album for the Young,* Op. 39, No. 20, "The Witch" (12-24).

Schubert, *Impromptu*, Op. 90, No. 2, B Minor section.
2. *Written dictation* (*quality, bass, melody, and name of chord*).
Bach, *371 Chorales*, No. 251 (phrases 1-2).
Grieg, *At Home*, Op. 43, No. 3 (1-8).
New Episcopal Hymnal, No. 1, *Stuttgart*,
No. 588, *Paradise*,
No. 63 (2), *Parker*,
No. 189, *Unde et Memores* (1-8).

IV — Assignment for Analysis

Bach, *371 Chorales*, No. 359.
Mozart, *G Minor Symphony*, K550, Allegro molto (1-9).
Schubert, *Serenade*.
Beethoven, *Piano Sonata*, Op. 10, No. 2, Trio (1-16),
Op. 27, No. 2, Adagio sostenuto (15-10
from end).
Schumann, *Vienna Carnival-Scene*, Op. 26, Allegro (1-16);
Novelletten, Op. 21, Trio II (1-8).
Chopin, *Mazurka*, Op. 41, No. 4 (17-24).
Dvořák, *Humoresque*, Op. 101, No. 7 (13-16).
Franck, *Symphonic Variations*, Allegro non troppo (1-6).
Grieg, *A Minor Waltz*, Op. 12, No. 2 (1-18).
Liszt, *Hungarian Rhapsody No. 2*, Tempo giusto vivace (1-8);
Les Préludes, F sharp Major section (1-4).
Sibelius, *Second Symphony*, Op. 43, Third Movement, Lento e
suave (1-4).

The following passages have been selected for analysis from the above
list. Identify the form, chords, and nonharmonic tones.

MOZART, *G Minor Symphony*, K550

Allegro molto

(a)

Moderato   SCHUBERT, *Serenade*

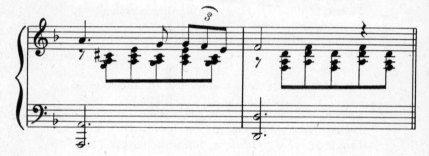

SCHUMANN, *Vienna Carnival-Scene,* Op. 26, No. 1 (Adapted)

Allegro, animato molto

SCHUMANN, *Novelletten*, Op. 21, No. 8

CHOPIN, *Mazurka*, Op. 41, No. 4

FRANCK, *Symphonic Variations*

Allegro non troppo

Melody in bass (octaves *ad lib.*)

LISZT, *Hungarian Rhapsody No. 2*

Tempo giusto vivace

Allegro marziale animato   LISZT, *Les Preludes*

SIBELIUS *Second Symphony*, Op. 43, Scherzo (Trio)

Lento e suave

(i)

Published by Breitkopf and Hartel and reprinted by permission of Associated Music Publishers, Inc.

Chapter XXIX

THE V₉ CHORD

Ex. 225   CHOPIN, (1810 — 1849) *Waltz*, Op. 64, No. 1 (Adapted)

Molto vivace

(Chromatic $^6_5$)

THIS WALTZ, often called the *Minute Waltz* because of the supposed performance time, was played by Chopin at his last Paris concert on February 16, 1848. The prevailing tonality is D flat major.[1] Another tonality is suggested at the beginning of

[1] Write the D flat major scale both in treble and bass, first using accidentals only, then with its signature of five flats. Note that the name of any flat major key corresponds to the next to last flat in the signature.

the second phrase (measures 13 and 14), but, since it is not confirmed by a cadence, the effect is merely that of chromatic embellishment.

There are a number of interesting new points about this waltz. Locate the cadences. Note how the semicadence in measure 12 is bridged over rhythmically. The accompaniment figure and chord sequence do not confirm the time signature. Evidently we have here a case of a larger meter ($^6_4$) than is indicated by the metric signature. Observe also the cross rhythm caused by the bracketed figure in measures 3 to 7 inclusive. This figure, in duple meter, is obviously derived from measures 1 and 2 and conflicts delightfully with the triple meter established by the accompaniment figure. Compare measure 13 with measure 1 and measures 13 and 14 with measures 15 and 16 for clues as to how Chopin secured unity as well as variety in the form.

Consider the form as a whole. There are two sections of equal length (including repetitions) which might be interpreted either as a large period with each phrase repeated, or as a repeated phrase followed by a parallel period. In either case, the effect is that of statement and conclusion.

Now in regard to the harmony: note the new chords in measures 9 and 11 that sound like a V_7 (see the accompaniment) but have an added B flat in the melody. Construct the V_7 upward from the root and add this new note. Following the same principle used in naming seventh-chords, this A flat–C–G flat–B flat is called a *ninth-chord* (V_9). Is it a consonant or dissonant chord, and why? Sing and resolve it to a I chord in *arpeggio* form, thus:

Ex. 226

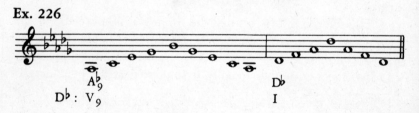

(Repeat in the enharmonic parallel minor key)

This new V_9 chord is used similarly to a fundamental V_7 resolving to the I. Since the V_9 is a five-tone chord, obviously one tone must be omitted in four-voice writing. This tone is usually the chord-fifth, as in Example 225, measure 9.

The chord-ninth resolves downward one degree as does the chord-seventh. Note that the chord-ninth of the V_9 is the sixth degree of the scale. Since this chord-ninth, being at least that far from its root, is usually in the soprano, the progression V_9–I may be used to harmonize the scale steps 6-5.

Unlike seventh-chords, the ninth-chord is rarely inverted. In fact, for all practical purposes, it may be considered only in the fundamental position. Ninth-chords built on scale degrees other than the fifth are theoretically possible (especially that on the II in either mode), but are used too rarely to be considered here.

In minor, the V_9 is a sharper dissonance than in the major mode, since its ninth is a minor instead of a major interval. Play the second part of this Chopin waltz which continues as follows:

Ex. 227

(Chromatic $\frac{4}{2}$)

B♭ V₉

Chromatic V₉   V₉   D II₇

D.C. al Fine
(to Example 225)

Note the minor V₉ chord in measure 4 of the first ending (Example 227). There are also a number of chromatic chords that may be ignored for the present, except for observing the chromatic V₉ in the second measure of the second ending.

Theoretically, it is possible to add several additional thirds to a seventh-chord, naming the chord (as in the case of the seventh

and ninth) from the distance between the chord root and the
added tone, thus:

Ex. 228

D♭: V   V₇   V₉   V₁₁   V₁₃   V₁₅?

Obviously, the V_{13} is the limit,[2] but in any chord beyond a ninth
so many tones must be omitted in ordinary writing that those additions are probably best classified as nonharmonic tones unless
all the tones are present, and the resolution of the chord is directly
to the I chord.

Additional points should be noted in connection with this waltz
(Examples 225 and 227, pages 546 and 549), for example the foreign tones. The essential melodic tone in measures 1 to 7, Example 225, page 546, is A flat, since the harmonic background is
D flat major. This is clear when the accompaniment enters in
measure 5. Here the A flat is embellished by its upper and lower
neighbors, G natural and B flat, and the latter, in turn, is embellished by its upper neighbor, C. The G natural–B flat, preceding the chord tone A flat are known as *double neighboring
tones* (the C is a very exceptional embellishment of the upper
neighbor B flat, or possibly might be heard as a chord-seventh).
Such double neighbors are always followed by their chord tones,
A flat in this case. The rapidity of the tempo minimizes all these
details, and to our ears the melody tone in the first seven measures
sounds clearly as an embellished A flat.

Note the double neighbors in Example 227, page 549, measure
8, and elsewhere. As in the case of a single neighboring tone, the
lower neighbor is usually chromatic and the upper one diatonic.
(See Chapter III, page 32.)

Note the *Da Capo* at the end of Example 227, and identify the
form of the waltz as a whole (Examples 225 and 227).

In regard to the use of the V_9 chord, listen for the melodic

---

[2] Example 227, measure 6, might be construed as a V_{13}, but the nonharmonic
explanation of the F is probably better.

progression (6-5) in the following melody. Sing the tune first
alone, then with a single bass tone for each measure (except the
last), thus:

Ex. 229   English Folk Song

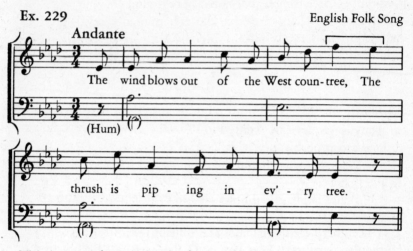

The wind blows out   of   the West coun-tree, The

thrush is   pip - ing   in   ev' - ry   tree.

This is a very bare, primitive bass and could be elaborated thus:

The wind blows out   of   the West coun-tree, The

thrush is   pip - ing   in   ev' - ry   tree.

Sing this harmonization, analyzing the effect of each part with the others. It is hardly to be expected that the student use all these dissonances, but the solution shows some of the inherent possibilities of a simple harmonic background.

Obviously C sharp major is the enharmonic equivalent of D flat major. It is rarely used, especially with its signature, but it is interesting to compare it with D flat major, thus:

Ex. 230

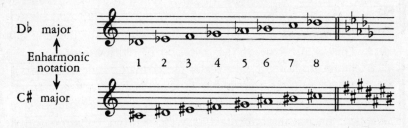

Hence, there are three major scales that may be written with enharmonic signatures: B as C flat; G flat as F sharp; and D flat as C sharp. Since the last concludes our study of major scales, we may now arrange the letter names of all the keys progressively according to the number of sharps or flats in their signatures, thus:

Ex. 231

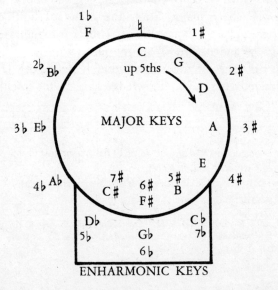

This figure shows why seven accidentals (one for each letter) are the practical limit for key signatures. The others, of course, are possible and are sometimes used in modulations (for example, G sharp major as the dominant of C sharp major), but they are rare.[3]

Review the major key signatures studied and recite them in clockwise order, giving the accidentals required for each.

To summarize: the melodic progression 6-5 may be harmonized by the V₉ chord followed by the I or V₇; and in the V₉, the chord-fifth is usually omitted and its dissonances (seventh and ninth) resolve downward one step. Other ninth-chords are possible but rare. This is also true of the inversion of ninth-chords.

A comparison of the new scale, D flat major scale (five flats), with its enharmonic equivalent, C sharp major (seven sharps), completes our study of the fifteen major scales. The scales having five, six, or seven accidentals may be written enharmonically, using either sharps or flats, but those using seven accidentals (C flat and C sharp) are rare.

The embellishment of a melody tone is accomplished by its upper diatonic and lower chromatic neighboring tones used consecutively. These *double neighbors* are immediately followed by their principal melodic tone.

Experiment using ninth-chords, double neighbors, and, also, the key of C sharp major. Study the *sound* of ninth-chords by playing, hearing, and singing them. They are romantic and emotional chords, and are most appropriate in music of that type. Embellish the tones of the V₉ with double neighbors. Depend on feeling derived from aural knowledge as a means to enlarge and enrich your musical vocabulary.

Review:

1. The construction and signature of D flat major and C sharp major.
2. The enharmonic major scales.
3. How many major scales may be written with signatures.
4. The parallel minor scale of C sharp major.

---

[3] See Wagner's *Rheingold* (B & H Piano Score), p. 25, where there are a few measures in B double flat (A) major. Also MacDowell's *To a Water Lily* which likewise touches A sharp (B flat) major.

5. How the V_7 and V_9 chords resemble each other in structure.

6. By what chord the V_9 is generally followed.

7. How the V_9 is used for harmonization.

8. What tone is omitted in the V_9 in four-voice writing, and why.

9. What is meant by double neighboring tone.

10. Another possible meter for Example 225.

For Further Study, Determine:

1. Whether D flat or C sharp major is most used, and why.

2. Why the parallel minor scale of D flat major is rarely used.

3. Why there are 15 major scales but only 12 different pitches in the octave.

4. The number of accidentals that would be required for G sharp and F flat majors.

5. How Example 225, measures 1 to 4, differs from a typical introduction.

6. The form of Examples 225 to 227.

7. Why the fifth is the best interval to omit in ninth-chords.

8. Whether the ninth of a chord ever occurs in an inner voice.

9. Whether the second inversion of the V_9 is possible, and why.

10. Why double neighbors must be followed by the tone between them.

11. Whether either phrase of a period may be repeated alone.

12. The difference between the repetition of each phrase in a period and the repetition of the entire period.

I — Assignment for Writing

1. Arrange Chopin's *A Major Prelude,* Op. 28, No. 7 (see *Assignment for Analysis*) for string quartet or for mixed voices. Make the vocal arrangement in E major, a fourth lower than printed, putting the melody either in the soprano or tenor. Add words and sing the arrangement in class.

2. Add the alto and tenor voices (in that order) to at least one of the following passages:

Figured basses:

LE JEUNE

(b)

WARD

Unfigured bass:

(c)

melody of first phrase

unison

3. Harmonize at least one of the following melodies for mixed voices:

Allegro

Bohemian Folk Song

BALFE, *Killarney*

Moderato

(V₉)

Moderato

Welsh Folk Tune

Fine

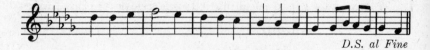

D.S. al Fine

Andante   Scotch Folk Song

(d)

IV   I   I₆ IV₇

The two preceding selections are reprinted by permission from A Book of Songs, Concord *Series No. 14. Published and copyrighted by the E. C. Schirmer Music Company.*

Allegretto   Esthonian Folk Song

(e)

2.

Alla marcia   Bulgarian National Anthem

(f)

Fine   D.S. al Fine

4. Harmonize at least one of the following melodies for piano. Identify
the form of each melody used.

Tempo di valse — HAIBEL (1795), *Tiroler*

(a)

Fine

1.   2.

D.C. al Fine

Moderato — German Folk Song

(b)

Quietly — MÜLLER (1828)

(c)

(VI)

Allegretto con brio   Hungarian Folk Song

(d)

Fine

D.S. al Fine

SCHUBERT, *Waltzes,* Op. 18a, No. 5

Tempo di valse

(e)

SCHUBERT, *Valses Sentimentales,* Op. 50, No. 6

Tempo di valse

(f)

SCHUBERT *Valses Sentamentales,* Op. 50, No. 4

Tempo di valse

(g)

Tempo di valse   SCHUBERT Op. 67, No. 4

(h)

(IV)

II — *Assignment for Playing*

1. Harmonize any of the melodies in the *Assignment for Writing* (3) and (4).

2. Complete the first phrase and improvise a second phrase, using these motives. Extend by repetition of each phrase. Note that the tonality differs from the key signature. (If a simpler motive is preferred, use an original one.)

Phrase 1   WEBER, *Invitation to the Dance,* Op. 65

Vivace

Phrase 2

3. Improvise melodies in D flat or C sharp major in period form extended by the repetition of each phrase. Repeat from memory and harmonize. (Optional.)

4. Play the melody of *America the Beautiful* by ear in the key of D flat major. Repeat with harmonization.

5. Transpose by ear familiar music into the keys of D flat or C sharp major. Continue reading simple music written in D and C major in the keys of D flat and C sharp to become familiar with these new keys. (See Chapters I to VIII, pages 3 to 107, and Chapter X, page 148.

6. Transpose the following modulatory chord patterns to all major keys. Then repeat, embellishing the repeated melodic tones in the first measure of each by double neighboring tones.

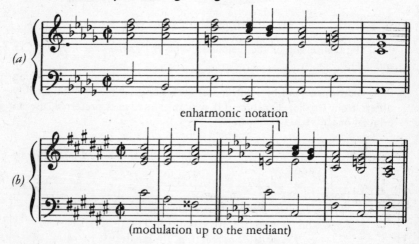

enharmonic notation

(modulation up to the mediant)

7. Continue the following sequential patterns through all major keys until C major is reached again:

   (*a*) Upward through the sharp keys using V$_7$:

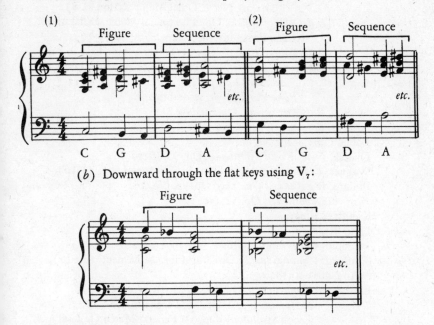

   (*b*) Downward through the flat keys using V$_7$:

8. Transpose simple melodic and harmonic passages in D flat major up a major second to E flat major, and down a minor third to B flat major. (Review notes on transposition.) Experiment transposing passages from these keys to D flat major.

III — Assignment for Listening

1. *Oral dictation:* harmonic recognition only. (Name chords by quality, letter, and Roman numeral.)

   (*a*) Examples in D flat major:

   Schubert, *Marche Militaire*, Op. 51, No. 1, principal theme;
   Unfinished Symphony, Andante con moto, D flat major section;
   Impromptu, Op. 142, No. 2, Trio.

   Donizetti, Sextette from *Lucia*.

   Weber, *Invitation to the Dance*, Op. 65.

   Schumann, *Novelletten*, Op. 21, No. 8, Trio (1-8);
   Symphonic Etudes, Op. 13, Finale.

Chopin, *Prelude,* Op. 28, No. 15, D flat section;
  Waltz, Op. 34, No. 1, second ending; D flat section;
  Mazurka, Op. 30, No. 3,
    Op. 50, No. 2, D flat Major section (1-8);
  B flat Minor Sonata, Op. 35, Funeral March, D flat Major
   section; First Movement, second theme (1-16);
  B flat Minor Scherzo, Op. 31, D flat section, Con anima.
Tchaikovsky, *String Quartet,* Op. 11, Andante cantabile, D flat
  section (1-25);
  Romeo and Juliet, second theme.
Sinding, *Rustle of Spring,* Op. 32, No. 3.
Sibelius, *Romance,* Op. 24, No. 9 (1-6).
Bohm, *Calm as the Night.*
Dvořák, *New World Symphony,* Op. 95, Largo.
Wagner, *Tannhauser,* Act. I, Scene 2, "Dir tone Lob!" (1-16).
Brahms, *We Walked One Day,* Op. 96, No. 2;
  Liebeslieder, Op. 52, No. 17.
Kjerulf, *Lullaby.*
Lack, *Madrigal.*

(*b*) Examples using ninth-chords:
Schubert, *Violin Sonata,* Op. 78, First Movement (10-15),
  Andante (30-34).
Beethoven, *Piano Sonata,* Op. 14, No. 1, Allegro (46-57);
  Symphony No. 2, Op. 36, Larghetto (68-75);
  Eroica Symphony, Op. 55, Funeral March (last 16
   measures);
  Sonata, Op. 13, Adagio (last 8 measures).
Chopin, *F Minor Fantasia,* Op. 49 (15-20);
  Mazurka, Op. 63, No. 1 (1-16).
Mendelssohn, *Songs Without Words,* No. 39 (21-25), No. 44
  (8-20).
Grieg, *At Home,* Op. 43, No. 3 (9-12).
Chaminade, *Scarf Dance* (1-16).

(*c*) Examples in C sharp major:
Haydn, *C sharp Minor Piano Sonata,* Trio.
Schubert, *Moment Musical,* Op. 94, No. 4;
  C Major Fantasia, Op. 15, Adagio (27-30).
Brahms, *Waltz,* Op. 39, No. 6.
Bach, *Well-Tempered Clavier,* I, Prelude 3.

(*d*) Examples using enharmonic keys:
Schubert, *Fantasie Sonata,* Op. 78, Trio (last 10).

Chopin, *Polonaise,* Op. 40, No. 1 (13-16);
  Nocturne, Op. 48, No. 2, Molto più lento;
  Mazurka, Op. 6, No. 2 (17-24),
    Op. 69, No. 1, G sharp Minor section.
Brahms, *Liebeslieder,* Op. 52, No. 15.

2. *Written dictation (quality, bass, melody, and name of chord).*
  Brown Book, Twice 55: No. 5, *America the Beautiful;*
    No. 37, *Auld Lang Syne;*
    No. 27, *Flow Gently, Sweet Afton.*
  New Episcopal Hymnal, No. 487, *Ellers,*
    No. 257, *Lancashire,*
    No. 416, *Beatitude.*
  Golden Book: Hail, Columbia, page 9,
    How Can I Leave Thee?, page 30.
  Mendelssohn, *Songs Without Words,* No. 48 (1-4) and (9-12).
  Wolf, *Prayer* (9-16).
  Schumann, *Night Piece,* Op. 23, No. 3, F sharp Minor section
    (1-8).

IV — Assignment for Analysis

Mozart, *F Major Piano Sonata,* K533, Rondo, F Minor section
  (1-8).
Beethoven, *E Major Piano Sonata,* Op. 14, No. 1, Allegro (30-38;
  46-57).
Schubert, *Hark, Hark, the Lark.*
Schumann, *Scenes from Childhood,* Op. 15, No. 2;
    Curious Story (1-4);
    Symphonic Etudes, Op. 13, Variation 4, Finale.
Weber, *Invitation to the Dance,* Op. 65, Coda;
    Rondo Brillant, Op. 62 (1-8).
Chopin, *Prelude,* Op. 28, No. 7 (complete); No. 15 (1-8), No. 16,
    Introduction; No. 18 (1);
    Waltz, Op. 34, No. 1, D flat section, pages 14-15;
    Mazurka, Op. 30, No. 3 (25-28; 47-64),
      Op. 33, No. 4, B flat Major section (last four
        measures),
      Op. 63, No. 2 (1-8).
Bohm, *Still as the Night* (1-5).
Mendelssohn, *Songs Without Words,* No. 20 (1-5); No. 48
    (1-18);
    Violin Concerto, Op. 64, Finale (8-12).

Bizet, *Carmen,* "Toreador Song" (1-8).
Brahms, *Hungarian Dance* No. 6,
                       No. 7, middle section,
                       No. 12, last 9 measures.
Franck, *Sonata for Violin and Piano,* First Movement (1-4).
Grieg, *G Minor Violin Sonata,* Op. 13, Allegretto, E Major section
     (1-4);
     Dance-Caprice, Op. 28, No. 3 (9-20);
     At Home, Op. 43, No. 3 (9-12).
Tchaikovsky, *Romeo and Juliet,* subordinate theme.

The following passages have been selected for analysis from the above list. Identify the form, chord, and nonharmonic tones.

(Introduction)

Allegretto   SCHUBERT, *Hark, Hark, the Lark*

(a)

SCHUMANN, Op. 15, No. 2

Allegro giojoso

V$_9$
inverted

WEBER, *Rondo Brillant,* Op. 62

Moderato e con grazia

Andantino

CHOPIN, *Prelude,* Op. 28, No. 7

Poco tranquillo

BOHM, *Still as the Night*

Chapter XXX

THE VII₇ CHORD

Ex. 232

CHOPIN, (1810 – 1849) *Polonaise*, Op. 26, No. 2 (Adapted)

As has been noted before (Chapter XVIII, page 302), Chopin was greatly influenced by the songs and dances of his native Poland. The *polonaise,* as its name indicates, is one of the most characteristic of these dances, having originated late in the 16th century as "processional music" for the opening of court ceremonies. It had no fixed steps or patterns, being more closely allied to the march than to a conventionalized dance. When used in court, only one step was taken for each full measure, thus giving an effect of great dignity. The characteristic melodic rhythm of the polonaise was an accented second beat (Example 232, measure 2) often over the accompaniment figure ¾ (♫♫♫♫), which, however, Chopin did not use in this instance. The last measure is the typical rhythmic and melodic ending.

Chopin wrote 11 polonaises whose general characteristics are either strong and martial, representing the pomp and splendor of the feudal Polish court (see the *Military Polonaise,* Op. 40, No. 1), or dreamy and sad, suggesting Poland in bondage (see Example 232). The *Polonaise-Fantasie* (Op. 61) is said to represent the struggle for national freedom ending in victory.

Play Example 232 again, listening for its key center and tonality. Observe the new key of E flat minor with its signature of six flats.[1] Name its relative and parallel major keys.

Listen once more to Example 232 for its harmonic background, noting the dissonant chord on the first beat of measure 2. Determine its root, and name the chord by letter and Roman numeral. Sing and resolve it in *arpeggio* form, thus:

Ex. 233

The symbol $^0_7$ is used to denote diminished quality. The VI⁶ is used here as a substitute for the I which would be the normal resolution.

Consider the construction of the VII$^0_7$. Since both its triad, D–F–A flat, and its seventh, D–C flat, are diminished, it is known as a *diminished seventh-chord.* (See Chapter XXVII, Example 214 (*e*), page 505, and Example 215 (*b*), page 505.) Let us consider its structure in more detail.

This diminished seventh-chord is made up of the minor thirds D–F, F–A flat, and A flat–C flat. This equality of interval construction makes the diminished seventh-chord unique because, as a result, all *inversions* sound like fundamental chords. This is

---

[1] Write the three forms of the E flat minor scale in treble and bass, first with accidentals, then with its key signature of six flats. Sing each from memory.

readily proved by writing the *inversions* of this diminished seventh
on D enharmonically, thus:

Ex. 234

In other words, *inversions* of diminished seventh-chords can
only be recognized through the eye, not through the ear. Consequently, all diminished seventh-chord sounds are spelled in reference to their chord of resolution. This means that the bass note
is regarded as the practical (aural) root, and that the spelling of
the other tones is determined by their resolution, not by purely
theoretical *inversions*.

It is this difference between the *sound* and the *sight* of a diminished seventh-chord that has made it known as the *enharmonic chord* — one of the most ambiguous chords in music.[2]
Its construction, however, makes it particularly useful in modulation. Test this by erecting a diminished $^6_5$, $^4_3$, and $^4_2$ chord on D.
(It is surprising to note the number of keys it is possible to enter
in this manner.)

Sing, an octave lower if necessary, this *Rheingold* motive from
the first of Wagner's music dramas known as "The Ring":

Ex. 235

Rhinegold!   Rhinegold!

Here is the same VII₇ chord in major, but how bright it sounds
in comparison with the same chord in minor. This is because the
chord-seventh has been changed from diminished to minor. Since
the triad remains diminished, however, the VII₇ in the major

---

[2] The augmented triad (III in harmonic minor), which is best treated as a
chromatic chord, shares this distinction for the same reason.

mode is called a *half-diminished seventh-chord,* symbolized $\varnothing$ 7. (See Chapter XXVII, Example 214 (*d*), and Example 215 (*a*), page 505.)

Each inversion of the VII$_7$ in major is distinctive and, unlike those of the diminished seventh-chord, can be both heard and seen. The inverted VII$_7$ in major is perhaps more used than is the fundamental form.

The VII$_7$ in both modes belongs to the dominant group of chords, and its technical treatment is, on the whole, similar to that of the V$_7$ and V$_9$ chords. The chord-seventh resolves downward stepwise and no interval is omitted or doubled. The VII$_7$ is usually followed by the I, as in Example 235, the resolution to the VI$_6$, in Example 232, being exceptional. In the progression VII$_7$–I, the third of the I chord is usually doubled.

In the major mode, the root of the VII$_7$ may also resolve down a fifth to the root of the III$_7$, especially in a series of sequential seventh-chords[3] (see Chapter XXVII, Example 214, page 504).

Note that in the VII$_7$–I progression, Example 235, each tone of the VII$_7$ is adjacent to at least one tone of the tonic chord. Consequently, this diatonic VII$_7$ sounds like an *embellishment* of the I chord in either mode. Chromatic diminished and half-diminished seventh-chords often embellish other diatonic chords. In fact, the diminished seventh is perhaps most often used chromatically, as in Example 232, last chord of measure 3, which embellishes the A flat$_6$ over the bar.

Identify the other chords in Example 232. The V$_9$ chord in the last measure shows the relationship between the V$_9$ and the VII$_7$ chords when the latter resolves to the I chord.[4] Melodically, this passage is developed from the pattern in measure 2.

Sing the following passage (Example 236), which shows the

---

[3] The progressions VII$_7$–III$_7$ are possible in the minor mode only when the natural form of the scale is used.

[4] The VII$_7$ is sometimes classified as an incomplete V$_9$ due to its frequent dominant function. However, it also functions as a real VII$_7$ by its resolution to the III$_7$ chord.

use of the diatonic VII₇ as a dominant substitute:

Ex. 236   MOZART, *Ave Verum* (1791)

Locate the diminished seventh-chords. In addition to these, there are many other interesting items worth noting. The passage begins and ends on the B flat major chord, which, however, is in different keys. Explain how this is possible. Study the chords and voice leading carefully through both singing and listening until you understand exactly how Mozart achieved his effects.

In Example 236, there are several instances of the points discussed in this chapter: the key of E flat minor, and the use of the diminished seventh-chord, both as a diatonic VII₇ and as a chromatic embellishment. In addition, it was noted that the principle of enharmonic notation could be used for both scales and chords. Applied to scales, it gave us three additional enharmonic minor scales of five, six, or seven accidentals each; and used for chords, it permitted free modulation by respelling the same diminished seventh-chord in different keys.

Note the difference in quality between the VII₇ in each mode. In minor, the VII₇ was a diminished seventh, whereas in major it was a half-diminished seventh-chord. Owing to its equal intervals, the *inverted* diminished seventh-chord always gave the effect of a fundamental chord.

Also, one observed the use of the diatonic VII₇ chord, either as a dominant substitute embellishing the I chord, or as a genuine seventh-chord resolving harmonically to the III₇. The chromatic use of the chord was also suggested. In all cases no interval was omitted or doubled, and the chord-seventh resolved downward one degree. These technical points emerged from analysis of the natural movement of the chord tones, especially as stepwise embellishments of the I chord.

It was noted in Chapters XXVII-XXIX, pages 499 to 546, that the three major keys having five, six, or seven accidentals could be written in two ways enharmonically, using either sharps or flats. That is, B major (five sharps) could also be written as C flat (seven flats), G flat major (six flats) as F sharp (six sharps), and D flat major (five flats) as C sharp major (seven sharps). These were called the *enharmonic* major scales.

This is also true of the corresponding minor scales using five, six, or seven accidentals. For example, Example 232, page 571, could be written in the key of D sharp minor rather than D flat minor without changing its sound. Compare the two scales, thus:

Ex. 237

Eb minor

Enharmonic notation

1 2 3 4 5 6 7 8

D# minor
(Harmonic form)

E flat minor and D sharp minor require the same number of accidentals, so that apparently there is no advantage in using one or the other signature. However, compositions using the signature of D sharp minor are very rare indeed, perhaps for psychological reasons.

Applying this principle of equivalent spelling to the minor

scales using five, six, and seven accidentals, we find that the enharmonic minor scales are:

Ex. 238

B♭ (5♭), or A♯ (7♯)

E♭ (6♭), or D♯ (6♯)

A♭ (7♭), or G♯ (5♯)

Construct and sing the other scales as already done with E flat and D sharp minors.

Since this concludes the study of minor scales, it is well to classify them according to their signatures by arranging them clockwise, thus:

Ex. 239*

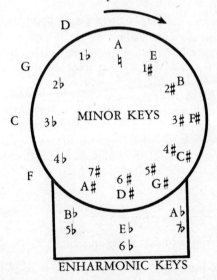

up 5ths

MINOR KEYS

ENHARMONIC KEYS

*The whole subject of the associations made with keys is interesting and complex. Keys are often regarded in terms of preference as to difficulty, mood, quality, and even color. Composers, as well as performers, have expressed themselves definitely on these points, though there is little agreement among them.

Now one can see more clearly why there are only three en-harmonic minor scales having signatures. Others could be written theoretically, but only by means of added accidentals, as the prac-tical limit of a key signature is seven sharps or flats. Those enhar-monic scales using more than seven occur very rarely in short modulatory passages.[5]

Review all the signatures and recite them in clockwise order, giving the required accidentals for each.

Finally, the study of minor scales was completed by classifying them according to their required sharps or flats. This gave 15 minor scales, including the three enharmonic scales, using five, six, or seven sharps or flats.

Much of the material in this chapter is given almost entirely for reference purposes. Use what you can, especially the diminished seventh-chord, but only when it can be done *musically,* not theoretically.

Review:

1. The construction and signature of E flat minor.
2. The enharmonic minor scales.
3. How many minor scales may be written with key signatures
4. The parallel and relative scales of E flat minor.
5. How the VII₇ resembles the V₉ in structure.
6. What chords usually follow the VII₇.
7. Whether any tones are omitted or doubled in the VII₇.
8. For what chord the VII₇ is sometimes substituted.
9. The difference in quality between the VII₇ in each mode.
10. Why the inversions of the diminished seventh-chord exist only on paper, that is, visually, not aurally.

For Further Study, Determine:

1. Which enharmonic minor scales are most used.

---

[5] See Bach, *Well-Tempered Clavier,* Vol. I, Fugue 3 (measures 19-22) which ends in E sharp (F) minor as the mediant key to the tonic key, C sharp major. A curious point regarding both enharmonic major and minor scales is the fact that certain scales have no parallel scale that can be written using a key signature (for example, D sharp minor, whose parallel must be written enharmonically as E flat, since D sharp major has no signature).

2. Examples of enharmonic minor scales requiring more than seven accidentals.

3. Why certain major and minor scales have no parallel scales which can be written using a key signature.

4. Why there are more written minor scales than there are pitches in the octave.

5. Why the VII_7 resembles the V_9 in structure but not always in function.

6. Why the root of the VII_7 is not doubled.

7. How the diminished seventh-chord (VII_7 in minor) can be used for modulation.

8. Why the resolution of the VII_7 to III_7 is called harmonic in contrast to its embellishing resolution to the I.

9. Why the natural form of the minor scale is preferable in the progression VII_7–III_7.

10. The most nearly related keys to E flat minor.

I — Assignment for Writing

1. Scan the following poem and set it to music for mixed voices. (Accompaniment optional.) Compare different versions by performance in class.

> The splendor falls on castle walls
> And snowy summits old in story:
> The long light shakes across the lakes,
> And the wild cataract leaps in glory.
> Blow, bugle, blow, set the wild echoes flying,
> Blow, bugle; answer, echoes, dying, dying, dying.
>
> *Blow, Bugle, Blow — Alfred, Lord Tennyson*

2. Add the alto and tenor voices (in that order) to at least one of the following passages:

BACH, *371 Chorales*

(a)

Soprano
Alto

Tenor
Bass 1

Bass 2

MENDELSSOHN, *Elijah,* No. 1, "Help, Lord"

MENDELSSOHN, *Elijah,* No. 22, "Be not afraid"

3. Harmonize at least one of the following melodies for mixed voices:

DOWLAND (1600), Excerpt from *Fine Knacks for Ladies*
Allegro moderato

(d)

(IV) (VII₇)

Andante maestoso MENDELSSOHN, *Elijah*, No. 42

(e)

(G: VII₃⁴)

WESLEY (1839)

(f)

(II₃⁴)

(E: VII₅⁶)

KUFFERATH

(g)

Lento WAGNER, *Rienzi*, Prayer

(h)

[melody in alto]

4. Harmonize at least one of the following melodies for piano. Identify the form of each melody used.

Allegro SCHARWENKA, *Polish Dance*, Op. 3, No. 1

(a)

Allegro SCHARWENKA, *Polish Dance*, Op. 3, No. 1

(b)

(G₇) (Cb)

(Cb) (Bb)

Allegretto giocoso Czech Folk Song

(c)

Fine

D.S. al Fine

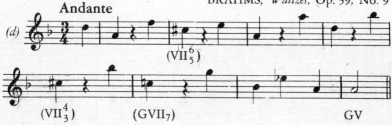

BRAHMS, *Waltzes*, Op. 39, No. 9

Andante

(d)

(VII⁶₅)

(VII⁴₃) (GVII₇) GV

Moderato SCHUBERT, *Ländler*, Op. 39, No. 9

(e)

Tempo di valse SCHUBERT, *Waltzes*, Op. 9a, No. 13

(f)

(VII₇)

II — Assignment for Playing

1. Harmonize any of the melodies in the *Assignment for Writing* (4).
2. Complete the following *A–B* form and extend by the repetition of each part.

Part I Moderato SCHUBERT, *Waltz*, Op. 18a, No. 17

Part II

chromatic
dim. 7th

3. Improvise melodies in B flat, E flat, or A flat minors in *A–B* form extended by the repetition of each part. (Harmonization optional.)

4. Transpose by ear familiar music into the enharmonic minor keys. Continue reading simple music in A, E, D, or B minors in the minor keys of the same letters, but with different signatures, for example, A and A flat minor. (See Chapters XXII-XXIV, pages 383-423.)

5. Transpose the following modulatory chord patterns to all minor keys. Note that they include all three types of the most used modulations from the enharmonic minor keys.

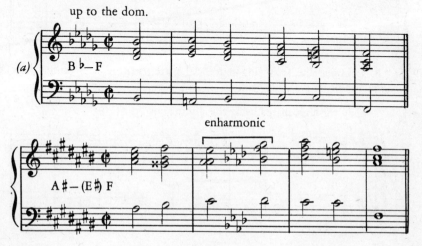

6. Continue the following sequential patterns through all minor keys until A minor is reached again.

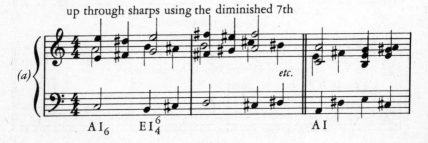

A I₆

down through flats using the diminished 7th

F V₆   I

7. Transpose simple melodic and harmonic passages in E flat minor down a minor third to C minor, and up a major second to F minor (review notes on transposition). Experiment transposing passages from these keys to E flat minor.

III — Assignment for Listening

1. *Oral dictation:* harmonic recognition only. (Name chords by quality, letter, or Roman numeral.)

Beethoven, *Sonata,* Op. 7, Allegro, Minore,
Op. 10, No. 1, First Movement (1-22),
Op. 10, No. 3, Largo (1-9),
Op. 13, Grave (1-10); Adagio cantabile (37-44),
Op. 26, Funeral March (1-30),
Op. 106, Adagio (1-13).
Schubert, *Waltzes,* Op. 18a, No. 2;
Ländler, Op. 171, Nos. 4, 5, 10,
Op. Post., No. 8.
Chopin, *Piano Sonata,* Op. 35, *Funeral March* (1-30);
Mazurka, Op. 24, No. 4, Con anima;
Polonaise, Op. 26, No. 2, Meno mosso.
Verdi, *Il Trovatore,* "Miserere."
Franck, *D Minor Symphony,* Allegretto.
Brahms, *Hungarian Dances,* No. 12, Presto; No. 15, Presto;
Waltz, Op. 39, Nos. 1, 3, 14.

Lack, *Madrigal,* Op. 136, Poco più animato (1-4).
Tchaikovsky, *Fourth Symphony,* Op. 36, Andantino (1-20);
　　　　　Nutcracker Suite, Op. 71*a,* "Danse des Miriltons."
Grieg, *Humoresque,* Op. 6, No. 2, D flat section;
　　　　Danse Caprice, Op. 28, No. 3, A Minor section.

2. *Written dictation (quality, bass, melody, and name of chord).*
New Episcopal Hymnal, No. 191, *Sacramentum Unitatis.*
Schumann, *Night Piece,* Op. 23, No. 1, Più tranquillo; No. 3, Più
　　mosso (9-16).
Chopin, *Rondo,* Op. 1, Più lento (1-24).
Mozart, *The Violet,* K476 (27-34).

IV — Assignment for Analysis

Bach, *Well-Tempered Clavier,* I, Prelude 3 (25-30),
　　　　　　　　　　II, Prelude 8 (11-16).
Play a Tune: Bourrée (Bach), page 32.
Beethoven, *Sonata,* Op. 26, Funeral March (1-30).
Verdi, *Il Trovatore,* "Miserere."
Schubert, *Ländler,* Op. 171, No. 7;
　　　　Waltz, Op. 9*b,* No. 4, second half.
Chopin, *Piano Sonata,* Op. 35, Funeral March (1-4);
　　　　F Minor Fantasia, Op. 49, Più mosso.
Brahms, *Faithfulness,* Op. 3, No. 1 (1-5).
Scharwenka, *Polish Dance,* Op. 3, No. 1.
Grieg, *Humoresque,* Op. 6, No. 2 (1-16).
Jadassohn, *Klavierstück,* (1-4).

The following passages have been selected for analysis from the above
list. Identify the form, chords, and nonharmonic tones.

BACH, *Well-Tempered Clavier,* Book I, Prelude III

Allegretto

(a)

BACH, *Well-Tempered Clavier*, Book II, Prelude VIII

Allegretto

VERDI, *Il Trovatore*, "Miserere"

Andante assai sostenuto

CHOPIN, *F Minor Fantaisie*, Op. 49

[Coda] **Tempo di marcia, più mosso**

octaves ad lib.

BRAHMS, *Faithfulness*, Op. 3, No. 1

Molto lento

GRIEG, *Humoreske*, Op. 6 No. 2

Tempo di minuetto

(f)

JADASSOHN, *Klavierstück*

Allegretto

(g)

(chromatic)
V₇

Summary IV

In the last four chapters examination of musical literature clarified certain details about the structure and the harmonic vocabulary of music.

First, in regard to scales, one important fact was the principle of *enharmonic notation,* which made it possible to complete the series of major and minor scales used today. By the term *enharmonic* is meant the use of different spellings for the same pitch, for example F sharp and G flat. Theoretically, all scales could thus be written in two ways, but, practically, only those requiring five, six, or seven accidentals were actually so notated. Hence, all major and minor keys are classified according to their signatures by arranging them clockwise, thus:

Ex. 240

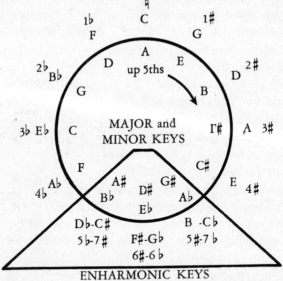

Second, the II₇, II⅚, II⅘, V₉, and VII₇ chords were added to our harmonic vocabulary, thus completing the study of the most frequently used diatonic chords. The II₇ and its inversion were similar to the V_7 as regards doubling and voice leading. Also, the other secondary second chords (III_7–IV_7–VI_7, and VII_7) were used chiefly in sequential passages, the root of each resolving down a fifth to the root of another seventh-chord. In these consecutive sevenths, the chord-fifth was usually omitted and the root doubled in alternate chords.

The VII_7 had a double function, through its resolution, either to the III_7 or to the I chord. Usually it resolved directly to the I, which gave it the effect of an embellishing chord, as all its tones were adjacent to those of the I chord. This resolution of the VII_7 to the I grouped it with the dominant chords. When the various seventh-chords were named according to their interval structure (Chapter XXVII, Examples 214, 215), the VII_7 was a *diminished seventh* in the minor mode and a *half-diminished seventh-chord* in the major mode. Since all intervals of the diminished seventh-chord were equal (minor thirds), all its "inversions" sounded like a fundamental chord. Hence, "inversions" of diminished seventh-chords were visual, not aural, and their spelling was determined entirely by their context.

The V_9 chord was heard as an extension of the familiar V_7 chord, and was most often used to harmonize the sixth scale step when followed by the fifth in the melody. The V_9 was usually found in fundamental position, and its five-voice structure made it necessary to omit one of its tones, the chord-fifth. Other ninth-chords, or further extension of the V_9 to V_{11} or V_{13}, were too infrequently used to warrant discussion at present.

Third, it was noted that the two-part (A–B) form was made up of two equal contrasting phrases or periods each ended by a perfect authentic cadence. The two parts often ended similarly, but there was no suggestion of a return to the beginning of part I. This form frequently was extended by repetition of each part (A–A–B–B). Also, the period form might be extended by the repetition of either the antecedent or consequent phrase, or both (Example 225, page 546), or by two different versions of either phrase (Example 218, page 525). It should be noted, however, that both these extensions are rare, and were discussed only because of the examples cited.

One new type of foreign tone was found: *double* neighboring tones, which were always followed (sometimes also preceded) by the intervening chord tone. These double neighbors were most useful as melodic embellishments. The lower neighbor was usually chromatic, and the upper neighbor diatonic as in the case of single neighboring tones.

Suggestions for Study

Find examples in musical literature of the following technical points discussed in Part IV:

(1) Chords.
  (*a*) The II_7, II_3^4, V_9, and VII_7.
  (*b*) Other seventh-chords cited in Chapter XXVII, Examples 214 and 215, pages 504-505.
(2) Nonharmonic tones.
  Double neighboring tones.
(3) Form.
  The extended binary (*A–B*) form.
(4) Enharmonic keys.
  The enharmonic major and minor keys omitted from Bach's *Well-Tempered Clavier*, Books I and II. (See Example 240, page 592.)

Appendix

SUMMARY OF NOTATION

TWO ELEMENTS are involved in the notation of music, tone and time. *Notes* are symbols of both tone and time; that is, both precise pitches and their duration are indicated by notes. Duration measured by regular pulsation is also shown by *time signatures*. Other symbols of notation affecting tone and time include staves, clefs, accidentals, rests, bar lines, dots, and ties. The purpose and use of these symbols may be summarized briefly as folows:

I — Tone (Pitch)

(a) The Staff

In western music the first seven letters of the alphabet are used to designate different pitches. These pitches are represented by notes written upon a *staff* (plural, *staves*) of five parallel equidistant lines and four spaces whose range may be extended by adding *leger lines* above and below the staff as needed. Each line and space of the staff represents a definite pitch (equivalent to the white keys of the piano), identified by a *clef* sign written at the beginning of the staff. Three clefs are in use: the *F or bass clef*, located on the fourth line of the lower staff; the *G or treble clef*, located on the second line of the upper staff; and the *C clef*, which may be placed on any line. The C clef is most often used today for orchestral instruments; when used by the viola, it appears on the third line and is known as the *alto clef*, and when used by the cello or trombone, it is found on the fourth line and is called the *tenor clef*. The C clef, wherever placed, always locates *middle C* or C[1] (one-line C) as shown in Example A.

The G (treble) and F (bass) clefs are most frequently used and, in piano music, are assigned to the right and left hands respectively. When combined, the treble and bass clefs form the *Great Staff,* shown in Example A.

Ex. *A* Octave Groups

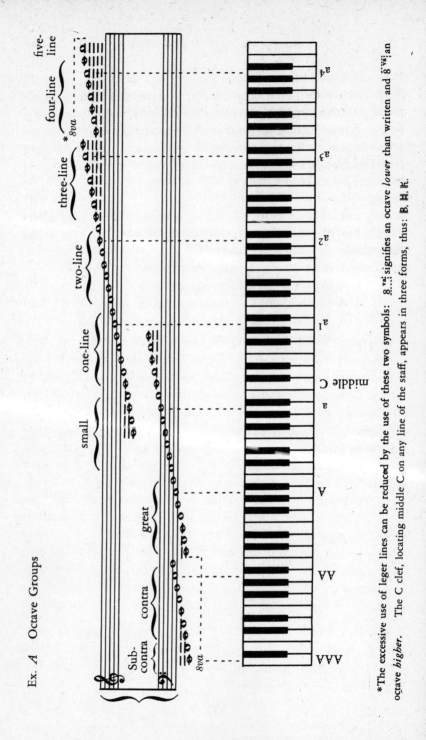

*The excessive use of leger lines can be reduced by the use of these two symbols: 8‥‥ signifies an octave *lower* than written and 8‥‥ an octave *higher*.   The C clef, locating middle C on any line of the staff, appears in three forms, thus: 𝕭, 𝕳, 𝕶.

596

Note the names of the *octave groups,* each beginning on C. A single pitch within each octave is named from the C immediately below it, thus: great E, small F, E¹ (one-line), A² (two-line), and so forth. Note also the use of abbreviations for pitches an octave higher or lower than written, used as a means of reducing the excessive and confusing use of leger lines.

(*b*) Accidentals

Any one of the following symbols placed before a note alters the pitch of the staff degrees represented by the white keys of the piano, thus:

> A sharp (♯), one half-tone upward
> A flat (♭), one half-tone downward
> A double sharp (✗), one whole tone upward
> A double flat (♭♭), one whole tone downward
> A natural (♮), restores the staff pitch.

II — Time[1]

(*a*) Note Values

Time in music is concerned both with notes of different duration and with recurrent pulses or beats. The note values in general use, with their equivalent rests, or periods of silence, are:

Ex. *B*	*Value*	*Note*	*Rest*
	whole	𝅝	▬
	half	𝅗𝅥	▬
	quarter	𝅘𝅥	𝄽
	eighth	𝅘𝅥𝅮	𝄾
	sixteenth	𝅘𝅥𝅯	𝄿
	thirty-second	𝅘𝅥𝅰	𝅀
	sixty-fourth	𝅘𝅥𝅱	𝅁

---

[1] For a discussion of the relation between time in poetry and music see Calvin S. Brown, *Music and Literature.* Athens, Ga.: University of Georgia Press, 1948.

The round part of the note is known as the *head*. The line drawn to the head is the *stem*. The curved line attached to the stem is the *hook*. A straight line connecting the stems of eighth notes or less is known as the *beam*. Thus ♪ ♪♪ , if occurring on one pulse may be written ♫♫ , the number of beams corresponding to that of the hooks. Any irregular division of a single time unit is indicated by writing the number contained in the group under it, thus: (triplet), (quintuplet).

A *dot* after a note or a rest increases its time-value one half; a double dot by three-fourths, thus: ♩. = ♩+♪   and   ♩.. = ♩ + ♪ + ♪

A *tie* is a curved line connecting the heads of two notes of the same pitch, the second of which is silent.

A *slur* is a curved line connecting the heads of two notes of different pitches indicating that the pitches are to be connected smoothly in performance.

The tie and the slur are shown in the following example:

Ex. *C*
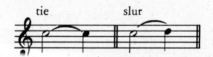

(*b*) Time Signatures

In addition to note values, time in music is measured by recurrent pulses, which occur in three basic patterns or meters:

> *Duple* — a strong and weak pulse or beat.
> *Triple* — a strong and two weak pulses or beats.
> *Quadruple* — a strong and three weak pulses or beats.

A perpendicular line, called a *bar*, is drawn across the staff before each strong beat. The space between two adjacent bar lines is called a visual *measure*. A *double bar* marks the end of a section or of a complete composition.

Two figures, written vertically, after the clef indicate the meter and the unit of note value used: that is, the upper figure indicates the number of pulses in the measure and the lower figure, the note value that is equivalent to one pulse or beat of the meter. These two figures together are known as the *time* or *metric signature*. Thus $\frac{2}{4}$ means that there are two pulses in the measure, each of which is represented by a quarter note.

Meters are classified as *simple* or *compound*.[2] The three basic
meters are *simple* when their pulses are subdivided by two or its
multiples. When their pulses are subdivided by three, or its multiples, the meter is said to be *compound*. The principal simple and
compound meters are represented by the following time signatures:

Table of Simple Meters

Ex. D

Duple $\frac{2}{16}\left(\frac{2}{♪}\right)$, $\frac{2}{8}\left(\frac{2}{♪}\right)$, $\frac{2}{4}\left(\frac{2}{♩}\right)$, $\frac{2}{2}$ or ¢ $\left(\frac{2}{𝅝}\right)$

Triple $\frac{3}{16}\left(\frac{3}{♪}\right)$, $\frac{3}{8}\left(\frac{3}{♪}\right)$, $\frac{3}{4}\left(\frac{3}{♩}\right)$, $\frac{3}{2}\left(\frac{3}{𝅝}\right)$

Quadruple $\frac{4}{16}\left(\frac{4}{♪}\right)$, $\frac{4}{8}\left(\frac{4}{♪}\right)$, $\frac{4}{4}$ or C $\left(\frac{4}{♩}\right)$, $\frac{4}{2}\left(\frac{4}{𝅝}\right)$

(Note the use of the symbol C for $\frac{4}{4}$ and of ¢ for $\frac{2}{2}$. It is important
to remember that these are different meters. The symbol C is a
relic of a medieval sign. Similarly the name for ¢ is *alla breve*,
referring to a medieval note value. Although incorrect, the collo-
quialisms for these signs, "common" and "cut" time persist.)

Table of Compound Meters

Ex. E

Duple $\frac{6}{16}\left(\frac{2}{♪.}\right)$, $\frac{6}{8}\left(\frac{2}{♩.}\right)$, $\frac{6}{4}\left(\frac{2}{𝅗𝅥.}\right)$

Triple $\frac{9}{16}\left(\frac{3}{♪.}\right)$, $\frac{9}{8}\left(\frac{3}{♩.}\right)$, $\frac{9}{4}\left(\frac{3}{𝅗𝅥.}\right)$

Quadruple $\frac{12}{16}\left(\frac{4}{♪.}\right)$, $\frac{12}{8}\left(\frac{4}{♩.}\right)$, $\frac{12}{4}\left(\frac{4}{𝅗𝅥.}\right)$

---

[2] Quadruple meter is sometimes classified as a compound meter.

Unusual time signatures such as $\frac{5}{4}$ and $\frac{7}{4}$ are sometimes used. Actually these signatures are a combination of duple or triple meters or of triple and quadruple meters, respectively, in either order.

All these facts regarding details of notation should be learned or reviewed primarily from the examination of music literature. Find examples in familiar music of each notational symbol defined above. For more detailed information, consult any standard dictionary of music.

INDEX

INDEX

(All references to musical compositions are indexed under the composer's name; references to chords under *Chords*.)

A

A–B, 55, 151, 527
  extended by repetition, 508
A–B–A, 36, 63, 82, 188, 527
  imperfect authentic cadence, 388
  length of parts, 387-389
  perfect authentic cadence, 388
  repetitions used, 388
  summary of variants, 388
Acciaccatura, 171
Accidentals:
  chromatic music, 33
  minor mode, 322
  neighboring tones, 32-33
  notation, 597
Accompaniment figures, 21-22
  alterations at cadences, 79
  broken-chord, 53-54, 79-80
  chord tones in right hand, 110, 111
  repeated chords, 67
  waltz, 35
Added sixth chords, 426
Adeste Fideles, 191
Aeolian minor scale (*see* Natural minor scale)
Aeolian mode, 340
Ain't Gonna Rain, 20-21
Alla breve, 599
Alto clef, 595
Alto voice (*see also* Inner voices):
  range, 247, 363
Amen cadence, 30
Annie Laurie, 49, 95
Antecedent group, 527
Antecedent phrase, 10
Anticipations, 94, 96
Appoggiatura, 170
Arensky, *Basso Ostinato,* 398
Arnoud, 215
Atonality, 4
Aubert, Jacques, 148-149
Augmented second, 304
  in harmonic minor scale, 321
Augmented fourth, 210
Augmented intervals, 210
Authentic cadence:
  imperfect, 93
    A–B–A form, 388
  perfect, 8
    A–B–A form, 388
    substitution of II₆ for IV, 47-48
Authentic modes, 340

B

Bach:
  cello suites:
    Third, 165
    Sixth, 168, 223
  chorales, 219, 351, 361, 390, 391, 410-411, 429, 450, 456, 479, 509, 530, 579-580
    My Soul, Now Bless Thy Maker, 111, 112
    No. 86, 271
    No. 106, 406
    No. 188, 223
    No. 234, 211, 212
    No. 336, 427-428
  English Suites, 319
  French Suites, 319
    Second, 319, 335
    Third, 418-419
    Fifth, 182-183
  Gavotte (Carroll I), 419
  Minuet (Carroll I), 360
  Praeludium (Peters Ed., Vol. VIII), 441-442
  style, 319-320
  Toccata, G Major, 405
  Two-Part Inventions, No. 8, 137
  Violin Sonata, Sixth, 171, 172
  Well-Tempered Clavier, 501
    Book I, Fugue II, 321-322, 323
    Book I, Prelude III, 588
    Book II, Prelude VIII, 589

Balfe:
  Bohemian Girl, The, 436
  Killarney, 557
Bar, 598
Baritone voice, range of, 247
Bass, stationary (see Pedal point)
Bass clef, 595
Basso continuo, 365
Bass voice, range of, 263, 363
Beam (note), 598
Beethoven:
  Op. 100, 141
  overtures:
    Coriolanus, 246
    Egmont, 301
    Fidelio, 16
  piano concertos:
    First, 131
    Fourth, 398
  piano sonatas:
    Moonlight, 258, 470, 471, 472, 473
    Pastoral, 61
    Pathetique, 275
    Op. 2, No. 1, 316-317
    Op. 2, No. 3, 44
    Op. 7, 184, 300-301
    Op. 10, No. 1, 166, 323
    Op. 10, No. 3, 204, 421
    Op. 13, 275
    Op. 14, No. 1, 488
    Op. 14, No. 2, 171
    Op. 27, No. 2, 258, 470, 471, 472,
      473
    Op. 28, 61
    Op. 31, No. 1, 515
    Op. 31, No. 2, 489
    Op. 49, 95
    Op. 79, 420
  quartets:
    Op. 18, No. 1, 166
    Op. 59, No. 3, 383
  Rondo, Op. 71, 259
  Ruins of Athens, 394
  Septet, Op. 20, 268
  Six Easy Variations, 274-275
  Sonatina, Op. 49, No. 1, 359
  style, 384, 470-471
  symphonies:
    Second, 261, 300
    Third, 6
    Fourth, 60-61, 178, 299

    Fifth, 28
    Seventh, 88, 383-384
    Eighth, 383-384
    Ninth, 6, 241, 384
  Violin Concerto, Op. 61, 378-379
  violin sonatas:
    Spring, 122-123, 224
    Op. 12, No. 2, 188
    Op. 23, 536
    Op. 24, 122-123, 224
Binary song form (see A–B)
Bizet, Carmen, "Toreador Song," 435
Boccherini:
  Minuet, 203
  Minuet in A Major, 257
Bohemian National Hymn, 482
Bohm, Still as the Night, 570
Bolero, 437
Bottomley, 404
Bourrée, 169
Brahms:
  Ballade, Op. 118, No. 3, 358
  Faithfulness, 590
  Folk Song, 511
  German Requiem:
    No. 2, 534
    No. 3, 533
    No. 4, 457
  How Art Thou Verily My Queen, 206
  Hungarian Dances:
    No. 4, 461
    No. 5, 447-448, 460-461
    No. 7, 461-462
    No. 9, 415
    No. 13, 463
    No. 15, 358
    No. 17, 467
  Intermezzo, Op. 118, No. 2, 467
  May Night, The, 535
  style, 448
  symphonies:
    First, 421, 466
    Third, 445
    Fourth, 123
  To an Aeolian Harp, 301
  Violin Sonata, Op. 100, 225, 380
  waltzes:
    Op. 39, No. 5, 522
    Op. 39, No. 9, 583
    Op. 39, No. 11, 516
    Op. 39, No. 15, 104

Broken-chord accompaniment figure, 53-54, 79-80
Bulgarian National Anthem, 558

C

C^1, 595, 596
Cadence, 8
  amen, 30
  authentic:
    imperfect, 93
      A–B–A form, 388
    perfect, 8
      A–B–A form, 388
      substitution of II_6 for IV, 47-48
  complete (*see* Cadence: perfect authentic)
  deceptive, 93
  evaded, 93
    substitute chords, 113
  half-cadence, 10
  imperfect authentic, 93
    A–B–A form, 388
  perfect authentic, 8
    A–B–A form, 388
    substitution of II_6 for IV, 47-48
  perfect plagal, 30
  plagal, 30
  semi-cadence, 10
    A–B–A form, 388
  surprise, 93
Cadential$^6_4$ chord, 65
  I^6_4 67
Calvisius, 197
Canon, 136-137, 173
Cantata, 188
Caron, 70
C clef, 595, 596
Cherubini, 268, 295
Chopin:
  ballades:
    Op. 23, 276
    Op. 47, 277
    Fantaisie in F Minor, 337, 590
  mazurkas:
    Op. 6, No. 2, 484
    Op. 7, No. 3, 147, 302
    Op. 17, No. 1, 32
    Op. 24, No. 3, 74
    Op. 41, No. 4, 543
    Op. 56, No. 2, 399
    Op. 67, No. 2, 357

  Op. 68, No. 3, 121
  polonaises:
    characteristics, 572
    Op. 26, No. 2, 571
  preludes:
    Op. 28, No. 7, 568
    Op. 28, No. 15, 569
  sonatas:
    Op. 35, 204-205
    Op. 58, 445
  style, 302
  waltzes:
    Minute (*see* Chopin: waltzes: *Op. 64, No. 1*)
    Op. 34, No. 1, 44, 146
    Op. 34, No. 4, 185
    Op. 64, No. 1, 546-547, 549-550
    Op. 64, No. 2, 484
    Op. 69, No. 2, 167
    Op. 70, No. 1, 59
Choral speech, 76
Chords, 3, 5 (*see also* Triads)
  added sixth, 426
  cadential$^6_4$, 65
    I^6_4, 67
  composer's choice of, 50-51
  dominant (*see* Chords: V)
  dynamic, 78
  eleventh, 551
  embellishing$^6_4$, 452
  fifteenth, 551
  first inversions, 47
    of sevenths, 150 (*see also* Chords: V^6_5 etc.)
    of triads, 407 (*see also* Chords: of the sixth; Chords: I_6, etc.)
  "gateway," 134
  inversions:
    first, 47
      of sevenths, 150 (*see also* Chords: V^6_5 etc.)
      of triads, 407 (*see also* Chords: of the sixth; Chords: I_6 etc.)
    second, 64
      of sevenths 189, 531 (*see also* Chords: V^4_3 etc.)
      of triads (*see* Chords: six-four; Chords: IV^6_4 etc.)
    third, 227-228, 528 (*see also* Chords: V^4_2 etc.)
  leading tone (*see* Chords: VII)

major, 92
  as ending for composition in
    minor, 362
mediant (*see* Chords: III)
names:
  descriptive, 133
  functional, 133
  letter, 5, 6
  number, 5, 6
ninth, 548-552
  quality, 549
of the sixth, 47 (*see also* Chords:
    I₆ etc.)
  consecutive, 406-407
  doubling, 364
  principles for use, 407
  to harmonize scale passage,
    405, 407
  voice leading, 406
passing $_4^6$ 472-477
  doubling, 473
  instrumental use, 470-473
  rhythmic location, 473
  vocal use, 473-474
  voice leading, 472-473
pivotal, 134
position, 363
quality in major and minor mode, 290
resolution, 19
second inversions, 64
  of sevenths, 189, 531 (*see also*
    Chords: V$_3^4$ etc.)
  of triads (*see* Chords: six-four;
    Chords: IV$_4^6$ etc.)
seventh, 20 (*see also* Chords: V₇ etc.)
  diminished, 572-576
  half-diminished, 573-574
  quality, 504-505
six-four, 64 (*see also* Chords: IV$_4^6$
    etc.)
  embellishing, 452
  passing (*see* Chords: passing$_4^6$)
static, 78
subdominant (*see* Chords: IV)
submediant (*see* Chords: VI)
substitute, 92, 109, 110, 113
  evaded cadence, 113
supertonic (*see* Chords: II)
third inversions, 227-228, 528
    (*see also* Chords: V⁴ etc.)
thirteenth, 551

tonal, 31
tonic (*see* Chords: I)
I, 6, 7-8, 31, 78
  cadential expansion by pedal point,
    427
  cadential use, 10
  minor mode, 290
  name, 133
  principal triad, 108
I₆, 53, 77-78
  substitute for I, 92
I$_4^6$, 65, 67
  at beginning, 385
  implied modulation, 261
  passing, 475
  substitute for V, 92
II:
  minor mode, 290
  name, 133
  subordinate triad, 108
  substitute for IV, 109, 110, 113
II$_2^4$, 528
II$_3^4$, 531
  doubling, 531
  II₆, 47-48
  substitute for IV, 92
    in perfect authentic cadence,
      47-48
II$_4^6$:
  embellishing, 475
  passing, 475
II$_4^6$, 425-426
  cadential use, 429
  doubling, 429
II₇:
  doubling, 503
  for II or IV, 507
  use, 506-508
III, 110
  augmented, 291
  in harmonic minor, 573
  minor mode, 290
  name, 133
  subordinate triad, 108
  substitute for V, 109, 110, 113
III₆, 404
III$_4^6$:
  embellishing, 475
  passing, 475
IV, 30-31
  minor mode, 290

name, 133
principal triad, 108
relation to II₆, 48
IV₆:
doubling, 403-404
substitute for IV, 403
IV₄⁶, 448-449, 451-452, 455
doubling, 451
passing, 475
use, 452
V, 7-8, 31
cadential use, 10
minor mode, 290
name, 133
principal triad, 108
V₂⁴, 227-228, 528
exceptional melodic resolution, 245-246
use, 228
V₃⁴, 189-190
use, 191, 211
V₆:
doubling, 386
substitute for V, 385
V₄⁶, passing, 474-475
V₅⁶, 150, 190
substitute for V₇, 151
V₇, 20
cadential expansion, 427
in modulation, 133
V₉, 548-552
use, 551-552
V₁₁, 551
V₁₃, 551
V₁₅, 551
VI, 91-93
minor mode, 290
name, 133
subordinate triad, 108
substitute for I, 92, 93, 109, 110, 113, 386
VI₆, 404
VI₄⁶:
embellishing, 475
passing, 475
VII:
minor mode, 290
name, 133
VII₆, 208
for V₄⁶ in chorales, 475
substitute for V₃⁴, 210-211

to harmonize leading tone, 212
VII₄⁶:
embellishing, 475
passing, 475
VII₇:
as embellishment, 574
classified as incomplete V₉, 574
difference in each mode, 575-576
doubling, 574
substitute for V, 575
VII₇⁰, 572-576
VII₇ᵈ, 573-574
Chromatic music, 33
Church modes, 339-340
Clefs, 595
Clef sign, 595
Clementi:
sonatinas:
  Op. 36, No. 1, 26
  Op. 36, No. 2, 161
Close harmony, 49
"Common" time, 599
Common tones, 364
Complete cadence (see Perfect authentic cadence)
Compound meters, 599
Concords, 19
Consequent group, 527
Consequent phrase, 10
Consonance, 19, 170, 210
Contra octave, 596
Contrary motion:
IV-V, 32
V-IV, 32
Contrasting period, 11
Corelli, Gigue, 152-153
Coron, 118, 134
Counterpoint, 78
Bach, 320
canons, 137
Criticism, stylistic, 364
Crüger, 374, 452-454
"Cut" time, 599
Czarist National Anthem, 344

D

Da capo, 14
Dal segno, 58
D.C. (see Da capo)
D.C. al fine, 36
Deceptive cadence, 93

Diabelli, *Sonatine, Op.* 151, *No.* 4, 60
Diatonic dissonances (*see* Seventh-
    chords; Ninth-chords; Chords:
    II₆; Chords: VII₆)
Diatonic music, 33
Diminished fifth, 209, 210
Diminished intervals, 210,
Diminished seventh-chord, 572-576
Diminished triad, 209
Discords, 19
Dissonance, 19, 170, 209, 210
Dominant, 133 (*see also* Chords: V)
Donizetti:
    "Il Nome," 260
    Lucia di Lammermoor, Sextette,
        135-136
    style, 260
Dorian mode, 340
    melody harmonized by Bach, 361
Dot, 598
Double bar, 598
Double dot, 598
Double flat, 597 (*see also* Accidentals)
Double neighboring tones, 551
Double pedal point, 427
Double sharp, 597 (*see also* Accidentals)
Doubling:
    chords of the sixth, 364
    consecutive seventh-chords, 504
    four-part vocal writing, 364
    passing $^6_4$ chords, 473
    II$^4_3$ 531
    II$^6_5$ 429
    II₇, 503
    IV₆, 403-404
    IV$^6_4$, 451
    V₆, 386
    VII₇, 574
Dowland, *Fine Knacks for Ladies,* 582
"Draw Nigh, Immanuel," 432
D.S. (*see Dal segno*)
Duple time, 598
Dussek, *Sonatina,* 180
Dvořák:
    Humoresque, 45
    Silhouette, 490
    Songs My Mother Taught Me, 104,
        511
Dykes, 234
Dynamic chords, 78

E

Echappée, 262
Eighth note and rest, 597
Elgar, *Salut d'Amour,* 524
Embellishing$^6_4$chord, 452
Embellishments:
    double neighboring tones, 551
    VII₇, 574
Emmett, *Dixie,* 4
Enharmonic chords, 573
Enharmonic keys, 553, 576-578
    minor, 577
Enharmonic notation, 501
    necessary for certain parallel scales,
        578
Equal temperament, 501
Evaded cadence, 93
    substitute chords, 113

F

F clef, 595
Fermata, 367
Fifths:
    diminished, 209, 210
    parallel:
        four-part vocal writing, 364
        organum, 362
    perfect, 91, 209
Figured bass, principles of, 365-366
Final, 340
Fine, 14, 36
First inversions, 47
    of sevenths, 150 (*see also* Chords:
        V$^6_5$ etc.)
    of triads, 407 (*see also* Chords: of
        the sixth; Chords: I₆ etc.)
Five-line C, 596
Flat, 597 (*see also* Accidentals)
Foreign tones (*see* Nonharmonic tones)
Forms (*see* Song forms)
Four-line octave, 596
Four-part vocal writing, 361-369
    compared with two- and three-part,
        368-369
    consecutive chords of the sixth, 406-
        407
    doubling, 364
    general principles, 363-364
    parallel fifths and octaves, 364
    position of chords, 363

procedure in adding inner voices, 366-367
progression, 363-364
spacing, 363
Fourths:
augmented, 210
parallel, in organum, 362
perfect, 209
Franck:
Organ Chorale, No. 1, 522
Violin Sonata, 158,569
Symphonic Variations, 544
Free nonharmonic tones, 49, 66
Freylinghausen, 431

G

Gabriel-Marie, *La Cinquantaine,* 400, 515
Ganne, *La Czarine,* 117
Gastorius, 312
"Gateway" chord, 134
Gavotte, 169
G clef, 595
Gibbons, Orlando, 475, 476, 477
Glareanus, 340
Glinka, 373
Gluck, 181
"God Rest Ye Merry Gentlemen," 402-403
Gounod:
Faust:
Ballet Music, 197
Waltz, 181
Funeral March of the Marionettes, 381-382
Gallia, "O Turn Thee," 512
Grainger, Percy, *Country Gardens,* 400
Graun, C. H., *The Death of Jesus,* 367-368
Great octave, 596
Great Staff, 595, 596
Gregorian Chant, 339-340
Grétry, *Lucile,* 327
Grieg:
Dance Caprice, 569
Humoresque, 591
Morning Mood, 105
Peer Gynt Suite, "Ase's Death," 524

H

Haibel, *Tiroler,* 559

Half-cadence, 10
Half-diminished seventh-chord, 573-574
Half note and rest, 597
Half steps, 132
Handel:
Elijah:
"Be Not Afraid," 580
"Help, Lord," 580
"Lift Thine Eyes," 179
Joshua, 219-220
"Joy to the World," 3
Judas Maccabaeus, 159, 480
"See the Conquering Hero Comes," 173, 368-369
Largo (see Handel: *Xerxes)*
Messiah:
"Comfort Ye," 419-420
"Every Valley," 443
"Hallelujah Chorus," 30, 76, 224
"I know that my Redeemer Liveth," 519
"Lift Up Your Heads," 216
Rinaldo, "Leave Me in Sorrow," 523
Saul, "Dead March," 305-306
style, 76-77
Xerxes, 49, 93, 95, 203
Hanes, 235
Harmonic interval, 210
Harmonic minor scale, 303-304
augmented second, 321
cadential origin, 505
Harmonic rhythm, 51
Harmonic sequence, 111
Harmonization *(see also* Vocal writing):
mixed voices, 363
Harmonizing melodies, 228
Harmony, 3
close, 49
open, 49
Haseler, 364
Hauser, *Cradle Song,* 396
Haydn:
Chorale of St. Anthony, 460
Creation, The, 374
"The Heavens Are Telling," 474
"With Verdure Clad," 241
Gypsy Rondo, 123
My Mother Bids Me Bind My Hair, 196-197
Sonata in E Minor, 415
style, 62, 244

symphonies:
  D Major, 271
  Drumroll, 77, 87
  London:
    No. 2, 207
    No. 4, 31
    No. 5, 240
    No. 7, 100, 420
  Military, 62
  Salomon (*see* Haydn: symphonies:
    London)
  Surprise, 46, 50
Hayes, 216
Head (note), 598
Heller, 415
Herbert, *Badinage,* 337
Himmel, *Mignon,* 236
Homophonic texture, 362
Hook (note), 598
Hopkins, *Three Kings of Orient,* 411
Humperdinck, 117
Hypo-dorian (-phrygian, etc.) modes,
  340

I

Imperfect authentic cadence, 93
A–B–A form, 388
Implied modulation, 261
Inharmonic tones (*see* Nonharmonic
  tones)
Inner voices, procedures in adding,
  366-367, 428
Intervals, 20
  diagram of relative size, 210
  names, 210
Inversions:
  first, 47
    of sevenths, 150 (*see also*
      Chords: V_5^6 etc.)
    of triads, 407 (*see also* Chords:
      of the sixth; Chords: I₆ etc.)
  second, 64
    of sevenths, 189, 531 (*see also*
      Chords: V_3^4 etc.)
    of triads (*see* Chords: six-four;
      Chords: IV_4^6 etc.)
  third, 227-228, 528 (*see also* Chords:
    V_2^4 etc.)
Ionian mode, 340
Isaac, Henrich, 528

J

Jacobsen, 84
Jadassohn, *Klavierstück,* 591
Johnstone, 250

K

Key, 3
Key associations, 577
Key signatures, 149, 150
  A flat major, 260
  A major, 169
  A minor, 384
  B flat major, 227
  B major, 501
  B minor, 424
  C flat major, 501
  C minor, 320
  C sharp major, 553
  C sharp minor, 471
  D flat major, 547, 553
  D major, 169
  D minor, 361
  D sharp minor, 576
  E flat major, 244
  E flat minor, 572, 576
  E major, 189
  E minor, 403
  F major, 208
  F minor, 289-290
  F sharp major, 528-529
  F sharp minor, 448
  G flat major, 526, 529
  G major, 149
  G minor, 341
  lack of, for certain parallel scales, 578
  major, summarized, 553
  minor:
    scale, 290
    summarized, 577
Key tone (*see* Tonic)
Kjerulf, 99
Komorowski, 143
König, 216
Kreipl, 142
Kreisler, *Caprice Viennois,* 499-500
Kücken, 57
Kufferath, 392, 482, 532, 533, 582
Kuhlau:
  Rondo, Op. 40, No. 2, 236-237

sonatinas:
  Op. 20, No. 1, 161
  Op. 55, No. 1, 29
  Op. 55, No. 4, 218
  Op. 55, No. 5, 70
  Op. 88, No. 2, 536
  Op. 88, No. 3, 503-504

L

Large second, 132
Large seventh, 170
Last Rose of Summer, The, 95
Latvian National Anthem, 581
Leading tone, 133 (*see also* Chords: VII)
  lowered, cadential use of, 339
  VII₆ to harmonize, 212
Leger lines, 595
Le Jeune, 556
Liadow, 360
Liszt:
  Hungarian Rhapsody, No. 2, 544
  Les Preludes, 544-545
Lwoff, Alexis T., 344
Lydian mode, 340

M

Major chord, 92
  as ending for composition in minor, 362
Major intervals, 210
Major mode, quality of chords in, 290
Major scale, 4-5
Major second, 132
Major seventh, 170
Major triad (*see* Major chord)
Martini, 162, 268
  Gavotte, 43-44
Mascagni, *Cavalleria Rusticana*, 523-524
Mason, Lowell, 457
Massenet, *Elégie*, 520
Mazurka, 302
Measure, 598
Mediant, 133 (*see also* Chords: III)
Mediant modulation, 343-346
Mehul, 71
Meisterchorales:
  No. 17, 371
  No. 19, 371
  No. 30, 371
  No. 32, 372
  No. 79, 382

Melodic interval, 210
Melodic minor scale, 320-323
Melodic repetitions, substitute
  chords for, 113
Melodic sequence, 111
Melody (*see also* Setting of words):
  harmonizing, 228
  obbligato, 78
  progressions, 6
Mendelssohn:
  Athalie, 411
  Elijah:
    "Behold, God the Lord," 520-521
    "It is Enough," 469
    No. 42, 582
    "Yet doth the Lord," 510
  Etude, 310-311
  Op. 50, No. 4, 433
  Piano Concerto, Op. 25, 444
  Song Without Words, No. 3, 17
  Winter Song, 331
Meter, 598-600
  poetic, 10
  relation to time signature, 502
Methfesel, 158
Metric signature (*see* Time signature)
Meves, 157
Meyerbeer, *The Prophet*, "Coronation
  March," 74-75, 381
Middle C, 595, 596
Minor chord, 92
Minor intervals, 210
Minor mode, 288-289
  major ending, 362
  modulation, 303
  quality of chords, 290
  quality of dominant key, 303
  summary of various forms, 342-343
Minor scale:
  Aeolian (*see* Minor scale: natural)
  altered from major, 289
  harmonic, 303-304
    augmented second, 321
    cadential origin, 505
  melodic, 320-323
  natural, 340-342
Minor second, 132
Minor seventh, 170
Minor triad, 92
Mixed voices (*see also* Vocal writing):
  harmonization, 363

three-part vocal writing, 230-231, 247-248, 262-265
Mixolydian mode, 340
Modal forms, 339-340
Modal triads, 108
Modes, 288
  Church, 339-340
Modulation, 132
  by thirds, from both modes, 345-346
  implied, 261
  mediant, 343-346
  minor mode, 303
  minor to its dominant, 387
  minor to relative major, 320
  relative use of types, 345-346
  sequence, 563, 586-587
Monk, 534
Monophonic texture, 362
Moskowski, *Spanish Dance*, 147, 437-438
Motive (*see* Sequence)
Movable C, 595, 596
Mozart:
  Ave Verum, 534-535, 575
  Berceuse, 39
  Fantasia, K475, 287, 288
  operas:
    Don Giovanni:
      "Deh vieni," 437
      "Il mio tesoro intanto," 85, 226
      "Minuet," 146
    Marriage of Figaro, 40, 70, 182
      "Ricevete, o padroncina," 157
      "Voi, che sapete," 165
  piano sonatas:
    K284, 100
    K330, 488
    K331, 190, 394, 462
    K332, 88
    K333, 123-124
    K457, 329
    K545, 124, 467
    K547, 20
  quartets:
    K428, 243
    K575, 468
  Requiem Mass:
    "Lacrymosa," 512
    "Offertorium," 341-342
    "Sanctus," 405, 535
  Rondo, 17-18
  violin sonatas:
    K303, 73
    K304, 6-7
    K379, 106
  style, 226, 288
  symphonies:
    G Major, 229-230, 400-401
    Haffner (*see* Mozart: symphonies: *K385*)
    Jupiter (*see* Mozart: symphonies: *K551*)
    K183, 258
    K385, 60
    K543, 276, 301
    K550, 541
    K551, 29, 446
  variations:
    on a Folk Song, 316
    on a French Theme, 335-336
    on a Theme by Grétry, 315-316
  Viennese Sonatinas, No. 2, 225, 386, 387
  Violet, The, 252
Müller, 559

N

Nageli, 25
Natural, 597 (*see also* Accidentals)
Natural minor scale, 340-342
Neander, 210
Neighboring tones, 32
  double, 551
Neumark, 385, 386
Ninth-chords, 548-552
  quality, 549
  use of V₉, 551-552
Nonharmonic tones, 23, 32, 112
  acciaccaturas, 171
  accidentals, 33
  anticipations, 94, 96
  appoggiaturas, 170
  composer's use of, 50-51
  double neighboring tones, 551
  échappée, 262
  free, 49
  organ point, 426-427
  pedal point, 426-427
  suspensions, 38, 49, 50, 94
  rhythmic location, 34
Notation (*see also* Enharmonic keys):
  enharmonic, 501

necessary for certain parallel
  scales, 578
summary, 595-600
Note values, 597-598
"Now Thank We All Our God," 453

O

Obbligato melody, 78
Octave groups, 596
Octaves, parallel, in four-part
  vocal writing, 364
Oh Sacred Head, 364
Oliver, 449
One-line C, 595, 596
One-line octave, 596
Open harmony, 49
Organ point (see Pedal point)
Organum, 362

P

P.A.C. (see Perfect authentic cadence)
Paderewski, Minuet in G, 332
Paisiello, 85
Parallel fourths, in organum, 362
Parallel fifths:
  four-part vocal writing, 364
  organum, 362
Parallel motion between voices, 264-265
Parallel octaves, in four-part vocal
  writing, 364
Parallel period, 11
  by inversion, 64
Parallel scales, 291
  historical background, 340
  lack of key signatures for
    certain scales, 578
Parallel sixths, in two-part vocal
  writing, 135-136
Parallel thirds, in two-part vocal
  writing, 135-136
Passing $\frac{6}{4}$ chords (see Chords: passing$\frac{6}{4}$)
Passing tones, 32
Passion Chorale, 364
Pastoral pedal point, 427
Pedal point, 426-427
  pastoral, 427
Perfect authentic cadence, 8
  A-B-A form, 388
  substitution of II₆ for IV, 47-48
Perfect fifths, 91, 209

Perfect fourths, 209
Perfect intervals, 210
Perfect plagal cadence, 30
Pergolesi, Stabat Mater, 317
Period, 10, 11
  A-B-A form, 388
  antecedent group, 527
  consequent group, 527
  extension, 527
  parallel, 11
    by inversion, 64
Phrase, 8, 10
  A-B-A form, 388
  antecedent, 10
  consequent, 10
Phrygian mode, 340
Picardian Third, 362
Pinsuti, Goodnight, Goodnight, Beloved,
  405
Pitch, 595-597
Pivotal chord, 134
Plagal cadence, perfect, 30
Plagal modes, 340
Plainsong, 339-340
  monophonic, 362
Polish National Anthem, 581
Polonaise, 302, 571
Polyphonic texture, 362
Position of chords, 363
Praetorius, 309, 451
Primary triads, 108
Principal triads, 108
Progressions (see also Voice leading):
  melodic, 6
  four-part vocal writing, 363-364
Purcell, Dido and Aeneas, 372

Q

Quadruple time, 598
Quality, 103, 108 (see also Major
    mode; Minor mode)
  ninth-chord, 549
  seventh-chords, 504-505
  triads, 290
  III in harmonic minor, 573
  VII₇, 575-576
Quarter note and rest, 597
Quintuplet, 598

R

Range of voices, 247, 283, 363
    alto, 247
    baritone, 247
    bass, 283
    soprano, 363
    tenor, 363
Reissiger, 328
Relative scales, 291
    historical background, 340
Repeated-chord accompaniment figure, 67
Repetition, 151, 226
    melodic, substitute chords for, 113
Resolution, 19
    of secondary seventh-chords, 531
Rests, 597
Retardations, 50
Rhythmic background (see
        Accompaniment figures)
Rimsky-Korsakov, Sadko, 375
Rodney, 413
Rondo, 131
Root, 5
Rossini, Barber of Seville, 40
Round, 136-137, 173

S

Sarabande, 376
S.C. (see Semi-cadence)
Scales, 4 (see also Key signatures)
    Aeolian minor (see Scales: natural
        minor)
    A minor, identical with Aeolian, 340
    C major, identical with Ionian, 340
    descending:
        harmonizing, 111, 342
        substitute chords, 113
    harmonic minor, 303-304
        augmented second, 321
        cadential origin, 505
    harmonizing with chords of the
        sixth, 405, 407
    major, 4-5
    melodic minor, 320-323
    minor, 289
        Aeolian (see Scales: minor: natural)
        harmonic, 303-304
            augmented second, 321
            cadential origin, 505
        natural, 340-342

    melodic, 320-323
    natural minor, 340-342
    parallel, 291
        historical background, 340
    relative, 291
        historical background, 340
    steps (see Scale steps)
    syllables, 4, 289
    twelve-tone, 428
Scale steps, 132, 133
    name, 133
    size, 132
Scansion, 8
Scharwenka:
    Moment Musical, 463
    Polish Dance, Op. 3, No. 1, 583
Schletterer, 177-178
Schubert, 268, 271
    By the Sea, 460
    Cathedral-Scene (Chorus), 581
    Crusaders, The, 481
    Death and the Maiden, 443
    Ecossaisen, Op. 18a, No. 3, 462
    Fantasia, Op. 15, 515
    Hark, Hark, the Lark, 566
    Hedge Roses, 525-526
    impromptus:
        Op. 90, No. 1, 44, 336
        Op. 90, No. 4, 110, 483
        Op. 142, No. 1, 45
        Op. 142, No. 2, 275-276
    In the Red of Evening, 460
    Ländler, Op. 39, No. 9, 584
    Maid of the Mill, The, 7
    Menuette No. 7, 436-437
    Moments Musicals:
        Op. 94, No. 2, 190
        Op. 94, No. 3, 336-337
    number of compositions, 526
    Op. 67, No. 4, 561
    Serenade, 542
    Slumber Song, 58
    sonatas:
        C Minor, 180, 484
        Op. 42, 400
        Op. 53, 185
        Op. 78, 399
        Op. 122, 256
        Op. 147, 538
    Spring Dreams, 90
    style, 90

symphonies:
 Unfinished, 28, 421
 Seventh, 421, 468-469
 Eighth (*see* Schubert: symphonies:
  Unfinished)
 Ninth (*see* Schubert: symphonies:
  Seventh)
To the Lyre, 536
Valses Nobles, 38, 41
Valses Sentimentales, 560-561
waltzes:
 Op. 9a, No. 13, 584
 Op. 18a, No. 1, 414
 Op. 18a, No. 2, 520
 Op. 18a, No. 5, 560
 Op. 18a, No. 10, 513
 Op. 18a, No. 11, 513
 Op. 18a, No. 17, 584-585
 Op. 91a, No. 12, 217
 Op. 127, No. 10, 414
Wanderer, The, 489
Whither?, 7
Who is Sylvia?, 49
Winter Journey, 90
Schultz, 109
Schulz, 118
Schumann:
 Album for the Young, 95
 Carnival, 205
  March, 469
 Landliche Lied, 137-138
 Lieder, No. 23, 538-539
 Little Lullaby, 116, 483
 Novelletten, 186-187, 543
 Op. 68, No. 29, 379-380
 Papillons, 186
 Scenes from Childhood:
  "A Curious Story," 567
  "Träumerei," 88-89
 Sonata, Op. 22, 256
 Spinning Song, 179
 Symphonic Etudes, 490
 symphonies:
  Spring (*see* Schumann: symphonies:
   First)
  First, 304
 Valse Noble, 538
 Vienna Carnival-Scene, 45, 275, 542
Secondary seventh-chords, 503, 504
Secondary triads (*see* Subordinate
 triads)

Second inversions, 64
 of sevenths, 189 (*see also* Chords:
  V$_3^4$ etc.)
 resolution of secondary
  seventh-chords, 531
 of triads (*see* Chords: six-four;
  Chords: IV$_4^6$ etc.)
Seconds, 132, 170
 augmented, 304
  in harmonic minor scale, 321
Semi-cadence, 10
 A–B–A form, 388
Sequence:
 harmonic, 111
 in Chopin, *Prelude, Op. 28, No. 7,*
  568
 melodic, 111
 modulatory, 563, 586-587
 seventh-chords, 504
 use of motive, 464, 486
Setting of words:
 procedure, 10-11
 three-part song form, 82
Seventh-chords, 20 (*see also* Chords:
   V$_7$ etc.)
 diminished, 572-576
  inversion, 573
 doubling, 364
 extension by thirds, 550-551
 first inversion, 150 (*see also* Chords:
   V$_5^6$ etc.)
 half-diminished, 573-574
 inversions:
  first, 150 (*see also* Chords: V$_5^6$ etc.)
  second, 189, 531 (*see also* Chords:
    V$_3^4$ etc.)
  third, 227-228, 528 (*see also*
    Chords: V$_2^4$ etc.)
 quality, 504-505
 secondary, 503, 504
  II$_7$, 503
 second inversion, 189, 531 (*see also*
   Chords: V$_3^4$ etc.)
 sequential movement, 504
 third inversion, 227-228, 528
   (*see also* Chords: V$_2^4$ etc.)
Sevenths, 170
Seventh step, harmonizing, 342
Sharp, 597 (*see also* Accidentals)
Sibelius:
 Finlandia, 278

616 INDEX

Second Symphony, 545
Signatures (*see* Key signatures)
Silcher, 459
Simple meters, 599
Six-four chords, 64 (*see also*
   Chords: IV⁶₄ etc.)
   embellishing, 452
   passing (*see* Chords: passing⁶₄)
Sixteenth note and rest, 597
Sixth, chords of the (*see* Chords: of the
   sixth)
Sixths, parallel, in two-part vocal
   writing, 135-136
Sixty-fourth note and rest, 597
Slur, 598
Small octave, 596
Small second, 132
Small seventh, 170
Sonata, 188
Sonata-allegro form, 188
Song forms:
   A-B (*see* A-B)
   A-B-A (*see* A-B-A)
   binary (*see* A-B)
   ternary (*see* A-B-A)
   three-part (*see* A-B-A)
   two-part (*see* A-B)
   typical, 527
Soprano voice, range of, 363
Spacing, in four-part vocal writing, 367
Speech, choral, 76
Spengel, 196
Staff, 595-597
Static chords, 78
Stationary bass (*see* Pedal point)
Stem (note), 598
Stozel, 410
Strauss, J., *You and You,* 354
Strophic form, 527
Stylistic criticism, 364
Sub-contra octave, 596
Subdominant, 133 (*see also* Chords: IV)
Submediant, 133 (*see also* Chords: VI)
Subordinate triads, 108
Substitute chords, 92, 109, 110, 113
   evaded cadence, 113
Sullivan, 262
   Gondoliers, 459
   Mikado, The, 270, 297, 433, 434
   Patience, 269, 270, 278-279
   Pirates of Penzance, 269, 270

Summaries:
   Part I, 125-127
   Part II, 280-283
   Part III, 491-496
   Part IV, 592-594
Supertonic, 133 (*see also* Chords: II)
Surprise cadence, 93
Suspensions, 38, 49, 50, 94
   use of, 50
Syllables:
   major scale, 4
   minor scale, 289
Symphony, 188

T

Tarantelle, 415
Tchaikovsky:
   Album for the Young, 312-313
   Fifth Symphony, 242
   Marche Slave, 344
   Op. 39, No. 9, 421
   Quartet, Op. 11, 242
   Romance, Op. 5, 256, 318
   Songs for Young People, "A Legend,"
      407, 408
Telemann, 350
Temperament, equal, 501
Tempo (*see* Harmonic rhythm)
Tenor clef, 595
Tenor voice (*see also* Inner voices):
   range, 363
Ternary song form (*see* A-B-A)
"The Campbells Are Coming," 22-23
Third inversions, 227-228, 528 (*see also*
   Chords: V⁴ etc.)
Thirds, 92
   parallel, in two-part vocal
      writing, 135-136
Thirty-second note and rest, 597
Thomas, *Mignon,* "Gavotte," 257-258
Thorough bass, 365-366
Three-line octave, 596
Three-part song form (*see* A-B-A)
Three-part vocal writing, 173-174
   compared with two- and four-part,
      368-369
   consecutive chords of the sixth, 408
   mixed groups, 230-231, 247-248,
      262-265
   VII₆, 212
Through-composed form, 527

Tie, 598
Tierce de Picardie, 362
Time, notation for, 597-600
Time signatures, 149, 598-600
  exceptional, 600
  relation to meter, 502
Tonal chords, 31
Tonality, 4
Tonal triads, 108
Tones:
  common, 364
  foreign (see Nonharmonic tones)
  key (see Tonic)
  names, descriptive or functional, 133
  nonharmonic (see Nonharmonic
    tones)
  notation, 595-597
  passing, 32
  pitch, 595-597
Tonic, 3, 33, 133 (see also Chords: I)
Transposing, 314
  method, 183
  reversal of clefs, 314
Treble clef, 595
Triads, 5, 20 (see also Chords)
  diminished, 209
  doubling, 364
  major, 92
  minor, 92
  modal, 108
  primary, 108
  principal, 108
  quality in major and minor mode, 290
  secondary, 108
  subordinate, 108
  tonal, 108
Trio, 62
Triplet, 598
Triple time, 598
Trotere, 435
Twelve-tone scale, 428
Two-line octave, 596
Two-part song form (see A–B)
Two-part vocal writing, 135-138
  compared with three- and four-part,
    368-369
  parallel thirds and sixths, 135-136

V

Verdi:
  Aida, "Grand March," 277-278

Il Trovatore:
  "Home to Our Mountains," 167
  "Miserere," 589
  No. 12, 436
Viennese waltz, 500
Vocal writing:
  four-part, 361-369
    compared with two- and
      three-part, 368-369
    consecutive chords of the sixth,
      406-407
    doubling, 364
    general principles, 363-364
    parallel fifths and octaves, 364
    position of chords, 363
    procedure in adding inner
      voices, 366-367
  progression, 363-364
    spacing, 363
  parallel motion between voices,
    264-265
  three-part, 173-174
    compared with two- and
      four-part, 368-369
    consecutive chords of the sixth, 408
    mixed groups, 230-231, 247-248,
      262-265
    VII$_6$, 212
  two-part, 135-138
    compared with three- and
      four-part, 368-369
    parallel thirds and sixths, 135-136
Voice, 174
Voice leading:
  chords of the sixth, 406
  four-part vocal writing, 363-364
  melodic progressions, 6
  passing $^6_4$ chords, 472-473
  II$_7$, 503
  IV$^6_4$, 451
Voices:
  inner (see Inner voices)
  range, 363
    alto, 247
    baritone, 247
    bass, 263
    soprano, 363
    tenor, 363
Von Flotow, Martha, "Ah! So Pure," 436

W

Wagner:
  Flying Dutchman, Motive of
    Redemption, 28
  Götterdämmerung, Siegfried Horn
    Motive, 522
  Lohengrin:
    Bridal Chorus, 235
    Prelude, 105
  Meistersinger, Eva's Motive, 225
  Parsifal:
    Act I, 122
    Faith Motive, 17, 106
    Motive, 259
  Rheingold, Motive, 573
  Rienzi:
    March, 198
    Prayer, 582
  Ring of the Nibelungs, 107
  Siegfried:
    Act III, 107
    Act III, Scene 3, 245
    style, 107-108
  Tannhauser:
    Act II, Scene 4, 513-514
    March, 513
    Pilgrims' Chorus, 241
  Tristan, 94
Waltz:
  Viennese, 500
  accompaniment, 35
Ward, 556
Wassileff, 376
Webbe, 178, 216
Weber, 141
  Invitation to the Dance, 41, 561-562
  Rondo Brillant, 567-568
We Gather Together, 506, 507
Wesley, 582
"When Johnny Comes Marching Home
    Again," 338-339
Whole note and rest, 597
Whole steps, 132
Wolf, Hugo:
  style, 424
  Goethe Songs, No. 35, 423-424

Z

Zarlino, 362
Zelter, 327
  Folk Song, 18